Lying for Unity

How Spain Uses Fake News and Disinformation to Block Catalonia's Independence

Michael Strubell

Lying for Unity

How Spain Uses Fake News and Disinformation to Block Catalonia's Independence

Michael Strubell

Published by Cookwood Press (USA)

ISBN (paperback): 978-1-61150-063-9

ISBN (EPUB): 978-1-61150-064-6

ISBN (Amazon/Kindle): 978-1-61150-065-3

Cover photograph: Image: https://www.freepik.com/free-photo/flying-catalan-flags_1489286.htm. This cover has been designed using resources from Freepik.com

Cover graphics: Pablo Strubell

Dedicated, with thanks, to the members of my family, for their patience and support during the various drafts of the book.

And to all those Catalans in prison or in exile, and all those who have suffered - or await trials before Spanish courts -, for defending a perfectly legitimate political aim of all peoples in the world: to be able to join, and make its contributions to, the international community, as a free nation.

"When Article 2 [of the Spanish Constitution] lays the constitutional foundation in the indissoluble unity of the Spanish Nation, it does not do so as a programmatic frontispiece, but as the ultimate, nuclear and irreducible foundation of all the Law of a State". Carlos Lesmes[1]

"[Josep Borrell defended that] the pro-independence leaders must be held accountable and assured that 'wounds have to be disinfected before they are stitched' and said a divided country like Catalonia is a 'sick' country". (La Vanguardia 2017) [2]

"Thanks to whom do ERC, Junts per Catalunya and the rest of the *independentistas* not have leaders right now, because they have been decapitated? Thanks to Mariano Rajoy and the PP". (La Vanguardia 2017) [3]

---

[1] Lesmes, Carlos (2017). *Discurso del Presidente del Tribunal Supremo y del Consejo General del Poder Judicial, Carlos Lesmes, en el acto de apertura del año judicial.* 5 September 2017. http://theobjective.com/wp-content/uploads/2017/09/20170905-Discurso-Carlos-Lesmes-apertura-an%CC%83o-judicial-2017-1.pdf

[2] La Vanguardia (2017). "Borrell apuesta por "desinfectar" las heridas de la sociedad catalana y "desprocesar" TV3", *La Vanguardia*, 16 December 2017. https://www.lavanguardia.com/politica/20171216/433655595420/elecciones-cataluna-21d-psc-josep-borrell-iceta-independentismo.html

[3] Europa Press (2017). "Sáenz de Santamaría presume de haber "descabezado" a ERC y Junts per Catalunya", *La Vanguardia*, 16 December 2017. https://www.lavanguardia.com/politica/20171216/433683114375/elecciones-cataluna-santamaria-presume-descabezado-erc-junts-per-catalunya.html

Contents

Acknowledgments

I am deeply indebted to my brother, Tony, for his encouragement and support. He read an early draft and made many suggestions, most of which I incorporated into a later draft. He also translated into English many of the quoted texts from their Spanish or Catalan originals. He also searched for potential publishers and put me in touch with a potential printing press.

I am likewise indebted to Professor Henry Ettinghausen, who also read a number of drafts painstakingly, tracking down typos and suggesting many improvements, and was kind enough to accept my invitation and write the Preface, which provides an excellent and extremely opportune introduction to the subject matter.

My son Pablo also gave me plenty of helpful advice - for which I am very grateful - on the world of digital editions, based on his experience as a publisher.

I am happy also to express my gratitude to the two peer reviewers for the Anglo-Catalan Society that suggested a number of insightful improvements, and to the Society's view - which I share - that the manuscript would not fit in its Occasional Papers collection (to which I have contributed on two occasions).

All of this would not have come to fruition without the enthusiastic and generous support of Liz Castro and her Catalonia Press.

I plead the indulgence of co-authors: I have only put into the index (which is probably too long for most readers anyway) the leading author of the cited articles, reports, chapters and books.

Finally, my thanks to the reader for saving me the references to the "Last accessed" date for URLs in the footnotes. To the best of my ability, I have checked that all were operative on December 31st, 2020.

Despite all the valuable contributions to the book, I take full responsibility for any errors or omissions in the text and/or index, and invite readers to contact me: m_strubell@yahoo.com.

Preface

Until Covid-19 hit the world's travel industry for six, Catalonia - with fewer than eight million inhabitants - was visited by nearly twenty million foreign tourists a year. Catalonia is that corner of Spain that attracts more foreign tourists than any other: the scene of brilliant holidays, notably in Barcelona, Catalonia's capital, on the Costa Brava and the Costa Daurada, in the Pyrenees and in its ancient towns and villages, amidst a remarkable variety of landscapes. For a far tinier number of people, however, Catalonia also figures as one of those many zones of discontent that manage to get a mention in a few of the world's more serious media from time to time.

Michael Strubell's book, *Lying for Unity. How Spain Uses Fake News and Disinformation to Block Catalonia's Independence,* examines how, especially - and ever more increasingly - in the course of the past decade, the Catalan independence movement has been deliberately and consistently persecuted and misrepresented by the entire panoply of powers wielded by the Spanish body politic. The Catalan people's very long-standing aspiration to be recognised as an independent state - an aspiration shared with millions of Scots - has served to exacerbate age-old hatreds and resentments within Spain which, in turn, have dramatically reinforced the emotional disconnection with Spain on the part of a huge number of Catalans. The precise number - as is the case in Scotland - can only be determined by a referendum.

In 2003 the supposedly Socialist Spanish Prime Minister, José-Luís Rodríguez-Zapatero, promised his support for a reform of the 1979 Catalan statute of autonomy. In 2006, after consideration by the Spanish Parliament's Constitutional Commission of the Catalan Parliament's proposed text, it was presented "planed down," as its supposedly Socialist chairman proudly proclaimed. The new text was nevertheless ratified by a referendum in Catalonia in which it received 74% support, and it obtained the official approval of the Prime Minister and King Juan Carlos. However, the Conservative 'Partido Popular' party challenged 128 of its 223 articles and collected signatures across Spain with a view to opposing the entire reform. In 2010 the Constitutional Court struck out some of its articles and reinterpreted many more in a restrictive way. The reaction in Catalonia to the butchering of the new statute was immediate and immense: on 10 July the largest demonstration ever held in contemporary Europe marched angrily, but peaceably, to the slogan "SOM UNA NACIÓ! NOSALTRES DECIDIM!" ("We are a Nation! We Decide!"). That reaction was repeated ever louder, year by year, in successive massive peaceful marches on 11 September, Catalonia's national day, as part of a popular operation that became known as "la revolta dels somriures" ('the revolt with smiles'), a movement that is wedded to multiculturality and a humane world view.

In 2014, the British government, under Conservative Prime Minister David Cameron, allowed an official referendum on independence to be held in Scotland, and the Catalans, who had been calling for a referendum for many years, attempted to follow suit. Their efforts were continuously vilified and deemed illegal by the Spanish state. Nonetheless, on 1 October 2017, well over two million Catalans (43% of the electorate) ignored the Constitutional Court's prohibition and took part in the referendum, with 92% of them voting for Catalonia to become an independent republic.

The then Conservative Spanish government, under Mariano Rajoy, had vowed to prevent the referendum taking place. The Spanish National Police and the Guardia Civil - 10,000 extra members of those forces were sent in from other parts of Spain - sought high and low for the special ballot boxes that would be used, but never found a single one. Instead, on the morning of 1 October they were ordered to enter the polling stations, by force if necessary, and to seize the boxes and the ballots. In the event, around a thousand voters and would-be voters were injured, some of them seriously. As the television newsreels showed, both in Catalonia and in much of the rest of the world, in very many cases the injuries were committed gratuitously and out of pure rage, using entirely unlawful means.

Only in Spain was the news of the police brutality deliberately and comprehensively falsified. The false news - that violence had been used by the voters against the armed and armoured police - was created by the Madrid media and was lapped up by a Spanish public that had previously been shown on television and in the press the resounding images of exultant police and Civil Guards being sent off in coaches from various parts of Spain to cries of "¡A POR ELLOS!" (i.e "Go get 'em!"). On 3 October, King Philip VI went on state television and declared himself horrified by the Catalan referendum and totally in sympathy with the way the police had attempted to put it down, thus earning for himself the immediate and permanent disaffection of a majority of Catalans.

Having failed to prevent the referendum taking place by suppressing it with brute force, the Spanish Conservative government, with the support of the so-called Socialist opposition, declared a state of emergency, dismissing Catalonia's legitimately elected semi-autonomous government, shutting down the Catalan Parliament, taking direct control of the Catalan administration, summarily arresting Catalonia's chief ministers and holding them for well over a year in pre-trial detention, charging them with rebellion or sedition and, in 2019, sentencing them to up to thirteen years in jail after a four-month-long trial. It was on the basis of the carefully selected images shown and the out and out lies told by witnesses for the prosecution, in many cases quite clearly learned by heart and repeated word for word, that the Supreme Court imposed its totally pernicious sentences on those senior ministers in the Catalan government who had not escaped injustice by seeking refuge abroad.

As of today, another nearly three thousand Catalans - from senior civil servants to mayors, rappers and even a clown - are still in the process of being tried for their part in the independence process as the repression goes on unrelentingly. The intention is, quite simply, to terrorise the independence movement into submission. The contrast with Britain's treatment of Scotland could not be more shocking. Oriol Junqueras, who was ousted after the referendum as Vice-President of Catalonia, is one of the political prisoners who have just spent their fourth Christmas in jail; several of the others have spent their third behind bars. Some of them have young families.

Catalonia's determination to free itself from the domination and exploitation of Spain goes back a very long way. A first crucial moment in its history was constituted by the Catalan War of Secession (1640-1652), a war that Portugal made use of in order to achieve its independence from Spain, but which left Barcelona starving and decimated by the plague during the fifteen-month siege mounted by the army of Philip IV. A second crucial moment was ended, in 1714, by another fifteen-month siege of Barcelona during the War of Spanish Succession, in which Philip V's troops rained down tens of thousands of cannonballs onto the city. Whereupon the Spanish state outlawed the centuries-old Catalan political and legal systems and banned the official use of the Catalan language. Thirdly, and still very much alive in Catalonia's collective memory, Franco ended his war on the Spanish Republic in 1939 by crushing Catalonia and instituting a thorough and long-drawn-out persecution of all those thought not to be wholly addicted to his Fascist regime. Hundreds of thousands of Catalans, and non-Catalans, fled across the border into France before the final onslaught, many of them ending up in the French Resistance, some of them being worked to death in Nazi extermination camps.

Franco's remorseless offensive against all things Catalan, again including the Catalan language and all expressions of Catalan culture, constituted an obsessive part of his persecution, both during the war and afterwards, of all forms of dissidence. Most notably, in 1940, Hitler handed over to him the Catalan President in exile in France, Lluís Companys, who was then tortured, condemned by a kangaroo court and shot by a firing squad in Barcelona - the only democratically elected president in the whole of Europe to be executed by the Fascists. For decades, the tons of documents looted by Franco's troops when they entered Catalonia at the beginning of 1939 and archived in Salamanca were systematically exploited by the secret police in order to denounce and persecute Catalans who had opposed or questioned the Franco regime.

In 1975, after three dozen years as dictator of a West European police state, Franco died in his bed. What would happen thereafter was an open question, with a huge groundswell of opposition to the regime on the one hand, but power still very firmly in the hands of Franco's diehard supporters, not least the military, on the other. In the event, under the symbolic aura of young, innocent-looking King Juan Carlos, whom the dictator had named and groomed as his successor, a process was put in place that became known as the 'Transición', an opening up of popular representation in the Spanish parliament to what had been underground opposition parties and the approval by referendum in 1978 of a new Constitution that included statutes of devolved powers to the regions. That much-trumpeted transition from dictatorship to democracy was, however, very far from being a total break with the Fascist past. It was concocted with the army making it clear that it was more than prepared to intervene if it thought fit. At no time in the ensuing decades has a single member of the Franco regime been charged with taking part in the persecution of the opposition - including arbitrary imprisonment, systematic torture and political executions - and there is still no prospect whatsoever of that occurring. What is more, there are still Francoist laws on the statute book.

What we are seeing in Spain today is the direct result of the Allies' tragic decision not to finish off the last Fascist dictator in Europe at the end of the Second World War, portraying him, instead, as a handy bulwark against the threat of Communism at the start of the Cold War, with Churchill describing him as "a gallant Christian gentleman." Whereas elsewhere in Europe hard-right parties have resurged in recent years, in Spain Franco is still alive and kicking. There are still thousands of unmarked graves where his opponents during the war, both military and civilian, were summarily executed and hurriedly buried. And Francoism expresses itself today unashamedly in the right-wing and hard-right Spanish parties, the 'Partido Popular' and the more recently formed 'Vox', as well as very often colouring the language and the messages of those parties supposedly in the middle or on the left of the political spectrum.

The show trial of the Catalan political prisoners by the Spanish Supreme Court in Madrid in 2019 was an exhibition by the heirs of the Franco regime, led by grotesquely right-wing prosecutors and the hard-right political party 'Vox' and tried by an unanimously reactionary string of judges, of their unquestioned domination of the Spanish judiciary. One of their most excruciating acts of injustice was the eleven-and-a-half-year prison sentence imposed on Carme Forcadell, the Speaker of the Catalan Parliament, for simply having allowed a debate to be held on the independence issue that had the backing of a majority of the MPs in the Catalan Parliament. Two other prodigiously savage violations of justice were the sentences of nine years meted out to two Catalan civic leaders, Jordi Cuixart and Jordi Sànchez, for supposedly inciting sedition on 20 September 2017, when what they actually did was climb on top of an empty

Guardia Civil vehicle in order to call on the crowd of tens of thousands to go home - a crowd that had gathered to protest at the police search of the Catalan Economics Ministry. The nine chief accused were sentenced by the Supreme Court to between nine and thirteen years in jail for sedition, an offence that has long dropped out of nearly all European legal systems, that being the reason why the Spanish prosecutors' desperate attempts to extradite the Catalan leaders who fled abroad, including President Carles Puigdemont and three other Catalan ministers, have again and again been rejected by the countries where they sought refuge.

Regarding the Spanish army, as came to light just a few days ago, last year young Spanish soldiers celebrated the feast of the 'Inmaculada Concepción' by singing Fascist anthems used by the 'División Azul', the force that Franco sent to back the Nazis against the USSR in 1940 as a token of his gratitude to Hitler for enabling him to crush the Spanish Republic. Earlier this month, a retired air force general had tweeted to his buddies that what is required now to save Spain from the reds and the independentists is a coup d'état and for twenty-six million Spaniards to be shot - which happens to be well over half of Spain's entire population. The supposedly Socialist Minister of Defence poo-pooed this as merely the opinion of a handful of moth-eaten military retirees. But, within days, a group of over a hundred artillery officers and NCOs still in service had WhatsApp-ed their support - and, they claimed, that of many of their colleagues - for those sentiments, which clearly regard Franco's armed rebellion against the Spanish Republic in 1936 as only the measly beginning of grossly unfinished business.

Just in case the claim that Spain has never made a clean break with Franco's Fascism sounds like an exaggeration, it is worth recalling that, a year after the dictator's death, the Francisco Franco National Foundation was established. Its aims were, and still are, to enhance and promote the dictator's memory and achievements. The Foundation received state funding until 2004, and private donations to it still attract tax relief. Its current President is General Juan Chicharro Ortega, who happens previously to have been an aide-de-camp to King Juan Carlos, Franco's appointed successor as head of state. King Juan Carlos, as is now well known, has lost for ever his aura as the revered keystone to the mythical 'Transición' by virtue of the spectacular financial scandals that have forced him to leave Spain in a hurry and take refuge in a hotel in Abu Dhabi that is said to be costing Spanish, and Catalan, taxpayers around £10,000 a day. Many years have gone by since the official Spanish government organisation that assesses public opinion last asked the citizens about their opinion of the monarchy.

As Michael Strubell demonstrates, the Spanish state's vengeful and unremitting repression of the Catalan independence movement over the past decade - first under the Conservative 'Partido Popular' and now under the coalition government of the supposedly Socialist 'Partido Socialista Obrero Español' and the supposedly further-left 'Unidos Podemos' - has relied very powerfully on disinformation. Disinformation, as he shows, has been meted out to Spain's and to the world's media from the start, and it continues by the day. It is a weapon that has been perfected over the centuries. Substantial anthologies exist of the denigration of Catalonia and its people that has been used over the ages by Spain's rulers. In 1557, a century before Catalonia's War of Secession, the exquisite Catalan writer, Cristòfol Despuig, complained at length that Spanish historians of his time knowingly ignored, distorted and perverted Catalonia's role in reconquering the Peninsula from the Moors with a view to making the reconquest a uniquely Castilian affair.

The current Prime Minister of Spain, the supposedly Socialist Pedro Sánchez, declared that the Catalan leaders had been tried for criminal conduct, and not for their political ideas, and insisted that his government would ensure the complete fulfilment of their sentences. Prisons in Spain are called 'Centros Penitenciarios' and are theoretically designed to make prisoners repent for their crimes. But none of the Catalan political prisoners has repented: on the contrary, they insist that they would do again what got them into jail. Which is the excuse for the judiciary's refusal to allow them any kind of leniency.

However, opposition to numerous aspects of Spain's handling of the Catalan Question has been publicly voiced by such international bodies as the Office of the United Nations High Commissioner for Human Rights, Amnesty International, the World

Organisation Against Torture, the International Association of Democratic Lawyers, PEN International, the Unrepresented Nations and Peoples Organization, the European Democratic Lawyers Association, the International Commission of Jurists, and the United Nations Working Group on Arbitrary Detention. None of their protests, however, has been echoed in the mainstream Spanish media. What has been greeted there with joy is the constant refusal of Spain's judicial system to consider the political prisoners' requests for day release from jail, for amnesty or reprieve, for reform of the antiquated and inappropriate laws of sedition and rebellion, etc. And the current supposedly progressive 'Partido Socialista Obrero Español'/'Unidos Podemos' government's cowardly refusal to take note of international condemnation of the trial and the sentences has assuaged the forces of the right, with the judges insisting that the political prisoners' refusal to relinquish their aspirations to independence bars them from any lessening of their punitive conditions. As for Europe, the power exercised by the right-wing blocks in the European Parliament and institutions has served to perpetuate the dogma that the Catalan Question is simply an internal issue for Spain to sort out.

One of the very few interventions in the EU Parliament on Catalonia's behalf was voiced recently by Irish MEP Clare Daly. Speaking in part in Catalan, she denounced the European Union for avoiding the issue of Catalonia, criticising the fact that a report that dealt with freedom of expression had been redrafted because it had "the audacity to explain that there are parliamentarians in prison" in Europe for organizing a democratic vote. Spain has yet again used - misused - the law in order to avoid addressing a political issue.

Michael Strubell's book provides very timely proof of the extent to which the Spanish state has demonstrated its Francoist heritage, exploiting its power, in every sphere and at every stage, to distort and discredit the Catalan independence movement and to destroy the lives of its leaders and their families. This, obviously, is intended as a warning to any who might be tempted to take further what has been a wholly peaceful and democratic process. Together with the Basque independentists, and with smaller such movements in Galicia and Andalusia, the Catalans are portrayed by the Spanish state - as they have been for centuries - as forces of evil that seek to undermine the sacred doctrine of the Unity of Spain. They stand first and foremost amongst the twenty-six million that the more reactionary elements in the military have got firmly in their sights. But, for the moment, the military can take it easy. For the present, the Spanish state - most particularly, the right-wing, hard-right and centre parties, the self-proclaimed progressive government and the dyed-in-the-wool, self-perpetuating judiciary - makes out that it has the Catalan independence movement firmly under control. As Michael Strubell demonstrates, this is very largely thanks to its permanent campaign of disinformation.

Henry Ettinghausen
Emeritus Professor of Spanish
University of Southampton

31 December 2020

Chapter 1. Introduction

Fake news and disinformation are at the heart of what I perceive to be the main thrust of one of the strategies used by Spain to try and counter the Catalan independence movement, by influencing public opinion in Catalonia, in Spain, and abroad. It is an example of one of the features of how Spain, as a state - including the parliamentary opposition at each moment - and its accompanying media, has accused the leaders of the Catalan independence movement of the same defects and biases that I contend any impartial observer would in fact attribute to the accusers themselves: from drawing on Nazism[4] to lying about "the facts".

Moreover, the reader may be surprised that what even an organization as distant from the Catalonia-Spain conflict as "Juezas y Jueces para la Democracia" sees clearly as a political conflict has and continues to this day to be regarded as a problem to be resolved in the courts: as I write, hundreds of Catalans still face trials and sentences of up to ten years in gaol, while others are in exile. The organization wrote that

> "we consider that the mere application of laws is not going to solve the current conflict, so we call on the political parties to continue looking for ways to solve the problem that exists in Catalonia." (Juezas y Jueces para la Democracia 2017)[5]

---

[4] e.g. Francisco M. Aviles Nuevo (aka F. MAN) (2017). "The Rape of Democracy". *Vineyard of The Saker Blog*, October 2 2017. https://thesaker.is/catalonia-two-opposed-views/

"Looks like most of the journalist, politicians, and analyst of the entire World have miss this fact: that they are NATIONAL SOCIALIST (aka NAZI) in their Ideology, forgetting which were the results of the last National Socialist Experiment in the last century"

"They accuse their victims of their crimes"

[5] Juezas y Jueces para la Democracia (2017). "Garantías y Derechos". Website, 3 November 2017. http://www.juecesdemocracia.es/2017/11/03/garantias-y-derechos/

In this paper we shall look at fake news and disinformation in a brief historic perspective, before homing in to Europe (and its North American allies) and particularly as regards the Catalonia-Spain conflict. Some attention will be given to the existence, and possible scale, of Russian interference in the conflict through the social media, and the narrative built round this, largely - I hope to prove - on extremely flimsy evidence. Finally, we shall study how the movement is even being accused of utilising the Covid-19 pandemic to further its ends.

The book is structured in eight parts, starting with this brief introduction.

In Chapter 2, we shall see how fake news is not a new phenomenon and that in Spain, building on a tradition of discrimination and hate speech in the media, disinformation, in general, and as regards the Catalan independence process, has been easily introduced and accepted by nearly all sectors.

In Chapter 3, we shall see how fake news has come to be seen, in Europe and the western world as a whole, as part of a Russian strategy of psychological warfare and diplomacy, which has been a suitable distraction for Spain's disinformation strategy as regards Catalonia.

In Chapter 4, some elements of the Catalan independence process will be outlined, and how Spain from the start devoted considerable energy in its foreign policy to try and ensure that, if Catalonia decided to declare independence without Spain's acquiescence (that is, unilaterally), then it would receive little if any foreign support.

In Chapter 5, the Catalan independence process is highlighted as a "breeding-ground" for falsehoods, manipulation, fake news... and pitiless lawfare. This builds on long-standing catalanophobia in much of Spain. Several of the main episodes have been selected to underline the massive disinformation that has taken place as a deliberate Spanish strategy.

In Chapter 6, claims are discussed of Russian involvement in the Catalan independence process, power-driven by the newspaper *El País*, and their international repercussions.

In Chapter 7, the threat posed by the Covid-19 pandemic for democratic values, the exercise of fundamental rights, is described, as is the enormous amount of disinformation unleashed in the media regarding its causes, treatment and prevention.

In Chapter 8, The Covid-19 pandemic is clearly seen as a new excuse to hammer the Catalan independence process. Two particularly outspoken examples are discussed.

In the concluding Chapter 9, a number of issues raised during the book are either confirmed or dismissed.

Chapter 2. Fake news is not new. It goes well back in history

It is said that Erik the Red discovered and colonized a huge ice-ridden island in the north Atlantic, and called it "Greenland" as a clearly false marketing ploy to attract fellow Vikings to settle there.

Propaganda is a tool used primarily in wartime. The words of "George Orwell", recalling his experience of the Spanish Civil War, is far from irrelevant to this paper:

> "...in Spain, for the first time, I saw newspaper reports which did not bear any relation to the facts, not even the relationship which is implied in an ordinary lie. I saw great battles reported where there had been no fighting, and complete silence where hundreds of men had been killed. I saw troops who had fought bravely denounced as cowards and traitors, and others who had never seen a shot fired hailed as the heroes of imaginary victories; and I saw newspapers in London retailing these lies and eager intellectuals building emotional superstructures over events that had never happened. I saw, in fact, history being written not in terms of what happened but of what ought to have happened according to various 'party lines'."[6]

Closer to the present day, we were recently reminded that "The original falsehood behind the Iraq War was that Saddam Hussein had weapons of mass destruction and intended to use them against America either directly or by giving them to al-Qaeda".[7] A good example of fake news concerned the cormorant drenched in crude oil purportedly spilt by Saddam Hussein after invading Kuwait

---

[6] http://orwell.ru/library/essays/Spanish_War/english/esw_1

https://estudiscatalans.blogspot.com/search?q=Orwell

[7] UK Government, MI6 and "Integrity Initiative", Softpanorama, 2020. http://www.softpanorama.org/Skeptics/Political_skeptic/Propaganda/Neo_mccarthyism/integrity_initiative.shtml

in 1991. A Spanish paper swallowed the story hook, line and sinker on 10 February)[8], yet under four weeks later Juan Arias, in the same paper, and without offering any apology,[9] reported on “The lies of war. The image of the cormorant drenched in oil was a fake, according to ‘Il Manifesto’”.

Shortly before publishing a paper on disinformation on just one side of the social media impact of the Catalan independence process, Del Fresno (2019)[10] wrote:

> "The problem is not that the truth is the opposite of a lie, but that opinion is elevated to the category of truth. The risk is that opinions cannot bear out the democratic model because, as political scientist Hannah Arendt wrote, "freedom of opinion is a farce unless factual information is guaranteed and the facts themselves are not in dispute."

Martínez Bascuñán (2018)[11] also refers to the threat fake news and falsehoods pose to democracy:

---

[8] El País (1991) “La catástrofe ecológica del golfo Pérsico”, *El País,* 10 February 1991. https://elpais.com/diario/1991/02/10/sociedad/666140402_850215.html

[9] Arias, Juan (1991) “Las mentiras de la guerra. La imagen del cormorán empapado en petróleo fue un montaje, según 'Il Manifesto'. *El Pais*, 5 March 1991. https://elpais.com/diario/1991/03/05/internacional/668127612_850215.html

27 years later, the same paper still failed to apologize: see Ana Tudela (2018) Comunicación. Propaganda y ‘fake news’: con nosotros mucho antes de la tecnología. *El País*, 2 January 2018. https://retina.elpais.com/retina/2017/12/28/tendencias/1514460844_757457.html

[10] Del Fresno, Miguel (2018). “Posverdad y desinformación: guía para perplejos”, *El País*, 16 MAR 2018. https://elpais.com/elpais/2018/03/16/opinion/1521221740_078721.html

[11] Martínez-Bascuñán, Míriam (2018). «El nuevo opio del pueblo», *El País*, 24 February 2018. https://elpais.com/elpais/2018/02/23/opinion/1519390373_509411.html

"Deliberately misrepresenting the facts is not distinctive of our age. Its use is as old as the *arcana imperii*, conceived of as a legitimate means of concealing the "truth" for a political purpose. And it is something that should not be trivialized because, as Rafael del Águila has reasoned, 'the exception marks the limit; and the limit is there even if the exception does not appear...'. However, this awareness of a limit has disappeared, and with it the reflection on the effects of lies on our perception of the world and democracy."

There has long been concern in Catalonia about the issue of disinformation. In 1991, writing about the Gulf War, Udina used the word[12]:

> "From the lack of fiction-spectacle we went on to a lack of information regarding reality. The "hypermediatization" of war that French theorist Dominique Wolton feared has gone on to become "simple disinformation", according to Paul Fabra, of *Le Monde* "because of the always fragmentary value of images".

A couple of years later Francisca Garrido (1993)[13]wrote about official news coverage (the so-called No-Do cinema news bulletins) at the time, of the Eastern Front (in which a Spanish division fought alongside Hitler against the Allies) between 1943 and the end of World War II.

> "In the many items of news projected by NO-DO, the successes of the Russians and the turning of the tables in the struggle in their favour are not reflected but, on the contrary, they try to give the impression of a continuity of Nazi superiority over the "Bolsheviks". Here, the real war had nothing to do with the war on the screen.

---

[12] Udina, Ernest (1991). "Golf: de la guerra espectacle a la desinformació". *Capçalera,* [en línia], 1991, Núm. 20, https://www.raco.cat/index.php/Capcalera/article/view/323098/413722

[13] Garrido, Francisca (1993). El frente del Este en el NO-DO: desinformación y propaganda, 1943-1945, *Filmhistoria online*. Núm. 1. https://www.raco.cat/index.php/FilmhistoriaOnline/article/view/226192/331818

> Disinformation and propaganda, censorship and the omission of fundamental events for the development of the war, such as the recovery of Stalingrad, are flagrant. "

In 2010, extracts of a German book by Karl Otte (published in Spanish as *El crash de la información*, Ariel) in a Catalan translation, were published in the journal *Capçalera*, under the now-eerie title "La crisi i el virus de la desinformació": the crisis and the virus of disinformation.[14]

> "For some time now, a stealthy, malignant virus, the effects of which can be seen in the current financial crisis, has not only infected the whole of the economy but, in settling inside our heads, threatens society as a whole. It is the virus of disinformation, which is antagonistic to living together with some degree of harmony, be it civil, political, or social…
>
> The real crisis has yet to come, not just the economic one, but also the political, educational, health, social ones in general, which can lead to the disinformation virus. …" (p. 76)
>
> "The Socratic apothem has never as true as it is now: 'I only know that I know nothing'; and this is so not only because we were not accustomed to the current avalanche of information or the growing complexity of a globalized reality, but because in our society there are certain forces that are very interested in turning information into disinformation.» (p. 77)

It is also ironic, incidentally, that the word "viral" is used to refer to "an image, video, piece of information, etc. that is circulated rapidly and widely on the Internet" (Oxford Dictionaries, 2015).

Here is another, more recent local example. I never saw international coverage of a particularly serious manipulation of images of the 2013 "Dia de la Raza" 12 October Unionist demonstration in the Plaça de Catalunya, in the centre of Barcelona,

---

[14] https://www.raco.cat/index.php/Capcalera/article/view/324997

the following year, by none other than *La Vanguardia*. It was quickly pointed out by, among other media, *Ara* (2014)[15]:

> "The most surprising case, though, was that of *La Vanguardia*. In the photograph, a section of the square that is full of people can be seen. But the photograph is really one taken at the previous year's demonstration. It is indeed part of the same photograph they published on the front page on the 12th October rally of 2013. On the inner pages the photographs are this year's (where one can see, for example, the umbrellas that had not been seen the year before). In mid-morning, the newspaper did apologize to its readers via Twitter and attributed the incident to «a mistake in the edition of the graphics"."

I am not in a position to express an informed opinion as to whether the mistake was indeed an accidental slip.

Just a couple of years later, in 2016, Melissa Zimdars [16] uploaded a useful paper which referred to 13 tags to classify false or misleading information on the basis that "the credibility of information and of organizations exists on a continuum". These include not only the obvious "fake news" or "hate news", but also "junk science" or "satire", that speak for themselves. She credits Ed Brayton for one of her useful tips: "If the story makes you REALLY ANGRY it's probably a good idea to keep reading about the topic via other sources to make sure the story you read wasn't purposefully trying to make you angry (with potentially misleading or false information) in order to generate shares and ad revenue."

In actual fact the manipulation of social media, using such methods as "cybertroops", is not new. In a 2017 working paper,[17]

---

[15] Gutiérrez, Àlex (2014). "'La Vanguardia' posa en portada la foto del 12-O de l'any passat", *Ara*, 13/10/2014. https://www.ara.cat/premium/Vanguardia-portada-foto-lany-passat_0_1229877001.html

[16] Zimdars, Melissa (2016). "False, Misleading, Clickbait-y, and/or Satirical "News" Sources". https://docs.google.com/document/d/10eA5-mCZLSS4MQY5QGb5ewC3VAL6pLkT53V_81ZyitM/edit

[17] Bradshaw, Samantha & Philip H. Howard (2017). "Troops, Trolls and Troublemakers: A Global Inventory of Organized Social Media

“Troops, Trolls and Troublemakers: A Global Inventory of Organized Social Media Manipulation”, Bradshaw & Howard (2017) state:

> “In January 2015, the British Army announced that its 77th Brigade would “focus on non-lethal psychological operations using social networks like Facebook and Twitter to fight enemies by gaining control of the narrative in the information age” (Solon, 2015). The primary task of this unit is to shape public behavior through the use of “dynamic narratives” to combat the political propaganda disseminated by terrorist organizations. The United Kingdom is not alone in allocating troops and funding for influencing online political discourse. Instead, this is part of a larger phenomenon whereby governments are turning to Internet platforms to exert influence over information flows and communication channels to shape public opinion. We compare and summarize this phenomenon in the following 28 countries: Argentina, Azerbaijan, Australia, Bahrain, Brazil, China, the Czech Republic, Ecuador, Germany, India, Iran, Israel, Mexico, North Korea, the Philippines, Poland, Russia, Saudi Arabia, Serbia, South Korea, Syria, Taiwan, Turkey, Ukraine, the United Kingdom, the United States, Venezuela and Vietnam. (p. 4)
>
> “… We purposively selected the following keywords and used them in combination for our search: astroturf*; bot; Facebook; fake; fake account; government; information warfare; intelligent agent; military; persona management; pro-government; propaganda; psychological operations; psyops; socialmedia; sockpuppet*; troll*; Twitter.” (p.5)

Manipulation”, Working Paper No. 2017.12, Computational Propaganda Research Project (COMPROP), Oxford Internet Institute (OII). http://comprop.oii.ox.ac.uk/wp-content/uploads/sites/89/2017/07/Troops-Trolls-and-Troublemakers.pdf

> "We conducted the research for this working paper in three stages. First, we conducted a systematic content analysis of news media articles. Second, we supplemented the content analysis with other sources from think tanks, government agencies, civil society groups, universities and other sources of credible research. Finally, we consulted with country experts to check facts, find additional sources in multiple languages and assist in evaluating the quality of sources.
>
> "Looking across the 28 countries, every authoritarian regime has social media campaigns targeting their own populations, while only a few of them target foreign publics. In contrast, almost every democracy in this sample has organized social media campaigns that target foreign publics, while political-party-supported campaigns target domestic voters. Authoritarian regimes are not the only or even the best at organized social media manipulation. The earliest reports of government involvement in nudging public opinion involve democracies, and new innovations in political communication technologies often come from political parties and arise during high-profile elections." (p. 3)

Sadly, for the purposes of this paper, Spain was not included, though the large-scale use of (among others) the social media to disinform, that we shall talk about below, may well have started after the paper's fieldwork had been completed. Chomsky's ground-breaking analysis of media manipulation has presumably been carefully followed by many (though some, probably intuitively).

"Fortunately, Chomsky has been given the task of synthesizing and expose these practices, some more obvious and more sophisticated, but apparently all equally effective and, from a certain point of view, demeaning. Encourage stupidity, promote a sense of guilt, promote distraction, or construct artificial problems and then magically, solve them, are just some of these tactics". (Kovačević 2006)[18]

---

[18] Kovačević, Marina (2006) *Noam Chomsky – "10 strategies of manipulation" by the media*. University of Arts, Belgrade.

* 2.1 Discrimination and hate speech in the Spanish media

In an analysis, Media.cat's "Observatori dels discurs discriminatori als mitjans" looked at "*Estratègies del discurs discriminatori als mitjans*" in 2017.[19] It analysed 171 news items on the digital portals of nine media: *La Vanguardia, El País, 20 minutos, Nació Digital, El Español, eldiario.es,* TV3, La Sexta and Telecinco. *El Español* was singled out as being responsible for six of the seven recorded instances of hate speech.

Shortly before Media.cat had published another report, "*Resultats Observatori del discurs d'odi als mitjans de comunicació 2016-2107*".[20] It analysed 308 news items in eight Spain-wide digital media described as having rightist or extreme right-wing profiles: *Alerta Digital, Baluarte Digital, Dolça Catalunya, La Gaceta, Libertad Digital, Mediterráneo Digital, OK Diario* and *Periodista Digital.21* (Note, incidentally, that four of these media were included

---

https://www.academia.edu/24651906/Noam_Chomsky_10_strategies_of_manipulation_by_the_media

[19] *Estratègies del discurs discriminatori als mitjans* . Media.cat. https://www.media.cat/discursodimitjans/estrategies-discurs-discriminatori-als-mitjans/

[20] *Resultats Observatori del Discurs d'Odi als mitjans de comunicació 2016-2017.* Media.cat. https://www.media.cat/discursodimitjans/oo_2017/

[21] The perceived ideological positioning of a number of these media was established by fieldwork in Cardenal, Ana; Cristancho, Camilo; Galais, Carol; Moré, Joaquim & Majó-Vàzquez , Silvia (2018). "El repte de mesurar el biaix ideològic en els mitjans escrits digitals", *Quaderns del CAC* 44, vol. XXI - juliol 2018 https://www.cac.cat/sites/default/files/2019-01/Q44_Cardenal_etal_CA.pdf, Figure 1.

They studied all the tweets sent by people who were MPs in the period 2016-2019 and compared those of PP and Podemos, to extricate the frames each uses, defined by the frequency of use of particular concepts and terms. The frequency of these frames was then calculated for each of the written media. The use of irony and sarcasm tainted the results, and the authors hope artificial intelligence will help to iron these out.

by Fernando Peinado and Daniel Muela (2018)[22] on a list of eight biased, partisan or fake news or blogs or websites that are funded by the Google Display Network: *Periodista Digital*, *OK Diario*, *Esdiario*, *Gaceta*, *Caso Aislado*, *La Tribuna de Cartagena*, *Mediterráneo Digital* y *Digital Sevilla*). These news items were collected between 9 January and 9 February 2017.

The earlier Media.cat report highlighted the following:

- "The interpretation of hate speech that we have applied in this study is not the legal one, which we consider more restrictive, but rather the interpretation shared by human rights and anti-racist organizations.

- **"The eight discursive strategies detected are**: most of them make visible the origin, religion, skin color, ethnicity or culture in news in which this data is not relevant and the random choice of international news items that confirm the prejudices of the medium."[23]

After detecting the above eight strategies being used by these media, one of the conclusions was that...

> "*Periodista Digital* and *Dolça Catalunya* are the ones which convey most explicitly, resorting to insult if necessary, the prejudices and stereotypes of the medium, which correspond to those of the far right. The former uses techniques to compete in the so-called click war, while the latter, at the other extreme, does not even have advertising.

---

[22] Peinado, Fernando & Daniel Muela (2018). "El negocio de la manipulación digital en España. Cómo las páginas de desinformación y propaganda ganan dinero aprovechándose de Google y otras redes de publicidad 'online'", *El País*, 23 May 2018.
https://elpais.com/politica/2018/05/17/actualidad/1526571491_535772.html

[23] *Resultats Observatori del Discurs d'Odi als mitjans de comunicació 2016-2017*. Media.cat. https://www.media.cat/discursodimitjans/oo_2017/

Strategies which contribute to Catalanophobia: The discursive strategies we have detected in this axis are the first, the third, the sixth and seventh."

It ends with tips for journalists and the general public on preventing, and coping with, hate discourses:

> "We have drawn up a list of recommendations aimed at both professional journalists and the general public: we send journalists reflections so that they do not reproduce the practices of the media that we have analysed, while we make proposals to the public to detect, stop and deconstruct the dissemination of discriminatory news."[24]

* 2.2 Media and trust

In many countries, there has been a clear deterioration in the public's level of trust in the practices of the press, and strategies are needed for its restoration in a context of uncertainty (Nigro 2018)[25].

In 2015, the Reuters Institute's "Digital News Report" [26] reported that:

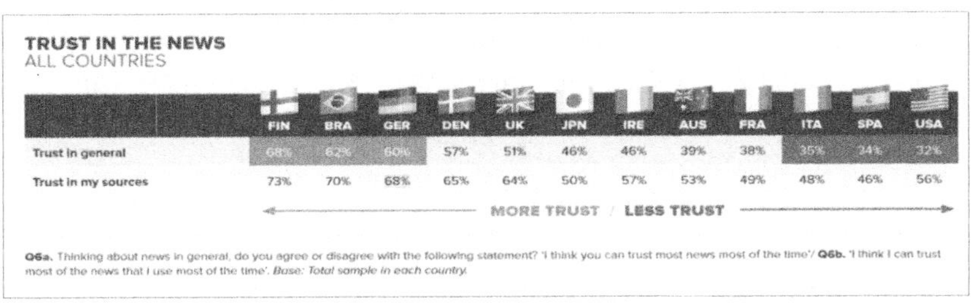

TRUST IN THE NEWS
ALL COUNTRIES

	FIN	BRA	GER	DEN	UK	JPN	IRE	AUS	FRA	ITA	SPA	USA
Trust in general	68%	62%	60%	57%	51%	46%	46%	39%	38%	35%	34%	32%
Trust in my sources	73%	70%	68%	65%	64%	50%	57%	53%	49%	48%	46%	56%

← MORE TRUST / LESS TRUST →

Q6a. Thinking about news in general, do you agree or disagree with the following statement? 'I think you can trust most news most of the time'/ **Q6b.** 'I think I can trust most of the news that I use most of the time'. *Base: Total sample in each country.*

---

[24] op. cit.

[25] Nigro, Patricia María (2018). "Causas de la pérdida de la confianza en la prensa y estrategias para su restablecimiento en un contexto de incertidumbre", *HIPERTEXT.NET,* Número 17, https://raco.cat/index.php/Hipertext/article/view/10.31009-hipertext.net.2018.i17.05/Nigro

[26] Reuters Institute (2015). "*Digital News Report 2015*". https://reutersinstitute.politics.ox.ac.uk/sites/default/files/research/files/Reuters%2520Institute%2520Digital%2520News%2520Report%25202015_Full%2520Report.pdf

"Overall we find significant differences in general trust, with over two-thirds (68%) agreeing that they trusted the media in Finland, compared with only one-third in the United States (32%), Spain (34%), and Italy (35%). Many of the countries with the highest levels of trust also have well-funded public service broadcasters." (p. 12)

The 2018 Reuters Institute's "Digital News Report" [27] reported on the public perception of fake news:

> "Over half (54%) agree or strongly agree that they are concerned about what is real and fake on the internet. This is highest in countries like Brazil (85%), Spain (69%), and the United States (64%) where polarised political situations combine with high social media use. It is lowest in Germany (37%) and the Netherlands (30%) where recent elections were largely untroubled by concerns over fake content."

In the item on the "Proportion that agree the Government should do more to combat misinformation - Selected Markets", Spain's tops the poll with 72% agreeing. "The Catalonia crisis and alleged use of Russian bots", we are told, has escalated the issue with politicians demanding action (p. 20).

> "[I]n Spain the situation is a little different. The weakness of mainstream media has spawned a large range of alternative political websites and blogs, some of which have existed for many years. *Libertad Digital* and *Periodista Digital* follow an anti-Podemos and anti-Catalan independence agenda. Other sites such as *Dolça Catalunya* (3%) and *Directe.cat* (3%) focus exclusively on the Catalan issue but from opposing perspectives. *OK Diario*, which styles itself as the 'website of the nonconformists', has featured in our list of main Spanish online sites for the last few years with 12% weekly reach." (p. 21)

---

[27] Reuters Institute (2018). "*Digital News Report 2018*". https://reutersinstitute.politics.ox.ac.uk/sites/default/files/digital-news-report-2018.pdf

As we shall see, some of these media are on lists of Spanish hate media and notorious disinformers we shall refer to again later.

> [A]cross a number of countries news brand trust differs by type. In the UK, Germany, Denmark, Italy, and Japan, the public service broadcaster is the most trusted type of brand. This is not the case in Spain, where TVE is one of the least trusted brands of those we asked about (5.54 average trust). Spain is also an outlier when it comes to trust in digital-born brands. While in every other country people tend to trust digital-born outlets less, in Spain they are trusted more on average (led by eldiario.es with 5.89 average trust). This is partly because of the low trust for traditional brands and partly because many digital brands in Spain were started by well-known journalists with a strong track record. (p. 41)

The lack of trust in RTVE is particularly marked among people who describe themselves as belonging to the left of the political arc.

Note also that “we observe large variations in brand trust from country to country. Even the lowest ranked Finnish news brands included in this study score higher than almost all Spanish news brands”.

AVERAGE LEVEL OF TRUST IN SELECTED NEWS BRANDS – FINLAND AND SPAIN

FINNISH BRANDS		SPANISH BRANDS	
YLE News	7.91	Antena 3	6.08
Kauppalehti	7.44	LaSexta	6.06
Helsingin Sanomat	7.42	El Pais	5.94
Suomen Kuvalehti	7.34	Cadena SER	5.92
Taloussanomat.f	7.33	Eldiario.es	5.89
Talouselämä	7.33	El Confdencial	5.85
Local Newspapers	7.31	Cuatro	5.84
Regional newspapers	7.27	El Mundo	5.84
MTV News	7.19	20 Minutos	5.78
Hufvudstadsbladet	7.02	El Periodico	5.76
Uusisuomi.f	6.56	La Vanguardia	5.61
Commercial radio news	6.54	TVE	5.54
Free newspapers	6.26	ABC	5.41
Ilta-Sanomat	6.12	COPE	5.32
Iltalehti	6.07	Telecinco	5.25

All in all, then, there is a dire need for the causes for the loss of trust in the practices of the press to be carefully analysed - WhatsApp and Twitter messages are a separate issue, given the very variable reliability of the sources - and for strategies to be developed for its successful restoration in the current context of uncertainty, which is likely to last into the future (Nigro 2018)[28].

* 2.3 What is disinformation?

To discuss the phenomenon of disinformation, a first task is to define it, to distinguish it from other forms of misuse of (in this case) the social media, and to describe its objectives. A paper by Dean Jackson (2017) helps to clarify the issues:[29]

---

[28] Nigro (2018). op. cit.

[29] Jackson, Dean (2017). Distinguishing Disinformation from Propaganda, Misinformation, and “Fake News”. National Endowment for Democracy, 17 October 2017. https://www.ned.org/issue-brief-distinguishing-disinformation-from-propaganda-misinformation-and-fake-new

"Disinformation is a relatively new word. Most observers trace it back to the Russian word *dezinformatsiya*, which Soviet planners in the 1950s defined as "dissemination (in the press, on the radio, etc.) of false reports intended to mislead public opinion." Others suggest that the earliest use of the term originated in 1930s Nazi Germany." (p. 1)

"One popular distinction holds that disinformation also describes politically motivated messaging designed explicitly to engender public cynicism, uncertainty, apathy, distrust, and paranoia, all of which disincentivize citizen engagement and mobilization for social or political change. "Misinformation," meanwhile, generally refers to the inadvertent sharing of false information." (p. 2)

"In the Russian context, observers have described its use to pursue Moscow's foreign policy goals through a "4D" offensive: dismiss an opponent's claims or allegations, distort events to serve political purposes, distract from one's own activities, and dismay those who might otherwise oppose one's goals." (p. 2)

"[A] growing consensus asserts that while the use of disinformation is not new, the digital revolution has greatly enhanced public vulnerability to manipulation by information—a trend which is predicted to continue. In part, these changes have been wrought by the advent of new social media platforms..." (p. 2)

"Fake news' political prominence does have lessons for analysts of disinformation. Fake news draws audiences because it validates their political preconceptions and worldviews, capitalizing on media consumers' confirmation bias. Many argue that because social media curates content according to user preferences, it has a polarizing effect that leaves consumers more vulnerable to manipulation in this way. Political actors have been able to use this to their advantage by producing incendiary content that spreads rapidly through grassroots online networks (some call this “political astroturfing”)." (p. 4)

As to its objectives, we can quote from another paper by Dean Jackson (2018):[30]

> "Disinformation has a wider variety of purposes, in a wider variety of settings, than is commonly appreciated. In the short term, it can be used to distract from an issue, obscure the truth, or to inspire its consumers to take a certain course of action. In the long-term, disinformation can be part of a strategy to shape the information environment in which individuals, governments, and other actors form beliefs and make decisions."

Along with useful ideas to help improve training in media and information literacy, López-Borrull et al. (2018) fear that radical polarisation creates a state of emotional tension that facilitates the spread of fake and manipulated news:

> It was necessary to study whether the radicalization of public opinion at certain times (US election campaign in 2016, Brexit referendum, Catalan referendum of October 1, 2017) generates a state of emotional tension that favours the dissemination of false or insufficiently crosschecked - or even distorted - content.[31]

The growing awareness of the need to monitor and report where necessary the development and spread of what has variously been called “fake news”, “post-truth” and “disinformation” has led to the setting up, in various countries, of organizations devoted to this activity.

---

[30] Jackson, Dean (2018), op.cit.

[31] López-Borrull, Alexandre; Josep Vives-Gràcia Joan & Isidre Badell (2018). “Fake News: ¿Amenaza o oportunidad para los profesionales de la información y la documentación? “ (Fake news, threat or opportunity for information professionals?), *El profesional de la información,* 2018, noviembre-diciembre, v. 27, n. 6: 1346-1356. eISSN: 1699-2407. https://recyt.fecyt.es/index.php/EPI/article/download/epi.2018.nov.17/41620

- FactCheck.org, a project of the Annenberg Public Policy Center of the University of Pennsylvania, "aims to reduce the level of deception and confusion in U.S. politics".

- The Poynter Institute for Media Studies32 (St. Petersburg, Florida), specializes, among other things, in Ethics and fact-checking. In 2017 it set up an International Fact-Checking Network (IFCN),33 which, among other activities, plans to "receive $1 million in funding from YouTube as part of the Google News Initiative (GNI) to support the fact-checking community in its battle against misinformation".34 To date, it has 71 verified signatories of the IFCN "Code of Principles", from many parts of the world, including two fact-checking organisations - to be mentioned in a moment - and a news agency, from Spain.35

- "stopfake.org" is another such organisation. Between September 2016 and October 2017 it hyperlinked to articles and summaries about Catalonia published in Disinfo, *El País*, and to an interesting piece originally published by the Atlantic Council in October 2017 36, on Catalonia and Crimea, from which I shall just quote this significant claim (as a foretaste of this issue, to be covered below): "Clearly", in the author's words,

  > "...the only linkage between Crimea and Catalonia may be the invisible hand of the Kremlin and its

---

[32] https://www.poynter.org/mission-vision/

[33] https://ifcncodeofprinciples.poynter.org/know-more

[34] https://www.poynter.org/fact-checking/2020/ifcn-is-receiving-1-million-from-youtube-to-support-fact-checkers/

[35] https://ifcncodeofprinciples.poynter.org/signatories

[36] Francis, Diane (2017). "The Only Thing Catalonia and Crimea Have in Common Is the Letter C". *UkraineAlert*, October 11 2017. http://www.atlanticcouncil.org/blogs/ukrainealert/the-only-thing-catalonia-and-crimea-have-in-common-is-the-letter-c

This was a response to a Bloomberg piece, "Why Catalonia Will Fail Where Crimea Succeeded" by Russian writer Leonid Bershidsky.

confederates who broke up Ukraine and are interested in destabilizing and atomizing Spain and other western nations".

• The Rand Corporation has located twenty "Tools That Fight Disinformation Online"[37]

In Spain, several fact-checking organisations exist.

> *"El País* and *El Mundo* were the first Spanish partners of The Trust Project, and, while *Público* launched a Transparent Journalism Tool, others focused on various fact-checking initiatives, with Facebook selecting Newtral, Maldita.es, and AFP as partners to identify disinformation in Spanish." (Negredo et al. 2019)[38]

> "Across all countries, the average level of trust in the news in general is down 2 percentage points to 42% and less than half (49%) agree that they trust the news media *they themselves* use. Trust levels in France have fallen to just 24% (-11) in the last year as the media have come under attack over their coverage of the Yellow Vests movement. Trust in the news found via search (33%) and social media remains stable but extremely low (23%)." (Negredo et al. 2019)[39]

- One is Newtral[40], www.newtral.es, which covers both true and fake news on the Covid-19 outbreak, in a slightly disorganised way.

---

[37] https://www.rand.org/research/projects/truth-decay/fighting-disinformation/search.html#q=fact-checking

[38] Negredo, Samuel, Alfonso Vara, Avelino Amoedo, & Elsa Moreno (2019). *Digital News Report. Spain.* http://www.digitalnewsreport.org/survey/2019/spain-2019/

[39] Negredo et al. (2019). op. cit.

[40] www.newtral.es/zona-verificacion/ and

https://www.newtral.es/topic/coronavirus/

- Another is “Maldito Bulo”, www.maldita.es, which was also overwhelmed with fake news when the Covid-19 outbreak hit Spain. Disinformation really took off, and the number of cases burgeoned. One of its founders, Clara Jiménez, told *El País* that since the outbreak began the daily number of reports they receive has risen from about 250 to between 1,500 and 2,000. By April 19, their website had exposed 432 lies connected with the coronavirus, as we shall see later on.41

- A third site, based in Madrid, is the recently-founded Observatorio Europeo de análisis y prevención de la Desinformación (ObEDes), The European Observatory of Analysis and Prevention of Disinformation, https://en.observatorioeuropeodes.org/. It is…

> "...a space for analysis and research on information and disinformation, within the European Union and internationally. The importance of ObEDes lies in the key role that Disinformation and Fake news have on public, economic, business, media, social, cultural and political activity. For this, the observatory has focused on the influence of education as a key tool for prevention, detection and analysis, promoting the development of critical thinking, collaboration and coexistence.”

Oddly enough, it hardly practises what it preaches, given its emergence on the slippery slope of detecting disinformation. We are not told who runs it (just that it has the institutional support of the Universidad Complutense de Madrid, the European Parliament and the European Commission) or how it is funded. According to another of its social media accounts42, there are agreements with the Office of the European Parliament in Spain (October 2019), and with the

---

[41] La pandemia se convierte en ‘infodemia’. La crisis del coronavirus dispara la difusión de bulos. El Gobierno identifica más de un millar. *El País,* 19 APR 2020. https://elpais.com/espana/2020-04-18/la-pandemia-se-convierte-en-infodemia.html

[42] https://es.linkedin.com/in/observatorio-europeo-15986b197

Universidad Complutense. I venture to surmise that someone somewhere will be suspecting that it is secretly funded by Mr. Putin, while someone else will be thinking of Mr. Soros! Its earliest posts are dated October 2019, and its website in 2020, and all we learn is that ObEDes has a "comité de expertos" chaired by a distinguished Partido Popular member and former (until 2019) MEP, Sr. Ramón Luis Valcárcel, "en" (= in) the Universidad Complutense de Madrid.

- An article by Lucía Abellán (2019) informs us that

> "The EU's unit against disinformation, created in 2015 and focusing mostly on campaigns coming from Russia, has already debunked 5,014 falsehoods, 1,166 in the last year alone, according to the database available on euvsdisinfo.eu. A small share of those cases - around 10 in the last 18 months - concern the conflict in Catalonia."[43]

- Catalonia also has a fake check site, Verificat, www.verificat.cat, which states that «We go back to the facts to face up to disinformation».

> "Verificat is the first verification platform in Catalonia. We were born in 2019, coinciding with International Fact-checking Day. We focus on combating disinformation circulating in Catalonia in Catalan and Spanish, and we do so because we want to reach everyone, and also the audience outside this territory that is interested in current affairs in Catalonia, one of the main foci of disinformation in Spain."

Disinformation and misinformation are inseparable, of course, from conspiracy theories. In this respect a Council of

---

[43] Abellán, Lucía (2019). "Spain launches unit to fight disinformation ahead of elections. Group includes experts from National Security Department and seeks to identify cyberterrorism threats", *El País*, 11 March 2019. https://english.elpais.com/elpais/2019/03/11/inenglish/1552290997_611483.html

Europe report by Wardelt and Derakhshan (2017)[44] is highly relevant:

> "We need to understand communication as something beyond just a transmission of messages. People's consumption of news and information is, first and foremost, a way to reaffirm their affinity with a larger dramatic narrative about the world and their place in it, and transcends facts and figures." (p. 76)

> "As D'Ancona underlines, conspiracy theories are effective because they are based on powerful narratives. They unconsciously tap into deep-seated fears. "Veracity will be drowned out unless it is resonant.".[45] There is research that shows that for false information to be challenged effectively, our brains need it to be replaced with an alternative narrative." (p. 76)

Of relevance is their Appendix, "European Fact-checking and Debunking Initiatives", in which they refer to a study published in 2016 by Lucas Graves and Federica Cherubini,[46]

> "There are 34 permanent fact checking operations that exist across 20 European countries. There are two different types: those attached to news organisations (around 40%) and those that operate as nonprofits (around 60%).[47]

---

[44] Wardle, Claire & Hossein Derakhshan (2017). *Toward an interdisciplinary framework for research and policy making*. DGI(2017)09. Council of Europe, Strasbourg. https://rm.coe.int/information-disorder-toward-an-interdisciplinary-framework-for-researc/168076277c

[45] D'Ancona, M. (2017) *Post-Truth*, Ebury Press.

[46] Graves, L.& F. Cherubini (2016). The rise of fact-checking sites in Europe. *Reuters Institute for the Study of Journalism*. http://reutersinstitute.politics.ox.ac.uk/publication/rise-fact-checking-sites-europe

[47] Nyan, B. & J. Reifler (2015) 'Displacing Mis-information about Events: An Experimental Test of Causal Corrections', *Journal of Experimental Political Science*, 2 (1): 81-93.

Much of the following information is drawn from the fact-checking database [48] created by Duke University's Reporter's Lab."

The information in the Appendix about Spain is even more relevant:

"❑ *El Objetivo con Ana Pastor* is a highly rated weekly public affairs programme on the Spanish television network La Sexta, which goes out to between 1.5 and 2 million viewers each Sunday.

❑ *Maldito Bulo* is an online-only fact-checking initiative linked to El Objetivo.

❑ *La Chistera* is a blog published by the data journalism unit at El Confidencial, a commercial digital news service based in Madrid and operated by Titania Compañía Editorial SL."

The Graves & Cherubini paper has useful sets of specific recommendations (pp. 80-85) for different targets, ranging from national governments to grant-making foundations.

Finally, an interesting study based on a survey and on a round table with specialists (Servimedia 2018)[49], on the subject of fake news in Spain, reached a number of sobering conclusions, among which the following:

"The online press (75.7%) is the medium in which, in the opinion of the interviewees, fake news is most likely to be generated. Official websites (55.9%) and the printed press (52.3%) [are] where it is generally considered least likely.

---

[48] https://reporterslab.org/fact-checking/

[49] Servimedia (2018). *Influencia de las noticias falsas en la opinión publica*, Estudio de Comunicación in collaboration with ServiMedia. September 2018. 44 p.
https://www.servimedia.es/sites/default/files/documentos/informe_sobre_fake_news.pdf

For participating journalists, the online press and television (69.2% in both cases) are the media where there is most likelihood of generating fake news. As far as television is concerned, this is the group where there is the greatest distrust, 19 points above the overall average."

Chapter 3. Fake News and Russian influence, a concern in Europe and beyond.

* 3.1 The European Union's actions to counter international disinformation

Let us look now at the European Union's position on disinformation, which is apparently a direct result of fears of Russian interference in the social media. The EU's concern with Russia's disinformation campaigns is documented. In the European Council Conclusions of March 19-20, 2015[50], conclusion 15 stated that:

> "13. The European Council stressed the need to challenge Russia's ongoing disinformation campaigns and invited the High Representative, in cooperation with Member States and EU institutions, to prepare by June an action plan on strategic communication. The establishment of a communication team is a first step in this regard."

The context referred to is the two Minsk Protocols to halt the war in the Donbass region of Ukraine, to be completely implemented by 31 December 2015).

Among the outcomes of this initiative are the Report of the High Level Expert Group (March 12 2018)[51], the European Commission Communication "Tackling online disinformation: a European approach" (26 April 2018)[52], the Council Conclusions of

---

[50] https://www.consilium.europa.eu/media/21888/european-council-conclusions-19-20-march-2015-en.pdf

[51] A multi-dimensional approach to disinformation. Report of the independent High level Group on fake news and online disinformation. March 2018. https://ec.europa.eu/digital-single-market/en/news/final-report-high-level-expert-group-fake-news-and-online-disinformation; http://ec.europa.eu/newsroom/dae/document.cfm?doc_id=50271

[52] 26 April 2018. http://ec.europa.eu/newsroom/dae/document.cfm?doc_id=51804

28 June 2018[53], the *"EU Code of Practice on Disinformation"*[54], opened to signatures in the latter part of 2018, and finally the December 2018 Action Plan. In October 2019, the first CODE OF PRACTICE ON DISINFORMATION ANNUAL REPORTS were published[55]. The Commission had received annual self-assessment reports from the online platforms and technology companies Google, Facebook, Twitter, Microsoft and Mozilla and from the trade association signatories to the Code of Practice detailing policies, processes and actions undertaken to implement their respective commitments under the Code during the Code's first year of operation. We can extract that:

> Google... reported that, between 1 September 2018 and 31 August 2019, it had removed over 10,842,500 YouTube channels for violation of its spam, misleading, and scams policy, and more than 56,500 channels for violation of its impersonation policy.
>
> Twitter... provided figures on actions taken to address spam, malicious automation and fake accounts: between 1 January and 31 August 2019, Twitter pro-actively challenged 126,025,294 accounts platform-wide. Twitter takes enforcement action against approximately 75% of the accounts challenged. In the same timeframe, users submitted some 4,544,096 reports of spam.

The European Union's "fact-checking team", East Stratcom Task Force, set up a website to monitor disinformation and to give guidance on detecting it: https://euvsdisinfo.eu. We shall discuss some of its revelations below.

So Europe has seriously moved towards addressing this issue, even though in the view of some, its interest has come very late:

---

[53] http://www.consilium.europa.eu//media/35936/28-euco-final-conclusions-en.pdf

[54] https://ec.europa.eu/digital-single-market/en/news/code-practice-disinformation

[55] https://ec.europa.eu/digital-single-market/en/news/annual-self-assessment-reports-signatories-code-practice-disinformation-2019

> "When the EU unveiled its Action Plan against Disinformation in December 2018, some experts welcomed the plan as a good first step toward a savvier and better-equipped West. Others, however, believe that the plan came too late and that the European Commission bears the blame for not treating the threat of disinformation with the urgency and gravity it deserved. (Janda 2019[56]

Another portal specifically aimed at Russia is DisinfoPortal.org, an interactive online portal that claims to be a guide to the Kremlin's information war. The portal aggregates open source research and journalism from the United States and Europe and presents it in a user-friendly way, with timely multimedia content produced by the Atlantic Council and its partners explaining Russia's ongoing influence operations. It claims to allow visitors to "Find and connect with experts by country, language, and expertise, view stories, reports, and videos from our partners, and explore in-depth country profiles". Among their experts are David Alandete and Nicolás de Pedro, both of whom we shall meet again later. And the Executive Director of the EU DisinfoLab is Alexandre Alaphilippe. On the website we are informed that ...

> "Russian disinformation has become a problem for European governments. In the last two years, Kremlin-backed campaigns have spread false stories alleging that French President Emmanuel Macron was backed by the "gay lobby," fabricated a story of a Russian-German girl raped by Arab migrants, and spread a litany of conspiracy theories about the Catalan independence referendum, among other efforts. Europe is finally taking action..." (Polyakova & Meserole 2018)[57]

---

[56] Janda, Jacub (2019). "#EUelections2019: The EU Must Take Disinformation Seriously". April 29, 2019 (Updated June 19, 2019). https://disinfoportal.org/euelections2019-the-eu-must-take-disinformation-seriously/

[57] Polyakova, Alina & Chris Meserole (2018). "The West is Ill-Prepared for the Wave of "Deep Fakes" that Artificial Intelligence could Unleash".

We shall discuss below the "litany of conspiracy theories", which turns out to be a list of 14 cases of what EUvsDisinfo regards as fake news that mention Catalonia, some just in passing, and that include sources that have nothing to do with Russia at all (such as an article in the Montreal-based "Centre for Research on Globalization").

There was visible interest in Spain, in the issue of Russia and disinformation, early in 2017, when a researcher at the "Real Instituto Elcano" published a paper (Milosevich-Juaristi 2017).[58]

Yet it hadn't crossed the mind of the same Instituto, in its 19 January 2017 update of its report *"Catalonia's independence bid: how did we get here? What is the European dimension? What next?"* (Real Instituto Elcano 2017)[59] to mention Russia.

In a study on the subject of Russian disinformation, Bodine-Baron et al. (2018: 17)[60] conclude that several needs emerge that cut across multiple links.

- "Establish clear and enforceable norms for acceptable behavior for states' and media entities' behavior on social media platforms.
- Coordinate U.S. executive and legislative branch activities.

---

https://disinfoportal.org/the-west-is-ill-prepared-for-the-wave-of-deep-fakes-that-artificial-intelligence-could-unleash/

[58] Milosevich-Juaristi, Mila (2017). "El poder de la influencia rusa: la desinformación", Real Instituto Elcano, ARI 7/2017. http://www.realinstituto-elcano.org/wps/portal/rielcano_es/contenido?WCM_GLOBAL_CONTEXT=/elcano/elcano_es/zonas_es/ari7-2017-milosevichjuaristi-poder-influencia-rusa-desinformacion

[59] Real Instituto Elcano (2017). "Catalonia's independence bid: how did we get here? What is the European dimension? What next?" https://web.archive.org/web/20180324125003/http://www.realinstitutoelcano.org/wps/portal/rielcano_en/contenido?WCM_GLOBAL_CONTEXT=/elcano/elcano_in/zonas_in/catalonia-dossier-elcano-october-2017

[60] Bodine-Baron, Elizabeth; Todd C. Helmus, Andrew Radin, Elina Treyger (2018). "*Countering Russian Social Media Influence*". Rand Corporation. 86 pp. https://www.rand.org/pubs/research_reports/RR2740.html

- Institute a formal mechanism for information-sharing that includes key players from the U.S. government and private social media companies.
- Increase the transparency of social media platform policies and algorithms for detecting and removing disinformation and malicious behavior. Encourage and fund academia to develop better tools for identifying and attributing disinformation on social media.
- Prioritize defensive activities over punishments to shape Moscow's decision-making.
- Continuously assess the cost and impact of proposed solutions relative to the effectiveness of Russia's activities."

* 3.2 Spain's actions to counter international disinformation

Poynter issued "A guide to anti-misinformation actions around the world" (Funcke & Flamini 2018)61 which covers 52 countries, including Spain, about which it reports as follows:

> "In early March 2018, the National Security Commission of the Congress of Deputies passed a proposal asking the government to take action against misinformation online.
>
> In the non-binding recommendation, the committee requested that the government cooperate with the EU in developing strategies against misinformation...
>
> In November 2018, Russia signed a pact with Spain62 to create a joint cybersecurity group aimed at preventing

---

[61] Funcke, Daniel & Flamini, Daniela (2018). "*A guide to anti-misinformation actions around the world*", Poynter. https://www.poynter.org/ifcn/anti-misinformation-actions/

[62] «Russia and Spain Agree to Cooperate on Cyber Security, Fight Fake News», The Moscow Times, 7 November 2018. https://www.themoscowtimes.com/2018/11/07/russia-and-spain-agree-to-cooperate-on-cyber-security-fight-fake-news-a63417

misinformation from affecting diplomatic relations between the two. The move came after Spanish ministers accused Russia of spreading misinformation about the Catalan referendum."

However, this agreement was acridly criticized by David Alandete (2019)[63] on the DisInfo portal:

"The Russian government scored a goal during their visit to Madrid last November. Foreign minister Sergei Lavrov somehow convinced his host to sign a mutual agreement to jointly fight disinformation. Several months have gone by and the agreement has been largely forgotten. However, the very signing of the agreement in the first place suggests that the Spanish state is unprepared for the ever-increasing threat of Russian hybrid warfare."

Spain has also acted against disinformation and cyberattacks. Note the reason for this action, which Baidez (2018: 18)[64] pointed out:

"In Spain, following the dissemination of false images and news on the day of the illegal referendum on the independence of Catalonia, "the government approved a National Security Strategy that for the first time included as threats cyber attacks and spreading fake news in the social media" (ABC, 2018). The Spanish Congress has recently set up a working group to study the problem in depth and seek solutions. This action has been rejected by

---

[63] Alandete, David (2019), "#EUelections2019: Spanish Weaknesses Against Kremlin Disinformation", Disinfo Portal, 29 April 2019. https://disinfoportal.org/euelections2019-spanish-weaknesses-against-russian-information-warfare/

[64] Baidez Guillen, Jessica Elena (2018) "*Fake News. Evolución, ámbitos de desarrollo y su repercusión en cibermedios nacionales. Casos: El País, El Confidencial, El Diario y Maldita*". Universidad Complutense de Madrid, BA dissertation. https://eprints.ucm.es/48123/1/TFG.pdf

the Federation of Journalist's Associations of Spain (FAPE)." (Prnoticias, 2018)[65].

Baidez merely voiced what was being said in various circles, including the Socialists (in March 2018):

> "The Socialist MP [PSOE spokesman César Luena] has defended that the proliferation of false news in cyberspace is a “reality” and has quoted several political events that have suffered these campaigns around the world: the US elections, Germany and Italy or Brexit. Luena recalled that these disinformation campaigns focused on Catalonia on the occasion of the illegal referendum on October 1 and the action of the State Security Forces". (Alberola 2018)66

This same article also describes the differing opinions of both Catalan pro-independence parties and Unidos-Podemos (at that time, in opposition):

> "The socialist initiative has also been supported by PDeCAT although, through MP Jordi Xuclà, it has questioned the alleged disinformation campaigns in favour of pro-independence interests in Catalonia. In this context, although rejecting the initiative, Unidos Podemos has criticized the PSOE for including fake news in favour of the independence movement and omitting those of the opposing side". Unidos Podemos, which has not voted in favour of the Socialist proposal, has presented its own bill, which has been rejected, to prevent the government from "attacking freedom of

---

[65] Prnoticias (2018). “La FAPE rechaza la creación de una comisión contra las ‘fake news’”, *Prnoticias,* 18 de Diciembre de 2018) https://prnoticias.com/periodismo/periodismo-pr/20166531-comision-fake-news-fape-rechazo

[66] Alberola, Miquel (2018). “El Congreso insta al Gobierno a reforzar los medios para frenar las ‘fake news’. Unidos Podemos rechaza la iniciativa porque ataca la libertad de expresión con la excusa de combatir bulos”, *El País*, 7 MAR 2018, https://elpais.com/politica/2018/03/07/actualidad/1520450353_962234.html

expression under the pretext of confronting opponents." (Alberola 2018)[67]

Daniel Funke and Daniela Flamini reported that

> "Before the April 2019 general election, Spain created a team of about 100 officials to scour social media for potentially false or misleading political posts[68]. It's unclear how that team addressed such posts during the election." (Funke & Flamini (2019)[69]

In a monographic issue on "La posverdad. Seguridad y defensa" of a Ministry of Defence publication, *Cuadernos de Estrategia,* Alfonso Merlos holds that "in general terms, the governments of various countries (including Spain) have been extremely cautious about attributing the authorship of this fake news to Moscow".[70] As we have seen, Spain has been an exception, and its backdown as regards its early accusations of Russian media interference in the Catalan independence referendum was regarded by Alandete as a humiliation. Indeed, Merlos makes the same affirmation:

> "Russia has actively intervened in the media and social networks through mechanisms for spreading false news in all relevant political processes in recent years, including the Catalan independence process".

We shall devote a whole section to alleged Russian interference in the Catalan independence process.

---

[67] Alberola (2018). op. cit.

[68] See Associated Press (2019). Spain fights cyberattacks, fake news ahead of key elections. *Fox News*, 15 March 2019. https://www.foxnews.com/world/spain-fights-cyberattacks-fake-news-ahead-of-key-elections

[69] Funke, Daniel & Daniela Flamini (2019). *A guide to anti-misinformation actions around the world.* Poynter. https://www.poynter.org/ifcn/anti-misinformation-actions/

[70] Merlos, Alfonso (2018). "La posverdad. Seguridad y defensa", *Cuadernos de Estrategia*, p. 83-106. Spanish Ministry of Defence. http://www.ieee.es/Galerias/fichero/cuadernos/CE_197.pdf

Over a year later, in March 2019, Spain was reported as officially continuing to voice its interest in countering cyberattacks and disinformation.

> "Spain fights cyberattacks, fake news ahead of key elections. Spain is joining Europe-wide efforts to fight disinformation and online sabotage with new resources ahead of elections" [...] "Spanish deputy prime minister, Carmen Calvo, announced Friday that the government has readied protocols to shield the April 28 general election from cyberattacks. That will take place one month before the May 26 European election" [...] "Calvo also said the government would fight intentionally misleading or wrongful information before, during or after voting".[71]

The Catalonia-Spain crisis first reached the table of the EU Council of Ministers on November 13 2017, a few days after the Spanish government had (without any legal basis, or even the green light of the Council of State, which is usually consulted on all significant political initiatives) established direct rule in Catalonia, dissolving the Catalan Parliament and (shortly afterwards) indicting and in nine cases imprisoning without bail the Government and a couple of social movement leaders.

> "The head of Spanish diplomacy, Alfonso Dastis, this Monday denounced before the other European partners the interference of the propaganda machinery of Russia and Venezuela in Catalonia. [It is] an interference based on the dissemination through social media of fake and manipulating messages in support of secessionists, with the aim of destabilizing the 1-O referendum."[72]

---

[71] Op. Cit.

[72] Sanhermelando, Juan (2017). "España denuncia en la UE la interferencia de Rusia en la crisis catalana. El ministro de Exteriores, Alfonso Dastis, dice que el Gobierno tiene datos de "manipulación" y "desinformación" desde

Spain's public accusations against Russia in relation to disinformation during the Catalan independence referendum explain why…

> "Russia and Spain Agree to Cooperate on Cyber Security, Fight Fake News *(in early November 2018)* [...] Spanish ministers said last November..." [73] that Russian-based groups had used online social media to heavily promote Catalonia's independence referendum in an attempt to destabilize Spain. Russian Foreign Minister Sergei Lavrov has dismissed the allegations as "hysteria."" [74]

This was regarded as a victory for Russia:

> "The Russian government scored a goal during their visit to Madrid last November. Foreign minister Sergei Lavrov somehow convinced his host to sign a mutual agreement to jointly fight disinformation."[75]

---

redes situadas en Moscú", *El Español,* 13 noviembre, 2017. https://www.elespanol.com/mundo/europa/20171113/261724021_0.html

[73] Reuters (2017). "Russia's Lavrov says allegations of meddling in Catalonia hysteria: Ifax". Reuters, 15 November 2017. https://www.reuters.com/article/us-spain-politics-catalonia-russia/russias-lavrov-says-allegations-of-meddling-in-catalonia-hysteria-ifax-idUSKBN1DF1AG

[74] Moscow Times (2017). "Russia and Spain Agree to Cooperate on Cyber Security, Fight Fake News", Moscow Times, 7 NOV 2017. https://www.themoscowtimes.com/2018/11/07/russia-and-spain-agree-to-cooperate-on-cyber-security-fight-fake-news-a63417

See also Emmott, Robin (2017). "Spain sees Russian interference in Catalonia separatist vote". Reuters, 13 NOV 2017. https://www.reuters.com/article/us-spain-politics-catalonia-russia/spain-sees-russian-interference-in-catalonia-separatist-vote-idUSKBN1DD20Y

[75] Alandete, David (2019)."#EUelections2019: Spanish Weaknesses Against Kremlin Disinformation". https://disinfoportal.org/euelections2019-spanish-weaknesses-against-russian-information-warfare/.

"David Alandete is the US correspondent for the Spanish newspaper ABC."

Some Catalan politicians, such as Ramon Tremosa MEP hotly denied such interference:

> "Ramon Tremosa, the EU lawmaker for the PDeCat party of Catalan separatist leader Carles Puigdemont, repeated on Monday that Russian interference had played no part in the referendum.
>
> "Those that say Russia is helping Catalonia are those that have helped the Russian fleet in recent years, despite the EU's boycott," Tremosa tweeted, referring to Spanish media reports that Spain was allowing Russian warships to refuel at its ports." (Emmott 2017).

Foreign Minister Dastis' claim about Russian interference in the independence process was the result of a concerted effort by people attached to the IfS (namely, Nicolás de Pedro), to the Madrid daily, *El País* (particularly, its deputy director David Alandete), and to the Real Instituto Elcano thanks to the timely contribution of Mira Milosevich-Juaristi, who conveniently (for the Spanish government) published a paper on what she saw as Russian involvement on November 7, a mere six days before the above-mentioned European Council meeting. And at 13:28 CET on the very same day of the Council meeting *El País* published in Spanish and English a text by David Alandete, "How the Russian meddling machine won the online battle of the illegal referendum"[76] in which we have to be grateful, at least, for his opinion that

> "A number of minority media outlets linked to Russia, such as *El Espía Digital*, which published stories from RT and Sputnik, have published stories that state, with no

[76] Alandete, David (2017). "La maquinaria rusa ganó la batalla 'online' del referéndum il·legal." *El País*, 13 NOV 2017 - 11:53 CET https://elpais.com/politica/2017/11/12/actualidad/1510500844_316723.html

https://english.elpais.com/elpais/2017/11/12/inenglish/1510478803_472085.html

El País has a sepcial permenent section on "Russian interference in Catalonia": https://elpais.com/agr/la_injerencia_rusa_en_cataluna/a

> convincing proof, that [George] Soros is financing the Catalan independence movement."

Alandete quotes in his article a paper published just a few weeks earlier by The Integrity Initiative (IfS), which shoved more ammunition in the same direction: "Framing Russian meddling in the Catalan question" (from which Alandete or his translator perhaps took a liking to the handy word "meddling").[77] Though the author does not figure on the text, this document (later leaked) would seem to be written by a Spanish-speaking hand - who knows if Nicolás de Pedro himself? It is certainly in the same visual style as his latest diatribe I shall mention later.

The international prestige of *El País*, built up over a period of decades; for example, a paper by Dean Jackson (2018) clearly bases his arguments on the position of *El País*:[78]

> "The Russian Federation stands out as the paramount example. Even a partial list of elections where Russian-produced or -supported disinformation has featured includes the French, German, and American elections in 2016 and 2017; the 2018 Czech presidential election; and the 2017 vote on Catalonian secession from Spain. In each of these cases, Moscow used a combination of state-owned international news outlets, smaller news sites linked to Moscow, and automated social media accounts, sometimes in tandem with leaks of stolen documents and communications."

As might be suspected, this reference to Catalonia is linked to an *El País* article, not long before McGrath shot the newspaper's evidence down in flames, as we shall see below.

---

[77] https://www.stopfake.org/content/uploads/2017/12/Framing-Russian-meddling-in-the-Catalan-question.compressed.pdf

[78] Jackson, Dean (2018). Issue Brief: How Disinformation Impacts Politics and Publics, National Endowment for Democracy, 29 May 2018. https://www.ned.org/issue-brief-how-disinformation-impacts-politics-and-publics/

Why *El País* jumped on the hobby-horse against Russia is a mystery, though the following claim allows one to conjecture an explanation:

> "Until 2016, Russia's propaganda network used Western media, including *El País,* to disseminate information favourable to the Kremlin's commercial and political interests. It did so through the joint printing and distribution of supplements that were sold monthly with *El País*. The newspaper of the Prisa group made a lot of money through this collaboration." (*El Diario* 2018)[79]

Not all the analysis in this field has been in written form. There have also been Seminars, such as the pompous-sounding one organised in Madrid on 31 January 2018 by the "European Council on Foreign Relations", an institution part-funded by governments and by the Soros foundation: "Disinformation, authoritarian fellow travelers & post-truth unbound".[80] The affiliation of the attendants is significant, as we shall later see: *El País,* CIDOB, ECFR, Real Instituto Elcano, London School of Economics.

Desperate to find concrete evidence - beyond mere idle speculation, which should be easy to shoot down in the courts - as regards a Russian link with the Catalan independence movement, Spain swooped onto Víctor Terradellas, director of a Foundation, Catalunya Món (López-Fonseca 2019) [81].

> "In Spain, the Civil Guard has found links between Russia and one of the Catalan separatists implicated in the

---

[79] El Diario (2017). El Kremlin pagó a El País y a otros medios por difundir propaganda rusa hasta 2016, *El Diario*, 20 November 2017. https://www.el-diario.es/rastreador/Rusia-Pais-medios-difundir-propa-ganda_6_710139001.html

[80] https://www.ecfr.eu/events/event/seminario_disinformation_authoritarian_fellow_travelers_post_truth_unbound

[81] López-Fonseca, Óscar (2019). "Spain's High Court opens investigation into Russian spying unit in Catalonia. Judge Manuel García-Castellón is probing whether an elite military group known as Unit 29155 carried out actions aimed at destabilizing the region during the separatist push", El País, 21 November 2019. https://english.elpais.com/elpais/2019/11/21/inenglish/1574324886_989244.html

secession drive: Víctor Terradellas, the former minister[82] of international relations from the now-dissolved political party the Democratic Convergence of Catalonia (CDC), and a very close associate of ousted Catalan premier Carles Puigdemont. Terradellas is under investigation for diverting subsidies from the Catalan regional government and Barcelona province. [83] Terradellas advised Puigdemont on international relations, pressured him to declare independence in Catalonia and also sent Puigdemont numerous WhatsApp messages.

"In a chat on October 26 - the day when the former premier had to decide whether to call new regional elections or declare independence - Terradellas suggested that Puigdemont should meet with him. He also told the former premier that an emissary of Russian President Vladimir Putin had confirmed that Russia would support a declaration of Catalan independence. When Puigdemont did not reply to the message, Terradellas sent another saying: "You haven't even listened to us. I think we deserved it." Puigdemont later said that declaring independence "could be devastating" for Catalonia, to which Terradellas replied that the emissary had "guaranteed" that former Russian leader Mikhail Gorbachev would back the declaration."

In another intercepted WhatsApp chat he jocularly claimed that the Russians were willing to send 10,000 troops to Catalonia! I am not in a position to judge whether all this is fake news, information leaked from a *sub judice* police investigation, or obtained through legally acceptable channels. What is objectively

[82] This is an incorrect translation. Political parties do not have "ministers" in their structure. He was presumably an advisor ("conseller" in Catalan, the same word used for referring to ministers).

[83] He hotly denied such claims, in an interview with *La Vanguardia*, on 26 November 2019. "Víctor Terradellas niega haber desviado fondos para financiar ni la vida de Puigdemont en Waterloo ni el 1-O". https://www.lavanguardia.com/politica/20191126/471878692424/victor-terradellas-niega-desvio-fondos-puigdemont-waterloo-referendum.html

clear is that this operation, called Operación Volhov", (Volkhov is a Russian river and city) received derisory and sarcastic comments not only from the Russian Embassy but also in many quarters, not just in Catalonia itself. Jon Inarritu MP was among them.[84]

Note that *El País* "adheres to The Trust Project", which explains that…

> "The Trust Project, a consortium of top news companies led by award-winning journalist Sally Lehrman, is developing transparency standards that help you easily assess the quality and credibility of journalism. Our original launch partners include the *dpa* news agency, *The Economist*, The Globe and Mail, Hearst Television, the Independent Journal Review, Haymarket Media, Institute for Nonprofit News, Italy's La Repubblica and La Stampa, Reach Plc and The Washington Post." "The El País website is among the first to display and test the Trust indicators".[85]

Ironically, perhaps, *El País* itself has been the focus of doubts on issues of trust: on October 27 2017 (the exact date is significant) Herman wrote about the sacking of John Carlin (after he published an essay (Carlin, 2017)[86] in another European paper, *The Times*, openly criticizing the Spanish government's hardline strategy to quash Catalonia's secession - which he himself would be sad to witness). Joan B. Culla and Francesc Serés also stopped contributing to the paper, amid claims that the unionist-leaning editors had

---

[84] CCMA (2020). "La xarxa es mofa de la suposada connexió entre l'independentisme i Rússia", CCMA, 29 October 2020 https://www.ccma.cat/324/la-xarxa-es-mofa-de-la-suposada-connexio-entre-lindependentisme-i-russia/noticia/3056186/

[85] https://thetrustproject.org/

[86] Carlin, John. (2017). "Catalan independence: arrogance of Madrid explains this chaos. Three centuries of Catalan grievances came to a head this week, but the intransigence of Spain's government is ultimately to blame for the crisis". *The Times,* 7 October 2017. https://www.thetimes.co.uk/article/catalan-independence-arrogance-of-madrid-explains-this-chaos-vmh7nnxsx

"censored" their criticisms. "Suspicion of El País", writes Mark Herman, "has left much of Spain and Spanish readers without a place to read even modestly neutral coverage of the complex Catalan crisis".

> "That sort of opacity in Spanish media, the newly sharp tone of El País' Catalan coverage, and events like star reporter Carlin's oddly-timed sacking, have only fueled the widely-held perception in Spain that El País is having its strings pulled. But the claims remain at best circumstantial."[87]

Earlier that very week, as Herman tells us, another long-standing *El País* contributor, Catalan political scientist Jordi Matas, said he had had an opinion piece blocked, and implied it had to do with the Catalan crisis. The paper's managing editor, David Alandete acknowledged that Spain's leading newspaper had positioned itself as a strong voice against Catalan secession — but that the paper's reporters were defending the Spanish constitution, not towing a government line. "We do not take the stance [that there is] a right to self-determination or the freedom to choose [to secede]", Herman reports him as saying. We can already see the key role Alandete and *El País* have tried to play in the campaign against Catalan independence.

[87] Herman, Marc (2017). Spain's most famous paper stumbles amid Catalonia independence crisis", *Columbia Journalism Review*, October 27 2017. https://www.cjr.org/business_of_news/catalonia-independence-el-pais-spain.php

Chapter 4. The Catalan independence process and Spain's foreign policy.

For lack of space we shall not give an overview of Catalonia's independence process, though politically rooted for well over a century. Readers can find many such introductions, which often include reasons sustaining the pro-independence discourse, including Castro (2012)[88], Strubell (2016, 2019a, 2019b)[89], Dowling (2017)[90], Miley & Garvías (2019)[91]. Suffice it to recall a remark made in one of these papers (Strubell 2019a):

---

[88] Castro, Liz (2012). "194 Reasons for Catalan Independence #raons (and counting)". Blog. 2 Octubre 2012 (updated 5 October 2012). http://www.newscatalonia.com/2012/10/reasons-for-catalan-independence-raons.html

[89] Strubell, M. (2016). "The Catalan Independence Process and Cold Repression (2003-2016)". *Treatises and Documents. Journal of Ethnic Studies*, 77 (2016): 5–31. http://www.inv.si/DocDir/Publikacije-PDF/Razprave%20in%20gradivo/RIG%2077/RIG_77_final_2.pdf

Strubell, M. (2019a). The Whys and Wherefores of Spain's Current Political Crisis: Catalonia... Again. *IAFOR Journal of Cultural Studies, 4* (1). https://doi.org/10.22492/ijcs.4.1.02 http://iafor.org/archives/journals/iafor-journal-of-cultural-studies/10.22492.ijcs.4.1.02.pdf

Strubell, M. (2019b). So What's the Endgame Now in Catalonia? International Policy Digest, 20 December 2019. https://intpolicydigest.org/2019/12/20/so-what-s-the-endgame-now-in-catalonia/

[90] Dowling, Andrew (2017). "*The rise of Catalan independence: Spain's territorial crisis*". Federalism Studies, Abingdon and New York: Routledge. DOI: 10.4324/9781315570969. https://www.researchgate.net/publication/323110892_The_rise_of_catalan_independence_Spain%27s_territorial_crisis

[91] Miley, Thomas J. & Roberto Garvía (2019). "Conflict in Catalonia: A Sociological Approximation", *Genealogy*, 3, 56; doi:10.3390/genealogy3040056. https://www.mdpi.com/2313-5778/3/4/56/pdf

> "The motives for wanting independence (beyond the universal fact that all peoples have the right to freely determine their political future) and its probable consequences have been explained and discussed in literally hundreds of books and articles, and thousands of local debates and lectures, including hundreds abroad. As meticulously explained in a recent paper, the motives are much closer to a Lockean revolution of the US kind, than to an ethnic one (Vidal-Aparicio 2015)92. Many, many Catalans of whatever origin or language background, want good and fair governance."

This has been acknowledged even by opponents of Catalan independence:

> "The Catalan independence movement stopped using certain concepts long since, and has sponsored others. The nation is no longer so useful, now it is better to talk about the people, which has a more mundane nuance, or about identity, that is something that includes us all, even the *soi-disant* citizens of the world. Language, culture and history, which used to be at the heart of the discourse, have given way to the economy, strategic interests and opportunity costs. Talking about the right to self-determination sounds old-fashioned, it is a right of peoples, an abstract right, it is much better to talk about the right to decide; people decide, I may not be recognized as part of a certain people, but I am a person, as a person I can decide, I have the right to decide. The independence movement now uses economic, financial arguments; arguments of logic and efficiency; it has gone from nationality to rationality. And so concepts are used, as threads: freedom, democracy, aspirations, future…

---

[92] Vidal-Aparicio , Oriol (2015). "Catalonia and the United States: Two Lockean Revolutions 240 Years Apart". Blog post. https://catalunyapqespanya.wordpress.com/2015/04/21/catalonia-and-the-united-states-two-lockean-revolutions-240-years-apart/

and the cognitive framework is woven." (Mezquida 2014)93

As soon as Spain realised that Catalonia's bid for a referendum to decide on its independence was in earnest, the Spanish Government put in place an interdepartmental strategy to foil it by any means other than at the polls. In addition, it adopted a strict no-negotiation strategy from start to finish, refusing to contemplate any kind of referendum, binding or consultative, as many as 17 times… as of May 2017 (CCMA 2017).[94]

The interdepartmental strategy fitted in well with this summary: "To negotiate is to lose. All or nothing. This is how politics works in Spain" (Martínez 2019)[95]. Among its early efforts were the spread of disinformation on three alleged consequences of Catalonia's hypothetical independence: (1) Spaniards living in Catalonia would lose their Spanish ; (2) Pensioners in Catalonia would lose their (Spanish) pensions; and (3) the Catalan economy would collapse by up to 25% of GDP. Some of these claims were utterly false. As to the third one, Ayadi et al (2015)[96] concluded that

---

[93] Mezquida, Amadeu (2014). "España contra media España ". *El Diario*, 1 January 2014. https://www.eldiario.es/cv/opinion/Espana-media_6_213188688.html

[94] CCMA (2017). "17 "nos" en 5 anys: la negativa del govern espanyol a negociar el referèndum" Corporació Catalana de Mitjans Audiovisuals, 21 May 2017. https://www.ccma.cat/324/17-nos-en-5-anys-la-negativa-del-govern-espanyol-a-negociar-el-referendum/noticia/2789954/

[95] Martínez, Antonio (2020). "Bloqueo e incertidumbre: así ve la situación política de España el partido de Merkel. "Negociar es perder. Así funciona la política en España". Un demoledor informe del think tank ligado a la CDU de Merkel destaca la polarización, las mentiras y la incertidumbre". *El Confidencial*, 19 Februaruy 2019. https://www.elconfidencial.com/mundo/europa/2019-02-19/bloqueo-e-incertidumbre-asi-ve-la-situacion-politica-de-espana-el-partido-de-merkel_1834526/

[96] Ayadi, Rym; Leonidas Paroussos, Kostas Fragkiadakis, Stella Tsani, Pantelis Capros, Carlo Sessa, Riccardo Enei and Marc Gafarot (2015). Scenarios of Macro-economic Development for Catalonia on Horizon 2030. "*Economic effects of a potential secession of Catalonia from Spain and paths*

> "In view of the macro economic assessment of the scenarios of Catalonia as an independent state under mutual agreement or unilateral secession assumptions in horizon 2030, the study points to the macro-economic unsustainability of the status-quo scenario from growth and employment perspectives due to the high and sustained deficit of Catalonia.
>
> In the short run uncertainty, high interest rates and a volatile investment environment triggered by the decision to secede is found to slow the Catalan GDP growth rate; the effect is ore pronounced if the decision to secede is unilateral. However the structure of the Catalan economy and the pursuit of fiscal policy towards a balanced public budget can deliver higher than the reference GDP and employment growth rates, once the transition period to sovereignty is over." (Ayadi et al 2015, p. 16)

There was no gnashing of teeth or apologies on the Unionist side when these three false claims were shot down in flames, even though Prime Minister Rajoy made a fool of himself in front of the TV cameras during an interview in the first of these three assertions (Paradinas 2015)[97] (and this falsehood was still being churned out, alongside the other, two years later! (Centeno 2017)[98]. The second was defended by a Minister:

> "The Minister of Employment and Social Security, Fátima Báñez, decided to send a message of "calm and

---

for integration with the EU". Final Report. CIDOB. https://www.vilaweb.cat/media/continguts/000/104/312/312.pdf

[97] Paradinas, Marcos (2015). "Rajoy, en ridículo al demostrar su desconocimiento de la ley. Vea como Carlos Alsina pone al presidente del Gobierno contra las cuerdas", 22 September 2015. https://www.elplural.com/autonomias/cataluna/rajoy-en-ridiculo-al-demostrar-su-desconocimiento-de-la-ley_27039102

[98] Centeno, Roberto (2017). "El gran engaño del separatismo: perderían un tercio del PIB", *El Confidencial*, 18 SEP 2017. https://blogs.elconfidencial.com/economia/el-disparate-economico/2017-09-18/cataluna-independencia-economia_1445015/

> confidence" to the 1.5 million Catalan pensioners yesterday, but also warned of the risks of breaking the single fund in a region that accumulates 25% of the deficit in Spain. "No one is going to jeopardize their present and their future. Pensioners will receive their payments thanks to the solidarity guarantee of the single fund." she said." (Alcelay 2017)[99]

Catalans countered on several fronts: Tomàs (2017) [100] mentions several.

Significantly, the minister put at the helm of this initiative by the Partido Popular government was not the Interior Minister, or the Justice Minister, or the Minister for Regional Affairs, but José Manuel García-Margallo, minister for Foreign Affairs from 2011 to 2016. Sr. García-Margallo's diplomatic activity to counter the international impact of the Catalan independence process was intense. He had the consuls (several honorary) of Latvia, the Philippines, Bulgaria and Finland withdrawn, and his Socialist successor did the same with the Greek consul. In all these cases it was claimed they were not neutral in their political position (Faus 2019)[101]

As an example, Latvia's acquiescence before Spain's repression of Catalonia was bought for €63 million (almost as much as the pseudo-military operation by Spanish police, which cost €87 million), as

---

[99] Alcelay, Susana (2017). "Cataluña gasta en pensiones casi 4.700 millones más de lo que cotiza. La independencia haría perder a la región más de 250.000 empleos, lo que afectaría de lleno a la caja de las pensiones y a su déficit", *ABC*, 18 September 2017, https://www.abc.es/economia/abci-cataluna-gasta-pensiones-casi-4700-millones-mas-cotiza-201709182216_noticia.html

[100] Tomás, Nicolas (2017). "Los expertos sostienen que las pensiones están más garantizadas en una Catalunya independiente", *El Nacional*, 11 June 2017. https://www.elnacional.cat/es/politica/pensionistas-catalunya-autonomica-referendum_165162_102.html

[101] Faus, Joan (2019). "L'estrès de ser diplomàtic a Barcelona". *El País*, 9 August 2019.
https://cat.elpais.com/cat/2019/08/04/catalunya/1564940351_781295.html

revealed by *Público* (del Castillo 2018). 102 This fact openly contradicts the oft-repeated claim that the Catalan conflict (generally referred to as a "desafío", a challenge, not as a "problem") is a strictly internal affair (as Rajoy told Frau Merkel in October 2017). Castan Pinos & Sacramento (2019, 2020)[103] have summarised Spain's counter-paradiplomatic activity in the period 2012-2017.

Nevertheless, no-one doubts that the way Spain has managed the Spain-Catalonia conflict has damaged its international prestige:

> "Spain aspires to play a more assertive and influential role in the integration process for the legislature that starts after the election of a new European Parliament. This ambition is favoured by a number of objective factors but is also hampered by internal political instability and, above all, by the Catalan conflict." […] "Without having to dramatize the gravity of the matter, it is clear that the issue has damaged the image of Spain in the EU (largely due to lack of information or the bias with which it has been received)". (Molina & Martín 2019)[104]

---

[102] Del Castillo, Carlos (2018). El silencio de Letonia sobre Catalunya que Rajoy compró con tropas costó 63 millones», *Público,* 17 January 2018. https://www.publico.es/politica/silencio-letonia-catalunya-rajoy-compro-tropas-costo-63-millones.html

[103] Castan Pinos, Jaume & Sacramento, J. (2019). "L'Etat contre-attaque: un examen de la contra-paradiplomatie espagnole en Catalogne (2012-2017)", *Relations Internationales* 179 (3): 95-111. https://www.academia.edu/40688683/_L_Etat_contre-attaque_un_examen_de_la_contra-paradiplomatie_espagnole_en_Catalogne_2012-2017_

Castan Pinos, Jaume & Jeremy Sacramento (2020). "La contra-paradiplomàcia, fase superior de la diplomàcia espanyola", *Pensem.cat* website, 13 de febrer de 2020. https://www.pensem.cat/noticia/77/contra-paradiplomacia/fase/superior/diplomacia/espanyola?rlc=an

[104] Molina, Ignacio & Natalia Martín (2019) "La crisis catalana y la influencia de España en Bruselas". *Real Instituto Elcano*, ARI 42/2019, 25 APR 2019. http://www.realinstitutoelcano.org/wps/portal/rielcano_es/contenido?WCM_GLOBAL_CONTEXT=/elcano/elcano_es/zonas_es/politicaexteriorespanola/

Intense diplomatic activity aimed at pre-empting the Catalan government's efforts to explain its case abroad include the then-president of the European Commission Jean-Claude Juncker's refusal to meet president Puigdemont, or a similar rebuff by the UK government. The same source[105] explained that the then-deputy prime minister Soraya Sáenz de Santamaría was carrying out a "pedagogical" task with the foreign correspondents resident in Spain. It was widely rumoured at the time the plane that President Artur Mas was to take to New York to meet US government officials in Washington, and politicians, was held up for an unprecedented five hours by the Spanish authorities, so that his agenda would be thoroughly derailed.[106] Endless efforts were made to try and block seminars on the independence process in academic fora throughout the world, as early as 2014[107]: Lisbon[108], Sweden[109], Paris, Copenhagen[110], Mexico[111], etc. Even a book launch in Utrecht was

---

ari42-2019-molina-martin-la-crisis-catalana-y-la-influencia-de-espana-en-bruselas

[105] "Moragas y Margallo ponen freno al desafío independentista con reuniones de alto nivel en el exterior", OK Diario, 14 May 2016. https://okdiario.com/espana/viernes-noche-moragas-margallo-coordinan-reuniones-altos-cargos-exterior-contrarrestar-generalitat-134770

[106] https://www.nuvol.com/llibres/vicent-partal-i-marta-rojals-entre-els-mes-venuts-de-no-ficcio-per-sant-jordi-25337

[107] Homs afirma que a l'estranger "no entenen per què a Catalunya no ens deixen votar". *El Punt Avui,* 26 February 2014. http://www.elpuntavui.cat/politica/article/17-politica/720223-homs-afirma-que-a-lestranger-no-entenen-per-que-a-catalunya-no-ens-deixen-votar.html

[108] https://comunicacio.e-noticies.cat/pressions-contra-el-proces-sobiranista-a-portugal-83860.html

[109] Debat europeu a Suècia sobre "el procés" tot i la pressió de la diplomacia espanyola per impedir-lo. https://www.llibertat.cat/2016/07/les-institucions-europees-organitzen-un-debat-sobre-el-cas-catala-a-suecia-35665/Imprimir

[110] "Un diputat danès reconeix pressions espanyoles per frenar la visita de Carles Puigdemont". *Nació Digital,* 24 January 2018. https://www.naciodigital.cat/noticia/147260/diputat/danes/reconeix/pressions/espanyoles/frenar/visita/carles/puigdemont

[111] "Puigdemont denuncia pressions espanyoles per impedir la seva assistència a un acte a Mèxic". 5 April 2019.

torpedoed by the Spanish embassy: a historical novel set in the 18th century, and published in Spanish! [112] In March 2017, President Puigdemont said of Spain's pressure against the process, in Washington, that it had been evident "for a long, long time" and that "Countries are free and take their own decisions" (Ferragutcasas 2017)[113].

We mentioned earlier Spain's concern about Kosovo. Spain's FM of the day, Josep Borrell, (himself a Catalan) has claimed the following (Europa Press 2019)[114]:

> "Borrell said in Belgrade that the cases of Catalonia and Kosovo are not comparable.
>
> The Minister of Foreign Affairs, the EU and Cooperation, Josep Borrell, stated this Wednesday in Belgrade, together with his Serbian counterpart, that the situation in Catalonia is not comparable to the case of Kosovo. "Those comparisons fall on deaf ears, they have no weight, although supporters of Catalonia's independence like them", he told a news conference with Ivica Dacic, whom he met during his visit to Serbia."

Incidentally, it is ironic (or conveniently forgotten) that the Tribunal de Cuentas (in itself widely accused of nepotism and lack of transparency) mentions a Catalan Government Memorandum

---

https://www.naciodigital.cat/noticia/176989/puigdemont/denuncia/pressions/espanyoles/impedir/seva/assistencia/acte/mexic

[112] VilaWeb (2014). "La presentació de 'Victus' als Països Baixos, suspesa per pressions de l'ambaixada espanyola", VilaWeb, 4 September 2014. https://www.vilaweb.cat/noticia/4209435/20140904/presentacio-victus-paisos-baixos-suspesa-pressions-lambaixada-espanyola.html

[113] Ferragutcasas, Núria(2017). "Puigdemont, sobre les pressions d'Espanya contra el procés: "Els països són lliures i prenen les seves decisions. El president de la Generalitat afirma a Washington que les pressions "es noten des de fa molt i molt de temps" i que, tot i així, "nosaltres som aquí i el món sap com ha d'actuar"", *Ara,* 28 March 2017. https://www.ara.cat/politica/Puigdemont-pressions-dEspanya-lliures-decisions-independencia_0_1767423464.html

[114] Europa Press. «Borrell afirma en Belgrado que los casos de Cataluña y Kosovo no son comparables». *Europa Press,* 13 MAR 2019.

("No. 5") entitled "Cataluña no es Crimea" in a long report on Catalonia's activities abroad, issued on March 28 2019[115] which also mentions documents published in "Czechoslovakian" (sic).

This position as regards Kosovo has been repeated many times by successive Spanish governments of differing political persuasions. A year earlier PM Rajoy had played his cards carefully so that his name would not be included in a European Council statement on Kosovo.

> "The Spanish diplomacy has vetoed a joint statement that the European Union intended to sign with the countries of that region at the summit to be held in less than a month in Bulgaria. The reasons have little to do with EU foreign policy. It is a question of preventing Mariano Rajoy's name from appearing in the same document as that of the leader of Kosovo, which Spain does not recognize as a country. Following the Spanish blockade, Europe will attend a meeting with a statement issued exclusively by the European leaders, not including the Balkans."[116]

One may ask oneself, therefore: (1) why is Spain one of only five EU member States (alongside Greece, Cyprus - both with a Greek Orthodox majority, like Serbia -, Slovakia and Romania), not to have recognised Kosovo as an independent state? The answer is

---

[115] Tribunal de Cuentas (2019). Informe Nº 1.319. *Informe de fiscalización relativa al destino dado a los recursos asignados a la ejecución de las políticas de acción exterior de la comunidad autónoma de Cataluña, correspondientes a los ejercicios 2011-2017.* March 28 2019. 465 pp. plus annexes. https://www.tcu.es/repositorio/7b967dfb-a08f-493e-a159-a7cb7d1c4071/I1319.pdf

"Among the documents of some delegations a leaflet promoting Catalonia was found at least in English and Czechoslovakian"... " In the Austrian delegation there is evidence that 487,20 euros were paid in 2017 for the printing of this leaflet in Czechoslovakian (sic)."

[116] "España veta una declaración europea por incluir a Kosovo. La equiparación que tratan de hacer algunas fuerzas independentistas con Cataluña inquieta al Ejecutivo de Rajoy". 22 ABR 2018. El País, https://elpais.com/politica/2018/04/22/actualidad/1524410681_427374.html

crystal clear to many observers, including Sofía Sánchez Manzanaro (2019)[117]:

> "Because of its own domestic policy, Spain refuses to recognize Kosovo as independent. The Catalan conflict, between this autonomous community and the Spanish state , is the main reason why the government considers Kosovo as part of Serbia, as its recognition could set a precedent in the Catalan context.
>
> In May 2018, the then-Prime Minister Mariano Rajoy did not attend the EU-Balkans summit meeting held in Bulgaria, because of the presence of the political representatives of Kosovo. Spain was the only EU member state that was not present at the meeting for that reason". (Sánchez Manzanaro 2019)

*** 4.1 The Foreign Ministry's Reports**

As early as 2013, when the secret service of the Ministry of the Interior (the "CNI") reinforced its contingent of agents in Barcelona monitoring what was already being referred to as "el procés" (Sallés 2013)[118], the Ministry for Foreign Affairs began churning out reports, often in various languages, to try and counter the growing secessionist movement (Ministerio de Asuntos Exteriores 2013, 2014[119]. This author cannot claim to be neutral, so

---

[117] Sánchez Manzanaro, Sofía (2020). "Los cinco países de la Unión Europea que no reconocen la independencia de Kosovo y por qué", *Euronews*, 17/07/2019. https://es.euronews.com/2019/07/17/los-cinco-paises-de-la-union-europea-que-no-reconocen-la-independencia-de-kosovo-y-por-que

[118] Sallés, Quico (2013). Crits "d'independència" davant la seu del CNI a Catalunya", *Nació Digital*, 20 February 2013. https://www.naciodigital.cat/noticia/52012/crits/independencia/davant/seu/cni/catalunya

[119] Ministerio de Asuntos Exteriores, 2013. Consecuencias económicas de una hipotética independencia de Cataluña.13 March 2013. http://www.exteriores.gob.es/Portal/es/SalaDePrensa/ElMinisterioInforma/Paginas/Noticias/20130313_MINISTERIO7.aspx.

his opinion that they are full of a carefully built narrative largely based on hearsay, prejudice, half-truths and subjectivity is of questionable value: but he believes that a cold, academic analysis of the discourse and content of these and other such texts would be a fruitful exercise. The latter include a lush 2013 publication by the Partido Popular think-tank, FAES, "*20 Questions and Answers on the Secession of Catalonia*", which actually confesses to a government grant on page 2.[120] It includes pontifications in reply to such nebulous questions as "Can we rightly speak of a history of 'Spain against Catalonia'?" or "Is the so-called right to self-determination applicable to Catalonia?".

The first of these questions deserves a short aside. In December 2013 an academic symposium was held in the context of the tricentennial of the fall of Barcelona at the end of the War of Spanish Succession. It was announced in August as "Espanya contra Catalunya: una mirada històrica (1714-2014)".[121]

The bubble of hypersensitive, righteous indignation over the title burst in Madrid just a few weeks before the symposium was to be held:

> "The title of the symposium and some of the reports have made the PP threaten to break any possibility of dialogue

---

Ministerio de Asuntos Exteriores, 2014. *Por la convivencia democrática*. 5 March 2014.
http://www.exteriores.gob.es/Portal/es/SalaDePrensa/ElMinisterioInforma/Paginas/Noticias/20140206_MINISTERIO1.aspx.

In English: Catalonia in Spain. For Democratic Co-existence. Ministerio de Asuntos Exteriores, Madrid.
http://www.exteriores.gob.es/Portal/es/SalaDePrensa/Multimedia/Publicaciones/Documents/Porlaconvivencia/por%20la%20convivencia%20democratica%20eng.pdf

[120] FAES (Fundación para el Análisis y los Estudios Sociales), 2013. *20 Questions and Answers on the Secession of Catalonia*. Madrid. English version: http://www.fundacionfaes.org/file_upload/news/pdfs/20140212192231.pdf

[121] VilaWeb (2013). "Espanya contra Catalunya: una mirada històrica (1714-2014)", VilaWeb, 17 August 2013.
https://www.vilaweb.cat/noticia/4139285/20130817/espanya-catalunya-mirada-historica-1714-2014.html

> between the Catalan President, Artur Mas, and the Spanish one, Mariano Rajoy. If the symposium is not suspended, the PP spokesman in the Parliament, Enric Millo, warned yesterday, Mas will have no legitimacy to dialogue with the Spanish government. The Minister of Foreign Affairs and Cooperation, José Manuel García-Margallo, was also adamant: from the title and the subtitle, he assured that it is a "flagrant falsification of history". He criticized the organizers: "They are exclusive nationalist pseudo-historians." "Josep Fontana will open the symposium with the paper "Spain and Catalonia: three hundred years of political conflict". The historian asks of those who criticize the symposium so much to wait to hear its contents. And that, when they criticize the papers, they do so with arguments and not with threats." (Marimon 2013)[122]

And on the very day it started, newspapers highlighted what they were calling "el simposio del odio", the symposium of hatred…

> "The inquisitorial and preventive diatribe over the symposium 'Espanya contra Catalunya' (Spain against Catalonia) that begins today in the Catalan capital, and the political controversy that accompanies it, is once again the common thread of the early editions of today's newspapers. Of the nine front pages of the Madrid and Barcelona press, it opens, actively or passively, four and is present on four more". (Campreciós 2013)[123]

Deep down, according to historian Àngel Casals (and this author agrees)…

---

[122] Marimon, Sílvia (2013). "Espanya contra Catalunya? El títol del congrés genera incomoditat a Barcelona i indignació a Madrid". *Ara*, 10 December 2013. https://www.ara.cat/premium/politica/Espanya-contra-Catalunya_0_1045095533.html

[123] Campreciós, Xavier (2013). "'Espanya contra Catalunya', verdades y mentiras". *El Periódido de Catalunya*, 12 December 2013. https://www.elperiodico.com/es/politica/20131212/espanya-contra-catalunya-otra-de-verdades-y-mentiras-2917849

"the symposium points to the need to confront «a very old and powerful ideological construction» that arose from the idea that «Castile is the legitimate heir to the Visigothic monarchy», a succession «given by providence» as from the 15th Century and the «Muslim invasion which created an anomalous situation» from which several circumstances arose, amongst which the «existence of the Catalans» that had to be put in doubt «once normality had been recovered».

Likewise, Casals has considered that it all reflects the «failure to achieve a culturally unified state», because it was impossible «to be efficient enough to make Spanish nationalism an attractive ideology»." (Palmer 2013)[124]

One of the convenors, Professor Jaume Sobrequés (2014)[125], later wrote an account of the knee-jerk reactions the very title of the symposium provoked in Spanish Nationalist circles, including even calls on the public prosecutor to have the symposium banned!

"The institutions were subjected to a lawsuit filed before the Public Prosecutor's office by several Catalan political parties, demanding that it be suspended, and to various parliamentary actions regarding this matter. Sectors of Catalan civil society and some intellectuals came out in support of the Spanish anti-Catalan offensive and, scandalized by the title of the symposium, called for its suspension. The book is a highly significant display of the ill-feeling the Catalan independence process is awakening in the Spanish intellectual, civic and media

---

[124] Palmer, Jordi (2013). "Tres segles d'Espanya contra Catalunya". *Nació Digital*, 18 August 2013. https://www.naciodigital.cat/noticia/92666/tres/segles/espanya/contra/catalunya

[125] Sobrequés, Jaume (2014). "Espanya Contra Catalunya: Crònica negra d'un simposi d'història". Barcelona, Editorial Base.

world, and of the moderation with which it is defended by some significant people in Catalan society.[126]

Each of the presentations, incidentally, can be seen in the set of videos: http://www.gxi.cat/espanya-contra-catalunya; and were published in book form as "*Vàrem mirar ben al lluny del desert. Actes del simposi "Espanya contra Catalunya: una mirada històrica (1714-2014)*"(2014).[127]

Returning to other activity by the Spanish , it has included distributing (or funding) "information" to try and shoot down all the "myths" that the Catalan independence movement has, according to them and despite all the efforts to silence it abroad, disseminated to explain their cause. One relatively recent example is a PowerPoint presentation[128], which according to a Catalan analyst contains seven manipulations. It claims that 1. International monitoring bodies approve of Spain's behaviour; 2. the Independence movement is comparable to Le Pen's National Front; 3. Independence is like Brexit; 4. Most Catalans are opposed to independence; 5. Barcelona is not Catalonia; 6. Police violence against 1-O voters was fake news; and 7. Separatism is nationalism, but Unionism is not. It was first used in public by Antonio María Bueno Armijo (Univ. of Cordoba, Spain) on September 28 inside the European Commission; he is reported as having said that separatism ("independentismo") is "morally bad", in line with several statements by the Spanish bishops. In the view of this author, the VilaWeb article shoots each alleged "manipulation" down in flames.

* 4.2 The Intelgiasp report

126 https://www.amazon.es/Espanya-Contra-Catalunya-Base-Hist%C3%B2rica/dp/8416166005

127 https://llibreria.gencat.cat/product_info.php?products_id=8463

128 https://www.vilaweb.cat/noticies/les-7-manipulacions-del-dossier-antiindependentista-de-josep-borrell/

Given Spain's apparent inability to accept that there are legitimate, rational arguments for Catalan independence, one should not be surprised to constantly stumble upon statements like the following:

> "... the foreign interference that seeks the political and economic instability of these international and national actors is fundamental for the maintenance of these movements (financed and with communication networks and logistics of violent action). But it has been the indoctrination in this ideology, facilitated by the Constitution and the territorial governance system in Spain with powers in Education, which has fed the basis of this ideology in recent years with manipulation of information, history and of thought."[129]

This particular source (the authors of which claim to have used Open Source Intelligence and Social Media Intelligence, programmes used - and taught in courses - by Spanish intelligence firms such as *Inteligencia más Liderazgo*130, set up up two army officers, inspired by Cicero's dictum: "A nation can survive its fools and even the ambitious. But it cannot survive *treachery from within*" and closely linked to Grupo GEES Spain)131 draws heavily on the colossal fake news narrative (that none of the fact-checkers has to my knowledge studied or exposed) built around a group of popular street firework throwers (known as "Diables") arrested by the Spanish police in "Operación Judas", treated as members of the CDR (*Comitès de Defensa de la República*) and initially accused of "terrorism" in a desperate attempt by the Spanish authorities, ahead of the Supreme Court sentence, to incriminate the independence movement as being violent, in spite of its firm commitment *ab initio* to non-violent, democratic methods of achieving its aim (e.g.

[129] GIASP (2019). "Comunicación estratégica y narrativa de los movimientos radicales independentistas de Cataluña", Intelgiasp website, 24 November 2019. https://intelgiasp.com/2019/11/24/comunicacion-estrategica-y-narrativa-de-los-movimientos-radicales-independentistas-de-cataluna/

[130] https://inteligenciayliderazgo.com

[131] GEES (Grupo Especial de Escoltas, Emergencias y Seguridad). https://www.gees-spain.org/inicio/actualidad-grupo/

Urreiztieta & Martialay 2019 in *El Mundo*)[132]. The colossal level of disinformation, in the form of outright lies, in the media coverage of this case (taking the title of the article just quoted as an excellent example), deserves the attention of researchers. Moreover, the cover-up by the Spanish government of details of this operation is exemplified by the fact that the question put to it on 5 February 2020 by Basque Bildu MP Jon Iñarritu García ("Guardia Civil officers taking part in Operation Judas, as well as the cost of this operation and chronology of each arrest made. (ref. 184/004229)") had not been answered at the end of August, over six months later (Iñarritu 2020)133. We shall return to a previous episode in the criminalisation of the CDRs) in the next sub-section.

The Intelgiasp report is packed with false and oft-repeated claims such as that the movement acts «"with a vision" of "genetic racism" and "racial superiority"» and quotes a long forgotten work allegedly written in the 19th century (actually, in 1903) and the title of which is not even correctly given. It also, naturally, refers to ASSENGE [sic]:

> "ASSENGE [sic] - Victim of "Spanish fascism" before the silence imposed on social networks in Ecuador at the request of the Spanish government, which protested against his tweets and influence on the Procés. "Without Assange, the Procés is not the same" (commented a pro-independence activist on Twitter, @Kaben_Zotz).

To gauge the validity of the report as a whole, let us just look into this quoted tweeter, described by the authors as being pro-

---

[132] Urreiztieta, Esteban & Martialay, Angela (2019). "La Audiencia Nacional descubre que los CDR reportaban a Carles Puigdemont". *El Mundo*, 29 October 2019.
https://www.elmundo.es/espana/2019/10/29/5db74fe6fc6c83b3438b48bc.html

133

http://www.congreso.es/portal/page/portal/Congreso/Congreso/Diputados/BusqForm?_piref73_1333155_73_1333154_1333154.next_page=/wc/servidorCGI&CMD=VERLST&BASE=IW14&PIECE=IWB4&FMT=INITXD1S.fmt&FORM1=INITXLDC.fmt&NUM1=62&DES1=I%C3%B1arritu+Garc%C3%ADa%2C+Jon&QUERY=202.ACIN3.+y+%2862+ADJ+D%29.SAUT.&DOCS=291-291.

independence. It should be clear to all and sundry that the author, who incidentally even today has but 8 followers (eight), was being sarcastic (in the same vein as the tweet being replied to). The text used in the report said as follows:

> "Quite some Francoists these Equadorians are. Torrent should send a CDR) commando to bale him out and grant him asylum (and a good 300 MB fibre) in the embassy of the tractor republik of Kataluña- Without Assange the "prusés" is not the same."[134]

The same tweeter, three months earlier, had announced his or her vote for Ciudadanos, and called independence supporters "Nazis" and "gentuza" (good-for-nothings)![135] Q.E.D.

All in all, there are plenty of examples in the text to support the idea that whoever commissioned this report wished above all to indulge in a massive exercise of disinformation directed against the Catalan independence movement.

* 4.3 Building a narrative of Catalan violence: large-scale anti-Catalan disinformation

As we have just said, one of the clear aims of the Spanish authorities and associated media has been and still is to convey to Spanish public opinion the impression that the movement's proclaimed non-violence is a myth. This was of particular interest in the months preceding the trial of the nine politicians and social leaders, accused of "rebellion" (by definition, a violent, armed uprising). Daniel Camon (2018)[136] undertook a study of the way the

---

[134] https://twitter.com/Kaben_Zotz/status/979150357464059904?s=20

[135] https://twitter.com/Kaben_Zotz/status/943226489109139457?s=20 (19 December 2017)

https://twitter.com/Kaben_Zotz/status/942616605992865793?s=20 (18 December 2017)

[136] Camon, Daniel (2018). "CDR, un relat de terrorisme". *Media.cat*, 26 abril 2018. https://www.media.cat/2018/04/26/cdr-terrorisme-criminalitzacio/

media, Nationalist politicians, the police and prosecutors demonised the CDR), from the moment they were set up, largely by parent-pupil associations, as “Comitès de Defensa del Referèndum” to try and make sure, using peaceful methods and by the sheer weight of numbers, that the polling stations (mostly in schools) would stay open on the voting day.

> "Not all the articles published by these three papers are analysed. Instead, the report focuses on what language is used to describe the CDR) in particular articles of the studied media and in other less-followed ones that might have had an influence on the language used by *El País, l'ABC* and *El Mundo*. That is why adjectives used to describe the CDRs) are also analysed in specific articles from other digital media such as *La Razón, El Español, Crónica Global, OK Diario* and *El Confidencial*.
>
> “The period analysed is from September 26 2017, when the first CDR) appeared in the newspapers studied, to April 12th, when the CDR member from Viladecans was freed and the judge reduced charges from terrorism to public disorders.
>
> “This report aims to show up the treatment that the mass media have given to the coverage of the activities of the CDRs). This is why we analyse the way in which the verbal escalation in the digital press has happened, but also in the public appearances of politicians, in the reports of the State police and in the texts of Spain’s National Public Prosecutor's Office, who have pointed to the CDR as an element of degradation of social coexistence in Catalan society and as generators of violence, up to the first arrests of some of their members, with accusations that go from "rebellion, sedition and terrorism to “assaults on the police, public disorders and disobedience."

In the conclusions of the report - published, incidentally, months before the arrests of the firework wielders, Camon says:

> "Maybe we should ask if this is the role that mass media should have in political conflicts. The press has a very important role in the emotional state of society, depending on the rigour, the storyline and the parameters used. It has the capacity to intensify conflict or calm down tension. To give an example, the fire affecting the Ateneu de Sarrià[137] in Barcelona - an attack the far right admitted having perpetrated with graffiti calling for "Death to the CDR" - took place on the night of 28 April, when the media analysed had for two days being ranting on about the Committees."
>
> "The creation of opinion in a society by means of a media storm to enable legislation or the application of laws in one sense or another is nothing new. Spain did not invent it, nor does it have an exclusive right to it, but, in this case, everything points towards an organized campaign to discredit the Committees for the Defence of the Republic, in particular, and the independence movement in general. This raises doubts, once again, about the independence of the mass media".
>
> Could it be that the State government - and, regrettably, here we have to include certain Spanish and Catalan media - is trying to achieve, by way of this strategy of criminalization, some people becoming dissociated from the Catalan independence movement and thus weaken the Republican cause? Or is it just a tactic to justify the repression applied so far and that they intend to continue applying?"

Spanish diplomacy has centred on the argument of pro-independence Catalans that after independence it would be in everyone's interest for there to be a seamless transition inside the EU. Catalonia's leaders have enthusiastically recalled the trans-Pyrenean, European origins of Catalonia's existence as a polity and until the recent snubs by the European Commission, pro-European feeling in Catalonia was preponderant, despite signs that euro-scepticism has

---

[137] A pro-independence organization

grown recently (Aumaitre 2018).[138] She refers, for instance, to successive results in EP elections, without bearing in mind that Spain refused Catalonia's almost unanimous request to be a constituency and to be able to vote in its own representatives. Nevertheless, she has to concede that...

> "The requests for mediation (or even activation of Article 7 of the treaties) addressed to the European institutions, the move of part of the former Catalan Government to Brussels, the demonstration that took place on December 7, 2017 in the Belgian capital and the issuance of European Arrest Warrants and the subsequent arrest of Carles Puigdemont in Germany are clear examples of the European dimension that the conflict has attained."

But long before that the Real Instituto Elcano seemed specially interested to focus upon data that suggested that pro-European sentiment in Catalonia was waning. Roig Madorran (2005)[139] said that in Catalonia, Flanders, Scotland and Baden-Württemberg, whose political leaders "proclaimed the virtues of the European integration process for regional entities with legislative powers", evidence had been found that

> "In short, according to the analyses carried out using ordinal logit regressions and probability simulations, it seems that in the mid-nineties a latent tendency was beginning to be found among individuals with strong

---

[138] Aumaitre Balado, Ariane (2018). "¿Un germen de euroescepticismo? El procés y las actitudes hacia la UE", Real Instituto Elcano, ARI 78/2018. 19 June 2018.
http://www.realinstitutoelcano.org/wps/portal/rielcano_es/contenido?WCM_GLOBAL_CONTEXT=/elcano/elcano_es/zonas_es/ari78-2018-aumaitrebalado-germen-euroescepticismo-proces-actitudes-hacia-ue

[139] Roig Madorran, Elan (2005). "El debate para la ratificación del proyecto de Constitución Europea en Cataluña, ¿Un conflicto de Cataluña con Europa?", Real Instituto Elcano, ARI Nº 6-2005, 18 January 2005.
http://www.realinstitutoelcano.org/wps/portal/rielcano_es/contenido/!ut/p/a1/04_Sj9CPykssy0xPLMnMz0vMAfGjzOKNQ1zcA73dDQ38_YKNDRwtfN1cnf2cDf1DjfULsh0VAepxmvs!/?WCM_GLOBAL_CONTEXT=/wps/wcm/connect/elcano/Elcano_es/Zonas_es/ARI%206-2005

regional identity, to reject the EU model that was being designed and that was to contrast with the discourse shown by political elites at the regional level."

Interest in reforming the European Union was nevertheless high in Catalonia, one of the few regions in Europe to organize a "Convention on the future of Europe". In the event, Roig Madorran pointed out that the "No" vote in the European Constitution referendum was higher in Catalonia than in most parts of Spain, but she ended her paper highlighting the view of a leading post-Communist:

> "...the Yes vote, the No vote, abstention and the blank vote are not only unquestionably legitimate proposals, but also reasonably defensible ones from pro-European positions, and to my mind, this disqualifies anyone claiming to have the monopoly of true Europeanism." (Gutiérrez Díaz 2004)[140]

* 4.4 Mr. Juncker's manipulated answer

One of the most grotesque examples of international disinformation relating to Catalonia, that I have not found mentioned by fact-checkers, was the written answer by the then President of the Commission Juncker, to a question asked by a PP MEP shortly before the 2014 non-binding poll, … The written answer in English was shorter than the answer in Spanish, which was immediately plastered across the front page of the rabidly nationalist Madrid newspaper *ABC* (see Figueres 1997,[141] Medina 1995[142]), before the Commission hastily claimed there had been an error. It refused to concede that this colossal blunder was in fact a deliberate ploy by high-placed Spanish officials within the Commission; and the European Ombudsperson

---

140 Gutiérrez Díaz, Antoni (2004). "Eurofestival constituyente", *El País-Cataluña*, 13 September 2004. Reproduced in http://www.alay.com/hist2021.html

141 Figueres Artigues, Josep Maria (1997). *Història de l'anticatalanisme. El diari ABC i els seus homes*. El Mèdol.

142 Medina, Jaume (1995). *L'anticatalanisme del diari ABC (1916-1936)*. Abadia de Montserrat.

did not query the official explanation. The newspaper's rectification was not plastered across the front page as had been the fake news, and this tends to happen all too often in media coverage of the Spain-Catalonia conflict. It was one of the examples chosen by Media.cat (2015).[143]

While we are on the subject of Mr. Juncker, another incident is relevant. The question put to him in a Euronews interview, was exactly this: "Will the Commission recognise and accept a 'yes' result in the 1st October referendum in Catalonia?". "We shall respect that choice" can clearly be heard in the original words of the video recording of the interview[144], and these same words are recorded even in the non-plussed Spanish nationalist press (e.g. *El Español*, who claims that unspecified sources in "el equipo de Juncker" were forced to "matizar")[145]. The interpreter was somewhat briefer (as tends to happen) and misinterprets "choix" as "opinion".

"If there were to be a "Yes" vote in favour of Catalan independence then we will respect that opinion, but Catalonia will not be able to become an EU Member State on the day after such a vote".[146]	"C'est évident que si ... l'indépendance de la Catalogne voyait le jour -à voire- nous respecterons ce choix, mais la Catalogne ne pourra pas devenir, le lendemain matin, le jour après le vote, membre de l'Union Européenne. La Catalogne sera soumise à

[143] Media.cat (2015). "Quatre exemples de discursos de la por amb arguments falsos mal rectificats", Media.cat, 24 September 2015. https://www.media.cat/2015/09/24/mitjans-que-propaguen-el-discurs-de-la-por-pero-no-les-rectificacions/

[144] Euronews. 14 September 2017. https://www.youtube.com/watch?v=4j6n0Z7XtvA

[145] "Juncker: "Respetaríamos la independencia de Cataluña pero estará fuera de la UE"". El Español, 14 September 2017. https://www.elespanol.com/espana/politica/20170914/246725893_0.html

[146] https://www.businessinsider.com/r-independent-catalonia-would-need-to-apply-to-join-eu-juncker-2017-9?IR=T

un processus
d'adhésion..."147

In section 6.6 more reference is made to Mr. Juncker's position on Catalonia, almost certainly following strong pressure by Spain.

*** 4.5 Will the truth out?**

In the end one wonders whether Spain actually wants the whole truth to be known, or even the conflict to be resolved. The way Josep Borrell got cornered, and then terminated the interview on the Deutsche Welle TV programme "Conflict Zone", was a classic example of arrogance.[148] Just a year and a half before that the Spanish Foreign Minister Alfonso Dastis had actually denied to BBC's Andrew Marr the veracity of "some" of the TV images of police violence (which he describes as having been "provoked" and used to try and highlight the issue of "fake news"[149]). This in turn provoked an indignant tweet[150] by a member of the BBC film crew that had recorded the scenes of violence shown during the interview. Not content with that, less than a month later, Minister Dastis lied without batting an eyelid to BBC's Gavin Lee, saying that Spain was

---

[147] https://www.youtube.com/watch?v=4j6n0Z7XtvA

[148] Conflict Zone (2019) "Borrell corta una entrevista en una televisión alemana al ser preguntado por Cataluña", *Deutsche Welle TV*, 28 March 2019. https://www.elindependiente.com/politica/2019/03/28/borrell-abandona-una-entrevista-una-television-alemana-al-preguntado-cataluna/

[149] CCMA (2017). "El ministre Dastis diu a la BBC que moltes de les imatges de l'1-O són "fake news"". CCMA, 22 October 2017. https://www.ccma.cat/324/el-ministre-dastis-diu-a-la-bbc-que-moltes-de-les-imatges-de-l1-o-son-fake/noticia/2816437/

[150] Esperanza Escribano: "Muy curioso porque la mayoría de las imágenes mostradas las grabamos un equipo de BBC en Pau Romeva [school] el #1O". 22 October 2017. https://twitter.com/esperanzaec/status/922097505394987009?s=20

considering constitutional changes that could allow its regions to hold referendums on independence in the future.[151]

Various commentators have kept voicing their opinion that the Spanish authorities have sought vengeance rather than a political solution (or even justice), with their implacable persecution-cum-prosecution of over 1,000 Catalans, mostly politicians and civil servants, for their role in organizing what after all is not a criminal offence (the 2005 Criminal Code reform dropped the organization of referenda from its list of offences). The incidents of civil unrest, particularly following the 2019 Supreme Court judgment, has increased to over 2,850. The following was written by Xavier Domènech (2019)[152]:

> "The prosecutors do not give in. It is shocking to see how they confirmed the charges of rebellion and sedition yesterday after viewing videos as evident as the ones shown at the *Procés* trial; and that they should do so on the same day that a UN working group declared that it considered the arrest of Oriol Junqueras, Jordi Sánchez and Jordi Cuixart- the ones so far examined - to be arbitrary".

Another spoke of a spirit of revenge (Lillo, 2018)[153]:

> "All of them, unexpectedly, experience what they consider to be the fraud of a system that they never imagined would react in such a disproportionate way. In such a vicious way. With such a spirit of revenge."

[151] "Spain FM Alfonso Dastis: Changes could allow referendums". *BBC*, 8 November 2017. https://www.bbc.com/news/av/world-europe-41918334/spain-fm-alfonso-dastis-changes-could-allow-referendums

[152] Xavier Domènech (2019). "Esperit de revenja", Regió 7, 30.05.2019. https://www.regio7.cat/opinio/2019/05/30/esperit-revenja/547785.html

[153] Lillo, Manuel (2018). "La cara B de la repressió", *El Temps*, No. 1790, 1 October 2018. https://www.eltemps.cat/article/5147/la-cara-b-de-la-repressio

So too did Sebastià Alzamora (2018)[154], among many others. Ada Colau, the Mayoress of Barcelona (who is not an advocate of Catalan independence), also spoke of the spirit of revenge and came out in strong protest against the incarceration of the Catalan political leaders (who joined the two Jordis) in November 2017:

> "Ada Colau, mayoress of Barcelona, visibly affected, calls the imprisonment of half the Catalan cabinet (added to those of Sànchez and Cuixart) the worst attack on the Catalan government in democracy and on the very democratic foundations of the Spanish State. (CCMA 2017)"[155]

Former Catalan President Artur Mas, also prosecuted on several scores for the 2014 popular poll, again described his prosecution as displaying a spirit of vengeance (Liñán 2018)156.

> "Artur Mas, Joana Ortega, Irene Rigau and Francesc Homs are already on the way to Barcelona, after reliving the events of the 9-N poll and the trial in which they were tried for disobedience, "satisfied" with their testimony and convinced that "there is not a single person responsible for any embezzlement".
>
> Mas spoke on behalf of the four defendants on leaving the Supreme Court and qualified the trial as a Spanish

---

[154] Alzamora, Sebastià (2019). "Esperit de revenja. Plana des del començament en tota la causa general contra l'independentisme i el republicanisme", *Ara*, 17 JAN 2019. https://www.ara.cat/opinio/Sebastia-Alzamora-Esperit-de-revenja_0_2163383836.html

[155] CCMA (2017). "Colau: "És una decisió que només s'explica amb l'esperit de revenja"". CCMA website, 2 November 2017. https://www.ccma.cat/catradio/alacarta/especial-2-n-catradio/ada-colau-es-una-decisio-que-nomes-sexplica-amb-lesperit-de-revenja/audio/980520/

[156] Gemma Liñán (2018). Artur Mas: "Som aquí per un esperit de revenja", *El Nacional*, 10 October 2018. https://www.elnacional.cat/ca/politica/artur-mas-revenja_312900_102.html

«revenge» operation by former ex-president[157] Soraya Sáenz de Santamaría, *Societat Civil Catalana* and *Advocats Catalans per la Constitució*, the last two of which head the prosecuting party.

The former president was adamant: "Embezzlement was dropped from the penal procedure and some unsatisfied people have carried the question further, to try to ensure that we are now condemned in a different court, when in the former procedure we were not. This is a case of revenge and I remember the words of Soraya Sáenz de Santamaría when she said that we and our families would pay for the 9-N poll in Catalonia out of our own pockets"."

Not least among their evidence is the meta-data description of the Public Prosecutors' charges laid against the political and social leadership of the independence movement. It read "Más dura será la caída" (The harder will be their fall). The revelation caused an understandable rumpus.[158]

---

[157] Her official post was in fact Deputy Prime Minister

[158] Infolibre (2020). "La Fiscalía dice que no pretendía "hacer escarnio" con el documento cuyo asunto era 'Más dura será la caída'". 31 October 2017. *InfoLibre*. https://www.infolibre.es/noticias/politica/2017/10/31/la_fiscalia_aclara_que_asunto_mas_dura_sera_caida_aludia_documento_anterior_no_querella_cataluna_71354_1012.html

Chapter 5. The Catalan independence process: a "breeding-ground" for falsehoods, manipulation, fake news... and unrelenting lawfare.

We are not going here into the pros and cons of Catalonia's independence (though it seems to be a general fact that, once declared, nations don't often reverse their decision later!).

Suffice it to refer to a statement (that many others would, I am sure, second) by Craig Murray, Britain's ambassador to from 2002 to 2004 but later expelled from the diplomatic service[159]. Murray has become, as we shall see, the scourge of many underhand diplomatic dealings and of the lack of accountability and transparency of many Government agencies and quangos. He stood up firmly, on the Referendum voting day, in defence of the Catalan people's right of self-determination:

> "When you see the right wing Establishment worldwide, plus the entire mainstream media, united against ordinary people as we see today in Catalonia, it's a no-brainer which side you should be on"... "The right of self-determination of peoples is inalienable, and the Catalan situation is a perfect illustration of the meaning of inalienable in this sense. In fact, by arguing that Catalonia specifically signed up to the current Spanish constitution, all the Spanish government and its supporters are doing is offering conclusive evidence that the Catalans are indeed a people with the right of self-determination.
>
> … The most extraordinary thing of all is the falling in line of the entire political Establishment, right across the EU, and all of its mainstream media, with the mantra that the Catalonian referendum is illegal. The right in international law of a people to self-determination cannot

[159] Norton, Ben (2020). "Dissident British ex-diplomat Craig Murray indicted for blog posts in Kafkaesque case". The Gray Zone, 27 April 2020. https://thegrayzone.com/2020/04/27/craig-murray-indicted-blog-posts/

be constrained by the domestic legislation of the larger state from which that people is seeking to secede".[160]

Similar statements were issued on various occasions by Alfred de Zayas, e.g.

> "In accordance with the Spanish Constitution, the right of self-determination must be applied in Spain in line with the provisions of international law. The current status of international law is developed in my "Notes". In this regard, it should be recalled that the holders of the right of self-determination are "all peoples" without exception, and that the principle of territorial integrity can only be invoked in the case of external interference by another State and not as a pretext to restrict said fundamental right. The validity of the right of self-determination established by the Spanish Constitution must prevail over the norms or resolutions of lower rank. [...]
>
> [A]ccording to international human rights law, the right of self-determination is inalienable and imprescriptible (like all fundamental rights), with which a theoretical renunciation by the Catalans of 1978 cannot deprive today's Catalan people (and future generations of Catalans) of their fundamental right of self-determination. Thus, today's Catalans are not legally bound by any theoretical renunciation made by a prior generation."[161]

---

[160] Murray, Craig (2017). "The Freedom of Courage", Blog, 1 Oct, 2017, https://www.craigmurray.org.uk/archives/2017/10/the-freedom-of-courage/

[161] De Zayas, Alfred (2018). Self-determination and Catalonia. Blog, 9 June 2018. https://dezayasalfred.wordpress.com/2018/06/09/self-determination-and-catalonia/

See also De Zayas (2017). Practical notes for the assessment of activities and allegations related to the peaceful and democratic exercise of the right of self-determination of peoples", December 2017. http://www.ohchr.org/EN/Issues/IntOrder/Pages/IEInternationalorderIndex.aspx

*** 5.1 Road maps**

Ahead of the 2017 referendum, the road map was laid down in two main documents - the highly detailed *Llibre Blanc de la Transició Nacional de Catalunya (White Paper on the National Transition of Catalonia)*, commissioned and published by the Catalan government[162]; and the "Junts pel Sí" coalition's 2017 election manifesto. Both documents were clear about the steps to be taken - if a majority of the Catalan electorate so chose - to attain national liberation.

Another 90-page report was published shortly before the referendum (IRAI 2017)[163]. The authors were Nina Caspersen (Professor, University of York), Matt Qvrotrup (Professor, Coventry University), Daniel Turp (Professor, University of Montreal), and Yanina Welp (Professor, University of Zurich). It includes in an annex the text of the Bill on the Self-determination Referendum that was to ignite the Spanish political world and media.

> "This report addresses different aspects of the proposed referendum in Catalonia. In chapter one, Professor Yanina Welp analyses and presents a political sociological perspective on the respective evolutions of the Catalan support for or rejection of independence. This chapter also summarizes the events that led to the demand for a referendum. In chapter two, Professor Nina

---

[162] Consell Assessor per a la Transició Nacional (2016). *Llibre Blanc de la Transició Nacional de Catalunya*. Generalitat de Catalunya. https://presidencia.gencat.cat/ca/ambits_d_actuacio/desenvolupament_autogovern/comissionat-de-la-presidencia-per-al-desplegament-de-lautogovern/llibre-blanc-de-la-transicio-nacional-de-catalunya/

A complete English version is available at the same URL, and a synthesis, in English, can be downloaded here: https://presidencia.gencat.cat/web/.content/ambits_actuacio/consells_assessors/catn/informes/llibre_blanc_angles.pdf

[163] IRAI (2017). Report of the International Group of Experts. The Catalan Independence Referendum: An Assessment of the Process of Self-Determination, IRAI (Institut de recherche sur l'autodétermination des peuples et les indépendances nationales), Montréal, Québec. https://irai.quebec/wp-content/uploads/2017/09/IRAI_Rapports-experts-Catalogne_EN_final.pdf

> Caspersen presents a comparative and historical overview of the political context of the demand for independence for Catalonia and draws up a number of scenarios for the future, depending on the outcome of the referendum. In the subsequent chapter, Professor Matt Qvrotrup analyses when referendums are held and what determines their outcome; as well, he analyses the legislation governing the conduct of the proposed referendums. He concludes, with some reservations, that the current legislation meets international standards. Finally, Professor Daniel Turp analyses and assesses the legality of the proposed referendum. [He] examines the right to decide of the people of Catalonia in light of rules found in international, European, Spanish, Catalan and comparative law".

Professor Qvrotrup, in hindsight, was well off target in predicting the likely reaction of the Spanish government to a Yes vote coupled with a declaration of independence:

> "The Spanish Government is initially likely to downplay the referendum result... and may react in a similar way to a declaration of independence, describing it as an act of protest, which is of no legal consequence." (p. 31)

One may suppose that the official referendum results were not published in the official Gazette (the *Diari Oficial de la Generalitat de Catalunya*), and the full text of the Resolution declaring independence was not published in the official journal of the *Parlament de Catalunya*, in order to forestall legal action against the Catalan Government and MPs. In the event, and the 9 to 13 years gaol sentences meted out in October 2019, such reasoning was to prove ingenuous, to say the least.

* 5.2 Catalonia: a pawn on the international chessboard?

We are not going to put Catalonia's bid into an international perspective, as does libertarian writer Justin Raimundo:

> "Catalonia's bid for self-determination is an ideological litmus test, one that tells us everything we need to know about the main forces contending for power in the world."[164]

Nevertheless, the Catalan independence process hit the media fan, as made clear by Negredo, Amoedo & Vara (2018):

> "Extensive coverage of the referendum in Catalonia and the response from the State - including police deployment, direct instructions to the Catalan government, judicial action, and a snap regional election - went on for months. Around this very divisive issue, the four Madrid-based newspapers and the two main titles in Catalonia joined the main Spanish political parties in defending the legal status quo. The leading and most moderate paper in *Catalonia, La Vanguardia* (50% total offline/online reach in this territory) called for dialogue in face of a 'devastating' situation. A broader spectrum of views was reflected by commercial TV and radio, where political talk shows dominated airtime, and by digital-native sites in Madrid and Barcelona."[165]

*** 5.3 Catalanophobia in Spain, and the myth of hispanophobia in Catalonia**

The Catalan independence process has long been under attack, politically, in the courts, and in the media. But this was made easier given Spain's long-standing view of Catalonia. The Catalan people have been often perceived in a negative light by Spaniards

---

[164] "In Catalonia: A Spanish Tiananmen Square?", 18 September 2017. https://original.antiwar.com/justin/2017/09/17/catalonia-spanish-tiananmen-square/

[165] Negredo, Samuel, Avelino Amoedo & Alfonso Vara (2018). "Spain", in *Digital News Report 2018,* Reuters Institute for the Study of Journalism: 102-103. https://reutersinstitute.politics.ox.ac.uk/sites/default/files/digital-news-report-2018.pdf

regardless of ideology, as attested in various sources, and this has greatly helped those opposed to the independence bid.[166]

> "Increasing antagonism between Catalonia and Spain has been brought about by several anti-Catalan campaigns in Spain. The newspaper "*El Mundo*"[167] proposed a poll among its readers in 2009 asking them if they felt hatred against the Catalans: the result was that 56% said yes. In a normal country, this poll would have been forbidden and this newspaper would have been closed down for inciting citizens towards hate attitudes. In Spain, there was not even a warning by the Spanish state or any court of justice against the newspaper *El Mundo*. The fact that 56% of the readers expressed hatred against Catalonia is obviously a result of false campaigns that are instigated from several Spanish institutions and news media." (Miralda 2010)[168]

26,648 people took part in this on-line survey.

Around that time, the Partido Popular, in particular, was blamed for the increase in catalanophobia, hate speech aimed at the Catalans, and the growing reaction in Catalonia against this, by the then Socialist President of Catalonia, Andalusian-born José Montilla (Ollés 2009)[169].

---

[166] For instance, "Base de Dades sobre la Catalanofòbia (B.D.C.)", https://wiki.vilaweb.cat/index.php/Base_de_Dades_sobre_la_Catalanof%C3%B2bia_(B.D.C.)

and the following set of blog entries with 300 examples all in recent years: https://estudiscatalans.blogspot.com/2015/06/herois_32.html

[167] "El Mundo justifica la catalanofobia". *E-Noticies*. 17 July 2009. https://comunicacion.e-noticies.es/el-mundo-justifica-la-catalanofobia-31183.html

[168] Miralda Escudé, Jordi "Why Catalonia's Independence is coming". Blog. April 2010. http://www.am.ub.edu/~jmiralda/catind.html

[169] Albert Ollés "(2009). "Montilla atribuye la desafección hacia España a los ataques del PP. Denuncia que los populares promueven el 'odio' al utilizar la 'catalanofobia' para castigar a Zapatero". 30 July 2009.

In another study (Brew 2020)[170] the author analysed available survey data to answer the question: "What is the degree of ‘hispanophobia’ in Catalonia, and of ‘catalanophobia’ in Spain?" It transpired that the Catalans liked people from each of the other "autonomous communities" clearly more than the Catalans were liked in return:

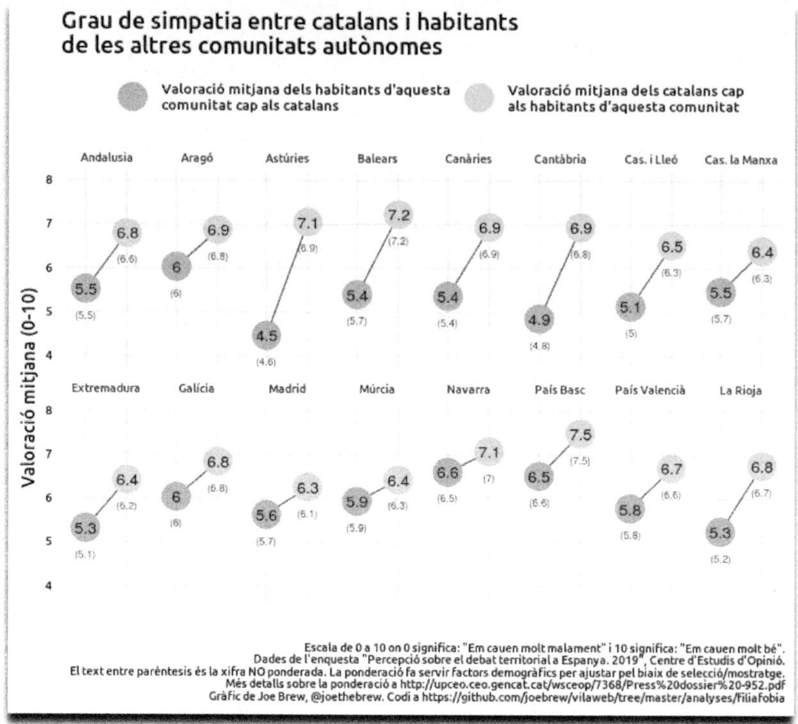

https://www.elperiodico.com/es/politica/20090730/montilla-atribuye-la-desafeccion-hacia-espana-a-los-ataques-del-pp-122028

[170] Joe Brew (2020). “La mentida de la xenofòbia independentista”, *VilaWeb*, 21 February 2020. https://www.vilaweb.cat/noticies/mentida-xenofobia-joe-brew/?f=rel

In English: “Phobia and philia: what Catalans and Spaniards think of one another. Catalanophobia is much more widespread than hispanophobia“. *VilaWeb,* 25 January 2020. https://english.vilaweb.cat/noticies/phobia-philia-catalans-spaniards-think-joe-brew/

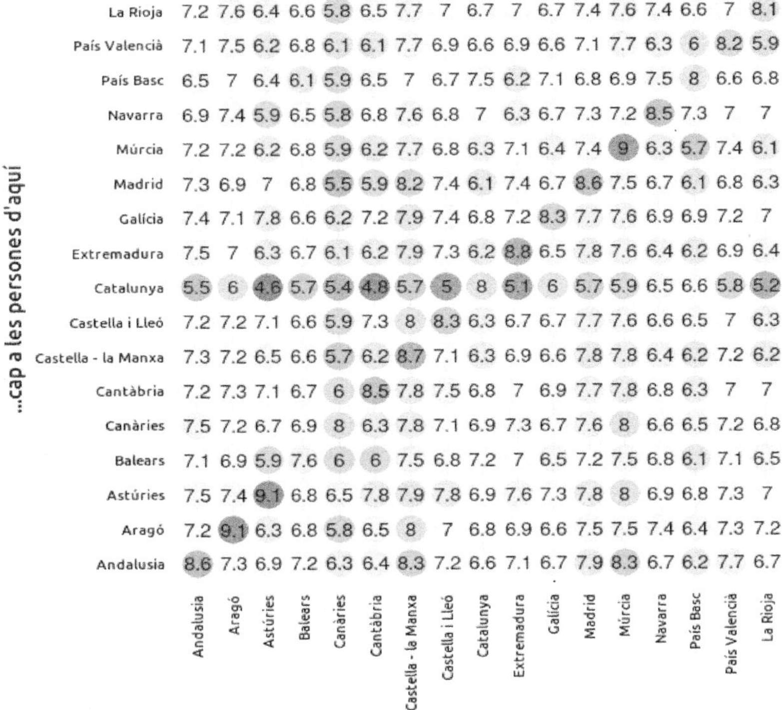

Grau de simpatia cap als habitants de les altres comunitats autònomes, segons comunitat autònoma

...cap a les persones d'aquí	Andalusia	Aragó	Astúries	Balears	Canàries	Cantàbria	Castella - la Manxa	Castella i Lleó	Catalunya	Extremadura	Galícia	Madrid	Múrcia	Navarra	País Basc	País Valencià	La Rioja
La Rioja	7.2	7.6	6.4	6.6	5.8	6.5	7.7	7	6.7	7	6.7	7.4	7.6	7.4	6.6	7	8.1
País Valencià	7.1	7.5	6.2	6.8	6.1	6.1	7.7	6.9	6.6	6.9	6.6	7.1	7.7	6.3	6	8.2	5.9
País Basc	6.5	7	6.4	6.1	5.9	6.5	7	6.7	7.5	6.2	7.1	6.8	6.9	7.5	8	6.6	6.8
Navarra	6.9	7.4	5.9	6.5	5.8	6.8	7.6	6.8	7	6.3	6.7	7.3	7.2	8.5	7.3	7	7
Múrcia	7.2	7.2	6.2	6.8	5.9	6.2	7.7	6.8	6.3	7.1	6.4	7.4	9	6.3	5.7	7.4	6.1
Madrid	7.3	6.9	7	6.8	5.5	5.9	8.2	7.4	6.1	7.4	6.7	8.6	7.5	6.7	6.1	6.8	6.3
Galícia	7.4	7.1	7.8	6.6	6.2	7.2	7.9	7.4	6.8	7.2	8.3	7.7	7.6	6.9	6.9	7.2	7
Extremadura	7.5	7	6.3	6.7	6.1	6.2	7.9	7.3	6.2	8.8	6.5	7.8	7.6	6.4	6.2	6.9	6.4
Catalunya	5.5	6	4.6	5.7	5.4	4.8	5.7	5	8	5.1	6	5.7	5.9	6.5	6.6	5.8	5.2
Castella i Lleó	7.2	7.2	7.1	6.6	5.9	7.3	8	8.3	6.3	6.7	6.7	7.7	7.6	6.6	6.5	7	6.3
Castella - la Manxa	7.3	7.2	6.5	6.6	5.7	6.2	8.7	7.1	6.3	6.9	6.6	7.8	7.8	6.4	6.2	7.2	6.2
Cantàbria	7.2	7.3	7.1	6.7	6	8.5	7.8	7.5	6.8	7	6.9	7.7	7.8	6.8	6.3	7	7
Canàries	7.5	7.2	6.7	6.9	8	6.3	7.8	7.1	6.9	7.3	6.7	7.6	8	6.6	6.5	7.2	6.8
Balears	7.1	6.9	5.9	7.6	6	6	7.5	6.8	7.2	7	6.5	7.2	7.5	6.8	6.1	7.1	6.5
Astúries	7.5	7.4	9.1	6.8	6.5	7.8	7.9	7.8	6.9	7.6	7.3	7.8	8	6.9	6.8	7.3	7
Aragó	7.2	9.1	6.3	6.8	5.8	6.5	8	7	6.8	6.9	6.6	7.5	7.5	7.4	6.4	7.3	7.2
Andalusia	8.6	7.3	6.9	7.2	6.3	6.4	8.3	7.2	6.6	7.1	6.7	7.9	8.3	6.7	6.2	7.7	6.7

Grau de simpatia de les persones d'aquí

Font de dades: Enquesta 'Percepció sobre el debat territorial a Espanya' del Centre d'Estudis d'Opinió.
Gràfic: @joethebrew

The Murcian, the Madrileño and Castilian (La Mancha) samples were the most empathetic in their scores of the others, while the Canary Islanders and, to a lesser extent, the Basques, were the least generous (vertical column). As shown before, the Catalans are seen as the least likeable by almost everyone. As might be expected, the degree of sympathy is much lower - 5.2 on average on a 0-10 scale - among people who have never been to Catalonia (and thus are fed solely on prejudice) than it is among people who have travelled to Catalonia 2-5 times (6.0), or more than 10 times (7.0).

These findings of "catalanophobia" are no surprise. In actual fact they replicate the findings of Sangrador made over 25 years ago, and so the independence process is not the reason for the low scores the Catalans get.[171]

Joe Brew's conclusion (whose data shows that the profile of supporters of Catalan independence is far removed, on several scores, from that of supporters of so-called "populist" parties across Europe) is devastating:

> "The rise in concern about hispanophobia in Catalonia is not reality-based. On average, most Catalans like Spaniards, and most Spaniards like Catalans. Where there are differences in the levels of sympathy and antipathy between Spaniards and Catalans, these are in the direction of *catalanophobia*, not *hispanophobia*. That is, 26.1% of Spaniards dislike (<5 on a 0-10 scale) Catalans, while only 10.2% of Catalans dislike Spaniards. By the same token, 9.6% of Spaniards 'don't like Catalans at all' (0 on a 0-10) scale, but only 1.3% of Catalans say that they think same about the inhabitants of the rest of the Spanish State.
>
> If the degree of catalanophobia in Spain is greater than the degree of hispanophobia, why does the latter get so much more attention from mainstream Spanish political groups? There are two possible explanations: (1) the myth of hispanophobia is a 'moral panic', a collective fair that has emerged *organically* out of some Spaniards' anxiety about their political future; or (2) hispanophobia is not an *organic* social phenomenon but rather an *intentionally artificial* one, engineered by political and social actors to justify interventionist/centralist policies. That is, questionable Spanish political decisions aimed at 'correcting' Catalan political decisions appear less questionable when framed in the (false but useful)

---

[171] See Strubell i Trueta, Miquel (2008). *Bulls and donkeys. National identity and symbols in Catalonia and Spain*. http://www.anglo-catalan.org/downloads/joan-gili-memorial-lectures/lecture10.pdf

See esp. pp. 24-26.

> context of a hispanophobic society which needs to be 'corrected'."

In this context, the Report of the Special Rapporteur on minority issues, Fernand de Varennes, on his visit to Spain[172] makes a disturbing statement:

> 41. The Special Rapporteur was informed that minorities such as Roma, people of African Descent, migrants, and religious minorities such as Muslims report that they sense that they remain the main targets and victims of intolerance expressed in hate speech. In addition, connected to events that took place in Catalonia in 2017, the Special Rapporteur received reports of an apparent increase in hate speech, vilification, vandalism, physical threats and even assaults against members of the Catalan minority and, to a lesser degree, other national minorities...

Readers may now understand the visceral language of the lecturer mentioned in the article referred to above (VilaWeb 2018) about a Spanish Foreign Ministry PowerPoint, when he said:

> Minute 47:30: "There is a conflict in Catalonia, but it is not a conflict between Catalonia and Spain... What we saw in Catalonia last year was probably just one of the heads of this monster called "nationalism". And we need to know the real nature of this enemy, because this nationalism is the real enemy, the main enemy of Europe, it has always been so. We need to know its real nature because we need to fight it."

My simple contention is that Spanish nationalism (which, being banal, in Billig's terms, is invisible to its bearers) is the origin of this visceral reaction, of the intolerant viciousness that any

---

[172] de Varennes, Fernand (2020). Report of the Special Rapporteur on minority issues, Visit to Spain. *Human Rights Council*. Forty-third session. 24 February–20 March 2020. Date: 9 March 2020. https://imatges.vilaweb.cat/nacional/wp-content/uploads/2020/03/A_HRC_43_47_Add.1_AdvanceEditedVersion.pdf

detached observer monitoring developments in the Catalonia-Spain conflict can see and hear in most of the Spanish media, day in day out.

Though the reader might think this paper is mainly about the social media, it is in fact a serious indictment of most of the Spanish press, which has often strayed far from neutrality and far from civility in its manners. In 2015, media.cat published an article[173] tearing to shreds four headlines in newspapers known for their belligerent opposition to Catalonia's quest for independence: *La Razón*[174], *El País, La Vanguardia* and *El Periódico de Catalunya.* Late in the previous year they had published a report, "L'espiral del silenci. El procés sobiranista a les tertúlies" ("The spiral of silence. The independence process in chat programmes"), [175] in which researchers compared the levels of plurality in newscasts in a range of Catalan and Spanish radio stations and television channels, both public and private, in the run-up to the non-binding poll on November 9 2014. Its devastating results made this report, with more than 14,000 visits, the most read article ever on the Media.cat web: as regards the supporters and opponents of the independence of Catalonia, in the Spanish media 97% defended Catalonia continuing inside Spain, while 2% were in favour of independence and 1% remained neutral. In the Catalan media, 55% were in favour of independence, while 38% opposed it and 7% remained uncommitted.

---

[173] "El perill del periodisme interpretatiu: quatre portades desmentides per la realitat", *Media.cat*, 9 September 2015.
https://www.media.cat/2015/09/09/el-perill-del-periodisme-interpretatiu-quatre-portades-desmentides-per-la-realitat/

[174] Carles Solà asked "La Razón, periodisme o propaganda?" in an article published on 10 March 2015 on the coverage of an incident in Solsona which, far from being organised by pro-independence supporters, was it transpired designed by a Unionist supporter to discredit them. The title speaks for itself. *Media.cat,* 10 March 2015,
https://www.media.cat/2015/03/10/la-razon-periodisme-o-propaganda/

[175] Martín, Sílvia &; Daniel Camon (2014), "L'espiral del silenci. El procés sobiranista a les tertúlies", Mèdia.cat,
http://www.media.cat/2014/11/06/informe-l%E2%80%99espiral-del-silenci-a-analisi/

The role of the media in the Spain-Catalonia conflict was stated in the harshest of terms by Xavier Díez (2019)[176]:

> "The conventional media, as well as a large proportion of the social networks, have concentrated on stirring up hatred against Catalonia and carrying out blatant operations involving information manipulation. Through programmes such as Espejo Público, the news of the generalist networks, the digital media, the Madrid press, a competition is rigged up to see who is the most anti-independence. In fact, pro-independence supporters are treated and distorted as "roaches" or "cockroaches", and, in fact, the topics used do not differ from the resources used by anti-Semites in Central Europe in the years leading up to the World War II. This is complemented by an information blackout on what is really happening in a Catalonia that, for its part, and in the face of the bacchanal of media lies, has turned its back on these media (the fall in television consumption of the Madrid-based broadcasters, as well as of the headlines of traditional newspapers, is of historical magnitudes). The offensive of hatred has managed to sever the cables that held a diverse citizenry united to a state that, given the repression of October 1 and thereafter, and the complicit silence of Spanish civil society, will be hard to rebuild. Mental divorce is already a reality…
>
> Of course, in order to dehumanize Catalans (as had been done before with the Basques, or with dissidents as regards the post-Franco Spain which controls the resources available to the State) a narrative that justifies hatred is needed..."

---

[176] Xavier Díez (2019). "Mentiras fundamentales sobre Cataluña". *Diario 16*, 19 November 2018. https://diario16.com/mentiras-fundamentales-cataluna/

Blog, 22 November 2018.
https://blocs.mesvilaweb.cat/xavierdiez/?p=270494

This was in the introduction to his article in which he singled out nine "Fundamental lies about Catalonia". The article is a scathing attack on Spanish disinformation:

1: Catalonia is divided

2: The independence cause is all about money

3: The independence movement is bourgeois

4: The independence movement is a *soufflé*

5: They are *putschistes*

6: Catalans can no longer live together

7: There are no political prisoners or exiles, just politicians in prison and outlaws

8: No one will recognize Catalonia / Catalonia will never be independent

9: Catalans are supremacists / nationalists/ nazis, …

The repression of Catalan leaders is part and parcel of Spain's attempts to put an end to the "Catalan problem" and complete the assimilation of the Catalan people. Díez continues:

> "If we talk about contemporary Catalonia, except for José Montilla (2006-2010), all, absolutely all Catalan Presidents have been victims of state repression. Prat de la Riba, first President of the "Mancomunitat" (a pre-autonomous regional administration prior to the Republic, between 1914 and 1924) died prematurely because of various incarcerations while he was a Catalan leader. Francesc Macià (1931-1933) was exiled and imprisoned several times. Lluís Companys (1933-1940) was imprisoned, exiled [in France], handed over by the Nazis to Spain, and finally shot. Josep Irla (1940-1954) was exiled and his assets were stolen by the Franco regime. Josep Tarradellas (1954-1980) spent 38 years in exile. Jordi Pujol (1980-2003) suffered the retaliation of the Franco regime and spent several years in prison.

> Pasqual Maragall (2003-2006) was ousted by the Socialist party, and cruelly defamed by the Spanish media. Artur Mas (2010-2016) has been prosecuted and his assets have finally been seized in an act of revenge by the state. And, Carles Puigdemont has also had to go into exile. What's Spain's problem with the Catalans?".

We can observe a constant propaganda campaign to portray the leaders and followers - of what, after all, is a perfectly legitimate aim for any self-respecting people - in a negative light by the Spanish authorities and many opinion leaders. The thrust of this campaign has been to persuade the outside world that Catalans have been deceived, manipulated, distracted from the "real problems", indoctrinated, promised the impossible, driven by non-applicable human values... No Catalan in their right mind would dream of such a thing. As Hispanist Thomas Harrington sarcastically put it, referring to David Alandete:

> "In his Spain, that is the real Spain run from Madrid and ever-prisoner to its own endlessly repeated mythologies about self and other, none of this is real. But what is real of course is Putin's evil hand.
>
> After all, what other reason could the Catalans, whom centralists like Alandete have always treated with mocking condescension despite their demonstrably higher levels of civic democracy and culture, have any reason to break up their perfect marriage?" (Harrington 2019)[177]

And in the presentation of a recent book of his[178] he says as follows:

---

[177] Harrington, Thomas A. (2017), "Largest Newspaper in Spain Blames Russia and Antiwar.com for Catalonia Pro-Independence News", Antiwar.com blog, September 23, 2017. https://www.antiwar.com/blog/2017/09/23/largest-newspaper-in-spain-blames-russia-and-antiwar-com-for-catalonia-pro-independence-news/

[178] Harrington, Thomas A. (2019), *A Citizen's Democracy in Authoritarian Times: An American View on the Catalan Drive for Independence*. Universitat de Valencia.

"Agents of sedition who are heedlessly destroying Spain's "consolidated democracy"? Xenophobes simply interested in protecting their own wealth who are, behind the rhetoric, not that different from the tribal authoritarians coming to the fore in Hungary and northern Italy? These are but two of the many narrative tropes the Spanish government and the establishment press in Europe and the US are rolling out to counter the rise of separatist sentiment in Catalonia. In this book, Thomas S. Harrington, an American with a deep familiarity with Catalan culture and history, argues that, far from being a threat to democracy in Europe, the scrupulously peaceful and people-driven movement for independence in Catalonia is, perhaps, the best hope we have for spurring its much hoped-for renewal."

Spain's propaganda machine, which relies on the powerful infrastructure of a Foreign Ministry built up (with the occasional civil war and coup changing its leadership) on regally-endowed think tanks who have been given the task not only of influencing international public opinion about the independence process, but also of monitoring it. In an article on Catalonia, entitled "Spain faces its worst constitutional crisis since the failed 1981 coup d'état, driven by Brexit-style populism" Francisco de Borja Lasheras,[179] Head of

[179] "Francisco de Borja Lasheras joined the European Council on Foreign Relations in October 2013 as Associate Director of the Madrid Office and Policy Fellow and assumed the position of Director in June 2016. Prior to ECFR, he served as the Spanish Permanent Representation to the OSCE, and spent several years in the Western Balkans, as seconded National Expert to the OSCE Missions in Bosnia and Herzegovina, in the field, as a human rights officer, and in Albania, with the Head of Mission. Between 2007 and 2009 he worked for the Fundación Alternativas' Observatory of Spanish Foreign Policy (Opex), as Coordinator on Security and Defence Policy, and taught comparative European politics at the George Washington University in Madrid. Borja graduated *summa cum laude* at the Deusto University´s Faculty of Law and holds a master's degree from Harvard University, where he studied international relations and politics. He has been published on multilateral diplomacy, the Western Balkans, Ukraine, institution-building, enlargement and security policy."
http://www.belgradeforum.org/speaker/francisco-de-borja-lasheras/

ECFR Madrid Office & Policy Fellow until he left in February 2018, wrote "Three myths about Catalonia's independence movement" in English, French and Spanish in September 2017.[180] While I disagree with its fundamental premises, including his claim that the independence movement is driven by "Brexit-style populism", I share his view that "I see some unsettling similarities in today's hate speech, stigmatizing of dissent, and the shaping of polarized political blocs in Catalonia, polarizing politics"... though I imagine we totally disagree about who and to what extent is using or promoting hate speech, who is stigmatizing dissent and who has been most keen to polarize political blocs. We need academic research to clarify this issue.

Opponents of the Catalan independence movement, that has from the outset of this phase stuck strictly to the belief that the aim is to be achieved not by violent means (like the IRA or ETA) but by peaceful, non-violent means and by the will of the majority of the electorate, that is, at the ballot box, claim that it is based on "populist" premises. Here is the view of an outspoken Socialist political scientist, Gabriel Colomé:

> Nobody was aware of what we were going through live, how they build an identity narrative through words: 'right to decide', 'voting is democratic', 'if you don't let me vote, you are not a democrat and you are authoritarian', 'tax spoliation', 'Spain steals from us'... The whole narrative is populism in its purest form. Populism like Trump, Pablo Iglesias. Moreover, it is post-truth. They use the same weapons."

---

180 https://www.ecfr.eu/article/commentary_three_myths_about_catalonias_independence_movement

In Spanish: https://www.ecfr.eu/madrid/post/tres_mitos_sobre_el_movimiento_independentista_de_cataluna

In French: https://www.ecfr.eu/paris/post/trois_mythes_a_propos_du_mouvement_independantiste_en_catalogne

Incidentally, the first of these slogans was used as early as the end of 2005, when the "Plataforma pel Dret a Decidir" was founded; and this author remembers no accusation of "populism" ever being directed at it. Be that as it may, do these allegedly populist slogans appeal to the segments of the Catalan population that are readily associated with populist movements? Joe Brew (2019)[181] provides plenty of empirical evidence that suggests quite the opposite. His analysis rejected, in supporters of the Catalan independence movement, the five main features of populism:

1. "*Low education*: Populism receives most support from those with low education (Waller et al. 2017).

2. *Low income*: Populism receives most support from those with low incomes (Pikkety 2018).

3. *Xenophobia*: Populism receives most support from those who are opposed to immigration and outsiders (Rydgren 2003).

4. *Unhappiness*: Populism receives most support from those who are discontent, not only with politics, but with life/society in general (Spruyt, Keppens, and Van Droogenbroeck 2016).

5. *Authoritarianism*: Populist movements often aspire for more 'mano dura' practices (penal populism), stemming from authoritarian attitudes about obedience and the law, etc. (Pratt and Miao 2018)"

Returning now to the whole issue of what constitutes "hate behaviour" and who engages in it in Catalonia, the issue has been grossly manipulated by the Spanish authorities, who around the time of the referendum began to prosecute Catalans (e.g. teachers, car mechanics, etc.) for so-called hate speech and behaviour aimed at...

---

[181] Brew, Joe (2019). "How 'populist' is the Catalan independence movement? Data analyst Joe Brew shows the five characteristics that confirm that independentism is not a populist movement", VilaWeb, 15 July 2019. https://english.vilaweb.cat/noticies/is-the-catalan-independence-movement-populist/

the Spanish police forces, hardly a defenceless, vulnerable minority, which is what the term is supposed to apply to (Amelang 2017).[182]

Though we shall not dwell on it, there has also been research on the use of the social media by politicians. One, specifically, was on their Instagram accounts. As we shall see below, in the Catalan conflict, all the perfect storm still needed was the active participation of the politicians involved. Carles Puigdemont (Junts x Cat), Oriol Junqueras (ERC), Albert Rivera (Ciudadanos), Pablo Iglesias (Podemos), Inés Arrimadas (Ciudadanos), Mariano Rajoy (PP), Gabriel Rufián (ERC), Pedro Sánchez (PSOE), Miquel Iceta (PSC) and Xavier Domènech (Catalunya en Comú) were all scrutinised by López Rabadán and Doménech Fabregat (2018).[183]

> "[N]ine thematic and formal categories associated with the spectacularization of politics during the most intense phase of the independence process in Catalonia, between June 2017 and April 2018, have been reviewed. The sample includes 188 images published by the top 10 leaders of the Catalan and Spanish political map, both in votes of their parties and followers on Instagram. The results show a regular political use characterized by intense personalization and orientation towards professional issues. In addition, a use of spectacular resources is detected, such as emotional appeal, the hybridization of spaces, and the experimentation with expressive filters." (p. 1013)

> "The empirical work of the research has focused on the most intense phase of the independence process in Catalonia: from the approval of the date and the question

---

[182] Amelang, Daniel (2017). "¿Pueden ser los cuerpos policiales víctimas de delitos de odio?", 3 October 2017, *El Salto Diario.* https://www.elsaltodiario.com/conquista-derecho/cuerpos-policiales-delitos-de-odio

[183] López-Rabadán, Pablo & Hugo Doménech-Fabregat (2018). "Instagram y la espectacularización de las crisis políticas. Las 5W de la imagen digital en el proceso independentista de Cataluña", *El Profesional de la Información,* Vol. 27, Núm. 5 (2018): 1013-1029. https://recyt.fecyt.es/index.php/EPI/article/view/epi.2018.sep.06/40850

in the (in June 2017) until the release of the President of the Generalitat Carles Puigdemont[184] in Germany (in April 2018). Within a process of institutional crisis that began in 2012, it is in this final phase that its most serious political, social and criminal consequences are concentrated. The sample includes 10 profiles of the main Catalan and state political leaders with a significant impact on Instagram. And their parties represent respectively 92.47% and 93.95% of the votes in the last general elections of 2016 and Catalan regional elections of 2017. (p. 1015)

*** 5.4 Fake news and the November 9 2014 non-binding poll on Catalan independence.**

In the run-up to what was to be a non-binding poll on independence (announced as an electoral pledge, and not challenged in the courts by the Spanish government or anyone else, to my knowledge), the Madrid newspaper *El Mundo* headlined "Investigan una cuenta de 12,9 millones de Xavier Trias en Andorra. Habría transferido el dinero desde Suiza al Principado en febrero de 2013" (Inda & Urreiztieta 2014)[185]. The headline takes for granted the veracity of the account's owner, and in the small print includes Sr. Trias' immediate and hot denial of the claim. Four days later the Swiss Bank (Catalan News 2014)[186] certifies the falsehood of the claim. The Anti-Corruption Public Prosecutor's Office decided not

[184] Carles Puigdemont had more than double the number of followers (225,000) than the next most popular leader, Oriol Junqueras (94,200). At the end of 2020, Sr. Puigdemont had no fewer than 795,700 followers.

[185] Inda, Eduardo; Esteban Urreiztieta & Fernando Lázaro (2014). "Investigan una cuenta de 12,9 millones de Xavier Trias en Andorra", *El Mundo*, 27/10/2014. https://www.elmundo.es/cataluna/2014/10/27/544dfbfa22601df70d8b456e.html

[186] Catalan News (/2014). "Swiss UBS guarantees that Mayor of Barcelona doesn't have any account, rejecting 'El Mundo' accusations", 31 Octobert 2014. https://www.catalannews.com/politics/item/swiss-ubs-guarantees-that-mayor-of-barcelona-doesn-t-have-any-account-rejecting-el-mundo-accusations

to push the case (Ajuntament de Barcelona 2014)187. In 2016 Núria Orriols[188] summarised some of the cases of fake news smeared against Catalan politicians up to that moment, often at critical moments in the run-up to elections of one sort or another (Xavier Trias narrowly failed to retain his mayorship of Barcelona in 2015, arguably because of the impact of one of these smear campaigns designed by the Spanish police and disseminated by the unscrupulous Madrid press):

> "Since 2012 the so-called Operation Catalonia has showed its hand via accusations of corruption against pro-independence leaders. Now, however, feuds within the Spanish police force have revealed the strategy — during a statement in court police Commissioner José Manuel Villarejo admitted to the existence of this operation— and leaked tapes from the Interior Minister's office brought it to light: the conversations between Jorge Fernández Díaz and Daniel de Alfonso, former head of the Anti-Fraud Office, have cast light on the conspiracy against Catalan leaders. Until now, the most well-known cases have been the appearance of a report about former President Artur Mas in the middle of the election campaign in 2012, the false Swiss bank accounts of former Barcelona Mayor Xavier Trias, and the alleged pressure on the BPA (Private Bank of Andorra) to obtain information on ex-Presidents Pujol and Mas and current Vice-President Oriol Junqueras." (Orriols 2016)

---

[187] Ajuntament de Barcelona (2014). "Public Prosecutor shelves case of Xavier Trias's alleged Swiss bank account, Barcelona City Council, December 2014. https://ajuntament.barcelona.cat/guardiaurbana/en/noticia/public-prosecutor-shelves-case-of-xavier-triass-alleged-swiss-bank-account_126785

[188] Orriols, Núria (2016). "Reports, fake accounts, and other attacks against the independence process. Since 2012, Spain has sought out scandals involving Catalan pro-independence leaders". Ara, 23 September 2016. https://www.ara.cat/en/Reports-accounts-attacks-independence-process_0_1655834483.html

These dirty tactics did not receive, and still do not receive, the attention that in my view they deserve from the media of democratic countries.

Just before the non-binding poll, it was described as "farcical" in an op-ed literally titled "A Threat to Spanish Democracy" by Cayetana (later to become PP spokesperson in the Spanish Congress), Núria Amat and Nobel-prize laureate Mario Vargas Llosa (2014)[189].

Back in 2012 (in an article allegedly dated 19 November 2013), Álvarez de Toledo had neatly summarised the bizarre position of the PP (the party that by challenging the 2006 Statute of Autonomy had unleashed the pro-independence movement):

> "Catalonia is once again the subject of curiosity and concern. The international media takes relish in portraying the heroic battle for independence waged by a postmodern Iberian Braveheart that is poised to take a step forward with Sunday's regional elections. The story is enthralling; an epic adventure worthy of sympathy and support. There is only one problem: it is not true." … "Sunday's regional elections may well deliver a majority for the separatist parties who will then no doubt claim a legitimacy to press for a referendum. This is something the central government will never accept - not least because, under current law, it cannot. The Spanish constitution, which Catalans have backed, rules out secession. For Catalonia to be independent, the constitution would have to be reformed. And that would mean calling a referendum, not just in Catalonia but in the whole of Spain."[190]

[189] Álvarez de Toledo, Cayetana; Núria Amat & Mario Vargas Llosa (2014). "A Threat to Spanish Democracy", New York Times, 4 November 2014. https://www.nytimes.com/2014/11/08/opinion/a-threat-to-spanish-democracy.html

[190] Álvarez de Toledo, Cayetana (2013). "The future of Catalonia is for all Spaniards to decide". Blog, 19 November 2013.

* 5.5 The 1 October 2017 Referendum and accusations of disinformation.

In the lead-up to the referendum (and thereafter) there were reports of journalists being harassed, both in the street and by the authorities. They have sometimes tended to be rather one-sided. Reporters Without Borders[191] issued a report in September 2017, shortly before the referendum. It was "produced by RSF's Spanish section as the region's separatist parties try to press ahead with the referendum although it has been banned by Spain's Constitutional Court." Note they apparently have no Catalonia branch.

> "The report describes the Catalan pro-independence government's constant pressure on local and foreign media, harassment of critical journalists by separatist movement "hooligans" on social networks, attempts by crowds of demonstrators to intimidate TV reporters, and the generally poisonous climate for press freedom.
>
> The report includes some of the many interviews that RSF has conducted with Catalan, Spanish and foreign journalists who have been the victims of harassment on social networks by Catalan government supporters. It draws attention to the pressure on media outlets that oppose independence and to the hostility they encounter on social networks.
>
> The accounts of foreign correspondents in Spain, especially those based in Barcelona, illustrate the

---

http://www.cayetanaalvarezdetoledo.com/2013/11/19/the-future-of-catalonia-is-for-all-spaniards-to-decide/#more-140

See also her article "Europe cannot afford to give in to the separatists", *Financial Times*, 18 February 2014. https://www.ft.com/content/bf93a536-988a-11e3-8503-00144feab7de, in which she can be seen to be blissfully oblivious of the existence of a deeply rooted, and potentially violent, Spanish nationalism.

[191] RSF Spanish section (2017). "Respect for media in Catalonia", Reporters Without Borders, September 28, 2017. https://rsf.org/en/news/rsf-publishes-report-respect-media-catalonia

> pro-independence movement's interest in the international media and the pressure it is putting on them because they are seen as a key element in the movement's visibility strategy.
>
> Catalan journalists working for media outlets that oppose independence told RSF that they have been the victims of intense harassment campaigns on social networks and of policies that deliberately draw attention to them."

The internet has been a battlefront for the Catalan independence issue. The director of research and information of the organization that runs the Catalan top-level domain .CAT, Pep Oliver, was detained on 20th September 2017] and retained in custody for 60 hours. As explained in English, French, Spanish and Catalan by Lundström & Xynou (2017)[192], in the run-up to the referendum on October 1 2017, which a Catalan Parliament Act had deemed binding, the Spanish government and the courts again forced servers such as Amazon and Google to block or neutralise websites related to the referendum. Many were blocked by the Spanish Guardia Civil (as if they were pornography or terrorism sites) and redirected to http://paginaintervenida.edgesuite.net. Of the 19 websites listed by Plataforma en Defensa de la Libertad de Expresión (2017)[193], eight (http://webdelsi.cat/, http://empaperem.cat/, http://joconvoco.cat/, http://vullvotar.cat/, http://Votaras1-o.cat, http://Sorayasaenz.cat, http://Marianorajoy.cat and http://Referendumcat.cat) are still blocked by the Spanish police as I write this section. Ironically enough, https://referendum.cat is once again active!

---

[192] Lundström, Tord & Xynou, Maria (2017). "Evidence of Internet Censorship during Catalonia's Independence Referendum", OONI website, October 3 2017. https://ooni.org/post/internet-censorship-catalonia-independence-referendum/

[193] Plataforma en Defensa de la Libertad de Expresión (2017), "Observatorio 1-O", 2 October 2017. http://libertadinformacion.cc/herramientas/observatorio-1-o/

Lundström & Xynou[194] explain that in the run-up to the 9 November 2014 non-binding poll, which the Catalan government started to organise and then found blocked by an automatic Constitutional court injunction, the Catalan government websites (including for essential emergency health services) were subjected to massive cyberattacks that were repulsed.

> "We confirm the blocking of at least 25 sites related to the Catalan referendum by means of DNS tampering and HTTP blocking, based on OONI Probe network measurements collected from three local networks195. OONI's data shows that these sites were blocked every day from (at least) 25th September 2017 (when the testing started) leading up to the referendum day, on 1st October 2017... Daniel Morales, 196 a freedom of expression activist who worked on the scripts to mirror the blocked sites, was called to appear in court on 22nd September and accused of being supported by Russian hackers by *El País*, one of Spain's largest media outlets." (Lundström & Xynou 2017, op. cit.)

Apart from censorship, there was massive disinformation on the Catalan conflict on or around the referendum day. The run-up to,

---

[194] (op. cit.)

[195] See https://explorer.ooni.org/country/ES.

[196] See also Pitarch, Sergi (2018). «El juez cita como imputado el 8 de febrero al hacker valenciano que replicó la web del referéndum de Catalunya». El Diario (Comunidad Valen ciana), 1 February, 2018. https://www.eldiario.es/comunitat-valenciana/imputado-valenciano-replico-referendum-catalunya_1_2816875.html

«Más de media docena de policías nacionales registraron la vivienda de los padres del joven de 21 años el pasado 22 de septiembre y se incautaron de su móvil personal y los discos duros, que no le han devuelto. Le imputan un delito de desobediencia y la policía lo considera el "cabecilla" de la red de piratas informáticos que publicitó el referéndum suspendido»

As reported by VilaWeb, that on 1 October 2019 published a list of 200 Catalans suffering or threatened by Spain's repressive campaign against the pro-independence movement (which totals 2,850 according to Òmnium Cultural), his case was dismissed by the court.

and aftermath of, the October 1 2017 self-determination referendum was a breeding-ground for fake news in the social media, both for and against Catalonia's independence. On the very same day, Maldito Bulo (2017) posted ten examples of fake news, in calling Catalonia "a battle-ground for dis/misinformation", a debatable affirmation inasmuch as it suggests that the examples form part of a deliberate, planned strategy; and the page was updated a year late197. This posting was reproduced the next day, together with a falsely-reported example of fake news (Plasencia 2017)198, and was the basis for a BBC article on the 21st[199]. Let us run through the examples, one by one. They were the following:

1. A 6-year-old child was allegedly (and falsely) rendered paralytic by the police, and a tweet to this effect got at least 7,248 RT according to the screen capture, and 9,153 in a later screen capture by Delgado (2019), and 8,427 on 12 May 2020. The Police's twitter account snidely added: "No todo lo que encuentres en las redes es verdad. NO hay ningún niño herido, a pesar de ser utilizados en las movilizaciones" ("Not all you find on the net is true. There is NO injured child, despite their being used used in demonstrations").200 The BBC (2017) chose this as one of four examples of fake news related to the October 1 referendum.

In actual fact the tweet may have nothing to do with October 1, though it WAS published that day. It was a comment (issued at "4.08 p.m.") to a Police tweet in which a young child (younger than six) is

---

[197] Maldito Bulo (2017). "10 bulos sobre el 1-O: Cataluña, campo de batalla de la desinformación", Maldito Bulo, upated 1 October 2018. https://maldita.es/malditobulo/2018/10/01/10-bulos-sobre-el-1-o-cataluna-campo-de-batalla-de-la-desinformacion/

[198] Plasencia, Marta (2017). "Los bulos que te colaron el 1-O y la foto real que te dijeron que era falsa", *El Español,* 2 October 2017. https://diariodeavisos.elespanol.com/2017/10/los-bulos-que-te-colaron-el-1-o-y-la-foto-real-que-te-dijeron-que-era-falsa/

[199] BBC Mundo (2017). 4 casos de noticias falsas que intoxicaron el debate sobre la independencia de Cataluña de España. BBC, 21 October 2017. https://www.bbc.com/mundo/noticias-internacional-41703119

[200] https://twitter.com/policia/status/914766615270559744?s=20

seen twisting its head at the sight of a policeman. The account holder seems to be very young ("si yo al instituto querer ir, pues quiero ir, pero si no me despiertan qé hago" ("In mistake-ridden Spanish: If I want to go to high school, well I want to go, but if they don't wake me, what shall I do?") she tweeted on 9 October 2017), to reside in Madrid to judge by the stripe on the taxi201) and not to have ever made any political tweets (unless they have diligently been deleted… except for this one)202.

Having said this, the BBC report (op. cit.) includes - at "15:51", that is, 17 minutes earlier - another tweet, by @vbmx_ - later deleted - that had made the same claim: "A policeman has crippled a six-year-old child..."

2. No Spanish policeman, while on duty in Barcelona for the referendum period, died of a heart attack. This fake news was written by a policeman203, who rectified the following day, but did not delete his original tweet (with 4,100 RTs). In their eagerness to attribute everything to the pro-independence side, *El Español* justified this by saying that he had indeed died at home in Valladolid (670 km away), but that "the policeman was said to have died as a result of a heart attack brought on by stress".

3. Policemen attacking firemen was another example of fake news. According to Maldito Bulo, it was disseminated by @tati6464, whose Twitter activity abruptly ceased on February 20 2018, and who often retweeted tweets by Izquierda Unida, and its leaders. It cannot be classified as pro- or anti-independence: it is simply an accusation of police violence… using a false image.204 The BBC (2017) chose

---

[201] https://twitter.com/lerrraagge/status/799745333660151808?s=20

[202] https://twitter.com/lerrraagge/status/914491902652813313?s=20

[203] https://twitter.com/PerdigueroSIPEp/status/914959311641726976?s=20

[204] https://twitter.com/malditobulo/status/914895472103493632?s=20 / https://twitter.com/tati6464/status/914862496242192386?s=20

this as one of four examples of fake news related to the October 1 referendum.

4. A policeman getting beaten up by demonstrators. The photograph had been taken in Andalusia nine years earlier. It was clearly disseminated by the Facebook account of a Unionist to portray Catalan voters as violent.205

5. The girl who said her fingers had been broken by a Spanish policeman (and, incidentally, her breasts fondled). In this author's opinion, (and I know Marta personally) the policemen snapped her fingers back, one by one, and she thought they had been broken, not just disjointed. She reported this as soon as she had the doctor's diagnosis. Unionists revelled in claiming this was "fake news", but I claim it was an understandable human error on her part, which got immediate dissemination on the pro-independence side and was nevertheless held up for months as evidence of fake news by the Unionist press.206

6. A white haired lady carried off by four policemen was not a friend of Basque independence activist Otegi. It was clearly disseminated by a Unionist.207

On 4 October, three days after being identified as fake news, the picture of the Basque lady with Otegi was still being held up as evidence that "La abuela 'buenista' independentista es admiradora del terrorista Arnaldo Otegi" ("The 'good' pro-independence grandma is an admirer of the terrorist, Arnaldo Otegi") in the "Caso Aislado" blog208 (that in the same article falsely accused Marta of

---

[205] https://twitter.com/malditobulo/status/914876899473727491?s=20

[206] https://www.lasexta.com/noticias/nacional/joven-que-denuncio-que-policia-habia-roto-dedos-admite-ahora-que-tiene-inflamacion_2017100359d3a8ad0cf2304a2736968c.html

[207] https://maldita.es/malditobulo/no-la-senora-desalojada-el-1o-no-es-la-misma-que-ha-sido-fotografiada-con-arnaldo-otegi/

[208] "La abuela 'buenista' independentista es admiradora del terrorista Arnaldo Otegi", "Caso Aislado" blog. https://casoaislado.com/la-abuela-buenista-independentista-admiradora-otegi/

“colaborando en el destrozo de uno de los coches de la Guardia Civil), and “El ‘show’ de la pacífica abuelita al descubierto: es amiga del terrorista Otegi” ("The 'show' of the peaceful grandmother is exposed: she is a friend of the terrorist Otegi") in *OK Diario*, which also got 752 RTs in a tweet that has not been deleted.[209]

7. A man with a bleeding face was in fact hurt in a miners’ demonstration in Madrid in 2012. That Twitter account, @Auraraluzile, which today has 98 followers, is protected, and seems only to have published 110 tweets since it was set up in May 2017. It immediately received a number of replies stating the tweet was false (among other things, as one pointed out, it was not sunny in Barcelona that day!).[210] The same day @Auroraluzile tweeted that he or she had actually just taken the picture[211], but the reply was to @Auraraluzile, so it would seem we are really looking at two accounts; and @Auroraluzile certainly does not exist today.

   @NormaBurguesa (87 followers), a Madrid-based bullfight-loving lawyer whose account has only been active from 17-29 May 2017, referred to @Auroraluzile (sic) as her daughter, in a tweet on 24 May 2017.[212] The BBC (2017) chose this as one of four examples of fake news related to the October 1 referendum.

---

[209] “El ‘show’ de la pacífica abuelita al descubierto: es amiga del terrorista Otegi“, 4 October 2017, 17:27h. https://okdiario.com/espana/show-pacifica-abuelita-descubierto-amiga-del-terrorista-arnaldo-otegi-1385729#link_time=1507132475

See also tweet: https://twitter.com/okdiario/status/915616984984932352?s=20

[210] See tweets on October 1 here: https://twitter.com/search?q=%40auroraluzile&src=typed_query

[211] See https://twitter.com/AlexisTw86/status/914465869325094913?s=20

[212] https://twitter.com/NormaBurguesa/status/867465416469356544?s=20

8. Someone claimed that only 92 polling stations had opened. It was clearly drafted by a Unionist.213

9. A pro-independence comedian tweeted a message with a picture of a teenager with a bleeding head, that turned out to have been taken in 2012.214 He later deleted the tweet. The picture was also used in Italy to illustrate a news item.215 The BBC (2017) chose this as one of four examples of fake news related to the October 1 referendum.

10. Another tweet, by someone claiming to be the Delegate of Catalonia in Estonia ("Antonio Sánchez", @ElinaStig - this account no longer exists; it may have belonged to Elina Born, a singer who opened an account around February 2015 and represented Estonia in the 2015 Eurovision Song Contest, alongside Stig Rästa; in October 2016 it apparently belonged to a Catalan-speaker claiming to be a *casteller*216; by 15 September 2017 he/she was reported as a troll issuing false tweets217; *El País* was apparently fooled, according to a tweet dated 14 October 2017218; a new account was open in the name of Antonio Sánchez on 14 October 2017: @TienesTipex, before temporarily renaming the account as "Karantiinis Antonio") claimed Estonia had said Catalonia has the right to decide its own future". This has been said by many others, including Nicola Sturgeon219

In conclusion, then, of the ten cases, numbers 2, 4, 6 and 8 clearly came from the Unionist side. Numbers 5 and 9 clearly came from the pro-independence side and were admitted as errors.

[213] https://twitter.com/malditobulo/status/914923349117194240?s=20

[214] https://twitter.com/malditobulo/status/914466436730507264?s=20

[215] https://www.teleclubitalia.it/82362/ancona-un-giovane-15enne-si-ritrova-con-un-coltello-in-fronte/1282362/

[216] https://twitter.com/finselscullons/status/787705510342590465?s=20

[217] https://twitter.com/denterd/status/908807468125442048?s=20

[218] https://twitter.com/Salvi_76/status/919105043051229184?s=20

[219] https://twitter.com/elpuntavui/status/923952498909605892?s=20

Numbers 1 and 3 were against police violence. Number 10 was by a troll supporting the pro-independence side. And No. 7 is in an elusive and fishy class of its own. All in all, three things are clear: (1) that fake news did circulate on the referendum day; (2) some of it (such as an independence flag painted into a scene showing police violence), should not distract one from the main conclusion, that there was a great deal of police violence that day; and (3) that the examples of fake news seem to have come from Unionist circles at least as much as from pro-independence circles (near to or far away from Catalonia).

France 24 reported the following220:

"- 'Censorship' -

The police crackdown against the referendum has also been covered in a radically different way by Spanish state television and Catalonia regional TV.

"Spanish television and Catalan television seem like different worlds," said University of Salamanca communications professor Carlos Arcila.

On October 1 TV3, which depends on the Catalan government, opened its main newscast with statements from Spanish government officials hailing the "professionalism" of security forces - followed by images of police beating would-be voters.

On Spanish public television TVE the images of police violence did not make the nightly news.

TVE journalists in Catalonia issued a statement condemning what they called "censorship of the facts"."

It is interesting to see how the Spanish police tried to defend themselves on the day, through their twitter account. *Voz Libre* ran

---

[220] France 24 (2017). "Fake news fuels Catalonia crisis tension", France24, 12/10/2017. https://www.france24.com/en/20171012-fake-news-fuels-catalonia-crisis-tension

an article221 on this on 2 October 2017. In the evening one of the official tweets stated that 19 Spanish policemen and 14 civil guards had required immediate medical attention that day. This figure was to be multiplied thirteenfold within a day, to 431! (La Vanguardia 2017).222 Incidentally, the person kicking a fence at the police is arguably the same man that later lost an eye to a rubber bullet shot straight at him by the Spanish police: one of many cases of police officers awaiting trial for violence… while he does as well.

Some of these items of fake news were among those handpicked by *El Español* (2017)223 as "Diez mentiras en diez fotos: la propaganda sobre la represión el 1-O".

We were informed by Poynter that "Online hoaxes about the Catalan referendum concentrated on police action in Barcelona" - Poynter. 4 October 2017.224

> "Local officials estimated that about 800 civilians were injured in the weekend's violence — during which police fired rubber bullets and beat back voters with batons — while the government estimated more than 400 police officers had been injured as of Tuesday."

Did any single journalist in the whole wide world do anything to confirm the latter claim, concocted AFTER the event merely to

---

[221] "La Policía y la Guardia Civil defienden a golpe de tuit su actuación en el 1-O. Destaca que su misión es "proteger la legalidad" pese a "provocaciones, insultos y agresiones"". Voz Libre, 2 October 2017. https://vozlibre.com/sin-categoria/la-policia-la-guardia-civil-defienden-golpe-tuit-actuacion-1-4789/

[222] La Vanguardia (2017). "Interior asegura que 431 policías y guardias civiles resultaron heridos en el dispositivo del 1-O. La cifra se eleva de los 39 agentes contabilizados anoche por el ministerio a los centenares que ha anunciado este lunes", La Vanguardia, 2 October 2017. https://www.lavanguardia.com/politica/20171002/431755741107/interior-policias-guaridas-civiles-heridos-1-o.html

[223] *El Español* (2017). "Diez mentiras en diez fotos: la propaganda sobre la represión el 1-O", 7 October 2017. https://www.elespanol.com/reportajes/20171006/252225238_0.html

[224] https://www.poynter.org/fact-checking/2017/online-hoaxes-about-the-catalan-referendum-concentrated-on-police-action-in-barcelona/

support the official narrative, that the voters were not peaceful? I fear not. Yet hundreds took sides, and let themselves be dragged into an absurd quest putting in doubt the official figures issued by the health authorities, as to civilian casualties. Peter Preston (2017)225 was one of them:

> "A failure to check pictures of those supposedly hurt in recent independence demonstrations did journalism no favours. […] When you plough through this account and many others, different perspectives begin to surface. Not that the civil guard's truncheon-wielding interventions weren't violent and frightening. But that the reporting of what happened - including the detail of those 893 injured voters - hadn't been independently checked."

True, but "journalism" could have taken just a little more notice of verified sources, such as

> (a) "805 Videos of the Repression lived in Catalonia caused by the Spanish Police in the Referendum of October 1, 2017",226 nearly all of which were posted within a few hours of the events recorded. How many journalists paid any attention to this material, which, moreover, discredits the narrative repeated parrot-fashion by dozens of Spanish policemen in order to get the Catalan political and social leaders of the independence movement locked away for years to come by the Supreme Court?

> (b) On the very same day the Council of Official Medical organisations (CCMC) issued a strongly worded protest at the violence of the police action.227 And a few days later they

---

[225] "Violence in Catalonia needed closer scrutiny in age of fake news", advised Peter Preston in the Guardian on October 8 2017. https://www.theguardian.com/world/2017/oct/08/catalonia-demo-injuries-fact-checking.

[226] "Spanish Police. 805 Videos of the Repression lived in Catalonia caused by the Spanish Police in the Referendum of October 1, 2017." #ThisIsTheRealSpain. https://spanishpolice.github.io/

[227] Comunicat del CCMC davant de les actuacions dels cossos policials de l'Estat durant la celebració del Referèndum https://www.comt.cat/actualitat-i-

threatened to sue media that still denied the evidence, both medical and visual, of that violence.228

(c) On October 19 2017 (after Mr. Preston's article, to be fair) a complete report was issued by the Press office of the Catalan government, a few days before the Government was sacked and direct rule imposed. This may explain why the hyperlink is now (23 April 2020) broken.229

(d) The in-depth study, case-by-case, by Dr. Núria Pujol-Moix,230 of the people treated by the public health services either on that day (93% of the total) or within the following three days (the remaining 7%), as a result of the police action. 137 were treated for injuries to the head and neck (which could only be caused by the police breaking international protocols).

---

publicacions/posicio-del-comt/3055-comunicat-del-ccmc-davant-de-les-actuacions-dels-cossos-policials-de-l-estat-durant-la-celebracio-del-referendum

[228] CCMA (2017). "Col·legis de Metges estudien denunciar els mitjans que qüestionen els ferits de l'1-O. Rebutgen que es posi en dubte la "seva professionalitat i independència" i recorden que actuen sota un codi deontològic". 13 October 2017. https://www.ccma.cat/324/collegis-de-metges-estudien-denunciar-els-mitjans-que-questionen-els-ferits-de-l1-o/noticia/2814681/

[229] https://govern.cat/salapremsapres_fsvp/docs/2017/10/20/11/15/232799c8-755f-4810-ba56-0a5bbb78609c.pdf

[230] Original: "Un estudi inèdit analitza cas per cas la gravetat dels 1.066 ferits de l'1-O. La metgessa i professora Núria Pujol-Moix ofereix en aquesta investigació científica més detalls sobre els ferits per la brutalitat de la policia". VilaWeb, 24 January 2019. https://www.vilaweb.cat/noticies/estudi-ferits-1-o/

Spanish translation: Estadística descriptiva de las personas atendidas por el Servei Català de la Salut a consecuencia de las cargas policiales del día del Referéndum de Autodeterminación de Cataluña, el 1 de octubre de 2017. Núria Pujol-Moix. https://comunicats.cat/estudio-inedito-de-los-heridos-del-1o/

Affirmations made by Gabriel Colomé, now an adviser for the Spanish government, were belied by her conclusions:231

> "An unpublished paper analyses the severity of 1,066 wounded on 1-O referendum day, case by case. Doctor and academic Núria Pujol-Moix offered more information on those injured by police brutality in this detailed scientific paper.
>
> Despite the evidence of the images and reports, representatives of the Spanish government and associated mass media immediately began to deny the facts, and a year later they still do so. For example, they said that the images were fake, that very few ballot stations had been intervened, that the majority of people affected only suffered psychological disorders, and even that the clinical reports did not reflect the truth. They also justified police violence by saying that the voters attacked the police officers. These statements have been used for the prosecution against people accused in relation to the referendum.
>
> On October 19, a report drawn up by the Catalan Health Service or CatSalut - the institution responsible for public health in Catalonia - stipulated that it had offered assistance to 1,066 people affected by the police attacks».

(e) Journalists might also have taken more notice of the harsh letter that the Commissioner for Human Rights of the Council of Europe, Mr. Nils Muižnieks, sent on 4 October 2017 to Sr.

---

[231] "Anyone who was struck was counted as injured," said Gabriel Colome, political science lecturer at Barcelona's Autonomous University.

"It is obvious that (the separatists) wanted those photos of violence," he added.

"Since you have won the media battle, you can say it was over 800, no one will question it. It is a post-truth battle, literally." (See France 24, 2017, op. cit.) https://www.france24.com/en/20171012-fake-news-fuels-catalonia-crisis-tension

Juan Ignacio Zoido Alvarez, Spain's Minister of the Interior, in which he wrote to convey his "concerns regarding allegations of disproportionate use of force by law enforcement authorities in Catalonia on 1 October 2017".232 The letter came into public knowledge on October 9, together with Sr. Zoido's reply, dated the 6th, and was quickly taken up by the press.

(f). Last but not least, the police violence has been taken to the courts. In actual fact, at least 110 Spanish policemen face charges (of whom three had been acquitted by 1 October 2019) for their actions on 1 October 2017 (Riart 2019).233

A Barcelona judge who was extremely critical of the police action on 1 October 2017 was actually fined €600 for expressing his views in private, and was also taken to court for slander by the public prosecutor:

> "The presiding judge of Barcelona Administrative court No. 17, Federico Vidal, sent an email from his official account to other judges and magistrates with expressions such as "police terrorism" or "uniformed terrorists" to refer to the actions of state security forces and police during the referendum on 1 October..
>
> The judge had already been punished in March by the Disciplinary Commission of the General Council of the Judiciary (CGPJ) with a fine of 600 euros for a serious case of "disdain" after a file was opened on 9 October following the publication of the content of the email in 'OK Diario'....
>
> In the messages, he also criticized the "police terrorism" that Catalonia "suffered." [...] "Has nobody anything to

---

[232] Muižnieks, Nils (2017). Letter from High Commission for Human Rights of the Council of Europe to the Spanish Foreign Minister Juan Ignacio ZOIDO, 4 October 2017. https://rm.coe.int/letter-to-the-spanish-authorities-concerning-disproportionate-use-of-f/168075ae1a

[233] Riart, Montse (2019). "Cent policies investigats per les càrregues de l'1-O". Ara, 01/10/2019. https://www.ara.cat/politica/Cent-policies-investigats-carregues_0_2318168202.html

say about the police terrorism that we suffered in Catalonia? Or about the 890 wounded caused by uniformed terrorists?" he asked in his messages, "or about the 2.3 million people who felt coerced, insulted and despised for wanting to vote? Is there really nothing to say?".

The judge continued his message with a reference to King Philip VI: "Let's do the same as his Bourbon Majesty and turn a blind eye so as not to lose our job or shall we bravely face up to harsh reality, or have indeed to deal with very real problems?". (ACN 2018)[234]

The fact that he was clearly accurate in his description may have been a factor in the case being dismissed in January 2019 by another Barcelona court (RB 2019)[235].

An important official complaint was addressed to Spain by the Council of Europe Commissioner for Human Rights, Nils Muižnieks on 4 October 2017.

1. Mr. Muižnieks' tweeted the following at 8:01 a.m., 9 October 2017:[236]

"See my exchange of letters with Minister of Interior of Spain on police conduct in Catalonia on 1 October".

His Press office issued a notice headlined "Commissioner calls on Spain to investigate allegations of disproportionate use of

---

[234] ACN (2018). "La Fiscalia denuncia per injúries el jutge de Barcelona que va criticar el "terrorisme policial" de l'1-O", *Diari de Girona*, 18 May 2018. https://www.diaridegirona.cat/catalunya/2018/05/18/fiscalia-denuncia-per-injuries-jutge/914380.html

[235] R.B. (2019) "Arxiven la causa per injúries contra el jutge que va afirmar que l'1-O s'havia fet "terrorisme policial"", *El Punt Avui*, 15 January 2019. https://www.elpuntavui.cat/politica/article/17-politica/1536310-arxiven-la-causa-per-injuries-contra-el-jutge-que-va-afirmar-que-l-1-o-s-havia-fet-terrorisme-policial.html

[236] https://twitter.com/CommissionerHR/status/917268728429142016?s=20

police force in Catalonia", with links to both letters (Council of Europe 2017).[237]

2. At 10:22 a.m. *EITB.EUS* (the Basque public broadcasting authority) announced on its website, quoting news agencies, "The European Human Rights commissioner asks Zoido to investigate 1-O police assaults on"[238]

The article ends quoting the minister's reply: "the first condition for the democratic system to function is the law", and that "outside the law there is no democracy".

3. 9 Oct, 2017 12:31 p.m. *RT* Wrote "Catalonia crisis: Council of Europe demands Spanish probe into 'police violence'".[239]

RT (which puts police violence in inverted commas, and includes a tweet with an example of serious violence by Spanish police) adds:

> In his response[240] [Sr. Zoido] noted that the police acted in accordance with the recommendations of Spain's constitutional court and in a "proportionate and appropriate manner."
>
> "Interventions were not aimed at citizens or their ideas, they were intended to prevent the holding of the referendum, the instructions transmitted by the highest court of the national territory," he said.

---

[237] Council of Europe (2017)."Commissioner calls on Spain to investigate allegations of disproportionate use of police force in Catalonia ", 9 October 2017. https://www.coe.int/en/web/commissioner/-/commissioner-calls-on-spain-to-investigate-allegations-of-disproportionate-use-of-police-force-in-catalonia

[238] https://www.eitb.eus/es/noticias/politica/detalle/5132693/cargas-policia-10-el-comisario-europeo-ddhh-pide-investigacion-zoido/

[239] https://www.rt.com/news/406121-council-europe-investigation-catalan-violence-police/

[240] https://rm.coe.int/reply-of-the-minister-of-interior-of-spain-to-the-commissioner-s-lette/168075ae31

4. For *La Vanguardia*, Luís B. García Arvelo published a piece on 09/10/2017[241]: “El Consejo de Europa pide investigar la violencia policial del 1-O.”

5. *Nueva Tribuna* wrote that "The European Human Rights commissioner calls for probe into 1-O police attacks" but notes that "The Spanish Government turns down the request ".[242]

This paper added further information, about the complaints and investigations by Rafael Ribó, the Catalan Ombudsman:

> "It has also come to the notice of the Ombudsman that Amnesty International concludes, in a report drawn up by observers, [243] that «there has been an excessive and unnecessary use of force by the police against defenceless people and the use of rubber bullets”, and that Human Rights Watch is also drawing up a report."

6. The English-language digital newspaper published in Spain, “*The Local*”, issued a piece by Lee Roden, on the 9th, 12:00 CEST+02:00 that “Council of Europe human rights chief urges Spain to launch probe into police action in Catalonia”. [244] After dealing with Mr. Muižnieks’s letter, Spain’s various responses were dealt with:

---

[241] La Vanguardia (2017). “El Consejo de Europa pide investigar la violencia policial del 1-O.” La Vanguardia, 9 October 2017. https://www.lavanguardia.com/politica/20171009/431919588840/consejo-de-europa-investigar-violencia-policial-1-o.html

[242] Nueva Tribuna. (2017). «El Comisario Europeo de Derechos Humanos pide que se investiguen las cargas policiales del 1-O». Nueva Tribuna, 9 October 2017. https://www.nuevatribuna.es/articulo/espana/comisario-europeo-derechos-humanos-pide-investiguen-cargas-policiales-1-o/20171009141344144201.html

[243] Amnesty International (2017). “Spain: Excessive use of force by National Police and Civil Guard in Catalonia”, 3 October 2017. https://www.amnesty.org/en/latest/news/2017/10/spain-excessive-use-of-force-by-national-police-and-civil-guard-in-catalonia/

[244] https://www.thelocal.es/20171009/council-of-europe-human-rights-chief-urges-spain-to-launch-probe-into-police-action-in-catalonia

"No democracy could "accept a challenge to its constitutional order and territorial integrity that seeks to impose a breakaway project by force," [Mr. Zoido] concluded.

On the same day Zoido's letter was written, the Spanish government's representative in Catalonia offered the first and to date only apology to Catalans injured by police during the independence vote.

> "I can do nothing but regret it, apologise on behalf of the officers who intervened. I am very sad, very sorry, we deeply regret that we have arrived at this situation, it has been very hard, everything that we have experienced and seen these past few days," Enric Millo said.

Spanish government spokesperson Ignacio Mendez de Vigo also later said he "regretted" the injuries."

7. Later that day, at 18:42 CEST, *El País* published a piece by their Brussels correspondent Lucía Abellán (oddly enough, given that the Council of Europe is based in Strasbourg): "The Council of Europe calls for an investigation into the October 1 police attacks". In her reference to the Minister's reply, "he underlines that the unilateral poll on independence does not coincide with the requirements the Venice Commission itself, which depends on the Council of Europe, lays down", without adding that it was Spain's threats, and the risk of civil servants being prosecuted, that made such compliance impossible. (Nevertheless, a group of academics and prominent legal practitioners have indeed been prosecuted, despite having resigned from what was to be the electoral commission on account of the crippling fines they faced unless they did so.). Sra. Abellán also drew readers' attention to the fact that the Parliamentary Assembly of the Council of Europe was due to meet that very week to discuss the situation arising out of the referendum.[245]

---

[245] Incidentally, organizing a referendum was dropped from the Criminal Code in 2005.

8. On the same day *Periodico Daily* included, at the end of a piece by Pietro Dragone misleadingly entitled "Catalonia proclaims its independence. Madrid: ready to use the bad guys!", a short reference to the exchange of letters.[246]

9. “The CE wants a thorough investigation into the police attacks in Barcelona” headlined a website, “*Periodistas en español.com*” on the 9th.[247] It also refers to the Catalan Ombudsman’s (Sr. Rafael Ribó) complaints and involvement. This website had devoted an article to police violence on the 2nd, the day after the referendum.[248]

10. On the 10th, the Navarra daily "*Diario de Noticias*" headlined a column on page 19 "Europe calls for a probe into the 1-O police attacks".[249] Towards the end it devotes a paragraph to the Minister’s reply, highlighting his view that the police "acted with prudence, appropriately and proportionately". On page 3 a newspaper staff comment underlined the "indignity" that "The PP threatens Puigdemont with the same end as Companys, arrested by the Nazis and shot [by the Franco regime]".

11. The Basque daily "*Deia*" issued the same headline on the same day on page 23.[250]

12. Also on the 10th, an Algerian newspaper covered the issue with a shortish piece on page 17:[251] "Government rejects EU [sic] request for an investigation". It devotes considerably

---

[246] https://www.periodicodaily.com/la-catalogna-proclama-lindipendenza-madrid-pronti-ad-usare-le-cattive/

[247] https://periodistas-es.com/la-ce-quiere-una-investigacion-efectiva-sobre-las-cargas-policiales-en-barcelona-92688

[248] “Cataluña: uso excesivo de la fuerza por la policía y guardia civil” https://periodistas-es.com/cataluna-uso-excesivo-la-fuerza-la-policia-guardia-civil-92391

[249] https://es.calameo.com/read/002698969f93b06d21c53

[250] https://es.calameo.com/read/002698969c73d855e55bb

[251] http://lechodalgerie-dz.com/wp-content/uploads/2017/10/n1607-du-10-octobre-2017.pdf

more attention to the Minister's reply than to Commissioner Muižnieks's request for an official inquiry into the allegations of police violence.

And that is all that a search will yield right now, running a Google search for "Muižnieks Zoido", for the period covering October 9-11 2017. Eight news pieces in the whole of Spain. My point here is that selective censorship imposed by media (at least those with an enduring presence on the net) is an important element which can help to gradually build a framework of disinformation.

(d) On October 12th, 2017 Human Rights Watch gave a good overall view of the assertions made both by the Spanish Government and independent observers and called for an independent enquiry.[252]

Incidentally, for anyone interested, as said above, all the "fake news" purportedly surrounding allegations of violence, even brutality by police (who according to the Minister "actuaron prudente, apropiada y proporcionadamente", that is, "acted with prudence, appropriately and proportionately") has ended up with at least 110 indicted policemen,[253] nearly all of whom who face trials in a number of courts in Catalonia, in many cases thanks to organisations such as the Associació d'Afectats 1-0[254]. Of the 110, 35 were prosecuted by 200 people injured in just three towns: Girona, Aiguaviva and Sant Julià de Ramis.[255] Fifty more have been prosecuted before a Barcelona court for their part in "policía nacional" action.

---

[252] "Spain: Police Used Excessive Force in Catalonia. Hold Independent Investigation into Violence During Referendum " Human Rights Watch, 17 October 2017. https://www.hrw.org/news/2017/10/12/spain-police-used-excessive-force-catalonia

[253] Riart, Montse (2019). "Cent policies investigats per les càrregues de l'1-O. Barcelona demana que declarin 28 agents més per completar tota la cadena d'ordres". *Ara*, 01/10/2019. https://www.ara.cat/politica/Cent-policies-investigats-carregues_0_2318168202.html

[254] https://www.afectats1o.cat/

[255] https://www.ccma.cat/324/declaren-els-primers-policies-investigats-per-les-carregues-de-l1-o-a-girona/noticia/2952571/

What really happened on October 1 2017, polling station by polling station, has been carefully mapped, locating 11,348 videos and photographs. In over 95% (where the police did not intervene) voting took place in totally ordinary fashion despite attacks on the internet coverage).[256]

In a "reality check" the BBC asked: "Did voters face worst police violence ever seen in the EU?" (BBC News 2017).[257] It recalls that "Speaking to the BBC on Sunday, Spain's foreign minister Alfonso Dastis, claimed images of police violence were "fake"". "It is true that fake photos have been used but virtually all of the media coverage showing police violence was real - including all of that shown by the BBC." … "[t]he Spanish Government accepts there was some violence - and has apologised for it."

> It is difficult to find examples where as many civilians were injured during clashes with police. Yet when assessing the level of violence, the degree of force is important, not just the number of injuries. There are various cases where police in EU member states used an equivalent or even higher degree of force in public.

However, it is worth noting that none of those other deeds took place at polling stations.

Other fake news, completely distorting a statement, also makes the Catalan independence movement the bad guys. There are plenty of well documented cases, but I have been unable to find a systematic listing of them, and they are not the main purpose of this paper. Suffice it to remember the case of Mr. Clayborne Carson, director of the Martin Luther King Institute, who in a statement denied having said that "El Instituto Luther King de EEUU pide que Torra deje de usar su figura: "Es hipócrita"" (that is, "USA's Luther King Institute calls upon Torra to stop using his figure: "He's a hypocrite""), according to El Confidencial. This article was widely tweeted, with

---

256 https://catmemoria.cat/poble-a-poble/

257 BBC News (2020). "Catalonia: Did voters face worst police violence ever seen in the EU?" *BBC News*, 27 October 2017. https://www.bbc.com/news/world-europe-41677911

aggressive comments, by plenty of Unionist leaders, as pointed out by Joe Brew.[258] The digital newspaper refused to apologize for the headline: in fact, Mr. Carson made no reference at all to Sr. Torra (the Catalan President), nor did he ask anyone anything, nor did he describe the Catalan government as hypocritical. As is always the case, the fake news spread like wildfire, but its readers probably never realised they had been disinformed.

Some initiatives cannot be classified as fake news, but rather as ways of winning a narrative. Take for instance, the constant repetition that the independence movement fostered "hatred" against the Spaniards (rather difficult to imagine, as at least three grandparents of most of the supporters of Catalan independence were born in the rest of Spain!) led to the Ministry of the Interior, after direct rule was imposed on Catalonia, to set up a special system for reporting "hate offences" in Catalonia: "Situación en Catalunya: protección de víctimas" (that is, "Situation in Catalonia: protection of victims" (*La Vanguardi*a 2017).[259]

On the other side of the balance, the general public has no real idea why so much fake news has emerged in relation to the Catalan independence movement. The International Press Institute, IPI, headlined a piece by Henri Mikael "In Spain, Catalonia crisis sparks 'fake news' debate", 24 January 2018.[260] Here the author voices serious doubts about the Spanish government's narrative about the impact of Russian bots in the Catalan referendum, quoting among others specialists in fact-checking.

> Journalists and media experts in Spain told the International Press Institute (IPI) that the concept of "fake news" reached a new level of publicity in 2017,

---

[258] https://threadreaderapp.com/thread/1040885600423952385.html

[259] La Vanguardia (2017). Interior abre un apartado en su web para denunciar delitos de odio en Catalunya, *La Vanguardia,* 25 November 2017. https://www.lavanguardia.com/politica/elecciones/20171125/433181272780/ministerio-interior-delitos-odio-catalunya.html

[260] Koponen, Henri Mikael (20918). "In Spain, Catalonia crisis sparks 'fake news' debate". IPI website, Jan 24, 2018. https://ipi.media/in-spain-catalonia-crisis-sparks-fake-news-debate/

> driven by the sharing of false stories on social media and the increasing efforts of media outlets to debunk hoaxes and misinformation on their websites." […] "according to [Clara Jiménez, co-founder of the website Maldita], "fake news" was "not a notable concern" in Spain at the site's outset. Last fall's political crisis in Catalonia, she said, "changed everything"...
>
> "In the aftermath of the Catalonia vote, political discourse in Spain resembled that of the United States in late 2016, with many fingers pointing at alleged Russian interference. A government-supported research institute suggested (White 2017)[261] [quoting Mira Milosevich, Real Instituto Elcano, soon to be shot down by McGrath] that Russia had deployed "trolls, bots and fake accounts" to further sow social division in Spain. In November, Spain's foreign minister raised the issue of Russian interference in Catalonia at a meeting of the EU's Council of Ministers (Sanhermelando 2017)[262].
>
> Many Spanish media outlets, such as *El País,* the most widely circulated daily newspaper in Spain, supported the narrative." …

The European Union's "fact-checking team", East Stratcom Task Force, found a few examples[263] of widely circulated pieces of disinformation originating from Russian sources, among which a handful relating to Catalonia[264]. One claimed that Catalonia planned to recognise Crimea as a legitimate part of Russia; another reported

---

[261] White, Todd (2017). "Russian Hackers Fueled Catalan Separatism, Madrid Institute Says". *Bloomberg,* 8 de novembre de 2017. https://www.bloomberg.com/news/articles/2017-11-08/russian-hackers-fueled-catalan-separatism-madrid-institute-says

[262] Sanhermelando, Juan (2017). "España denuncia en la UE la interferencia de Rusia en la crisis catalana", *El Español,* 13 NOV 2017. https://www.elespanol.com/mundo/europa/20171113/261724021_0.html

[263] https://euvsdisinfo.eu/disinformation-cases/?text=catalonia&disinfo_issue=&date=

[264] We have referred to this briefly above.

that EU officials supported violent measures in Catalonia; while another went so far as to claim that Spanish is being taught as a foreign language in Catalonia. We have mentioned one such case above (on the “domino effect”). To my knowledge, however, no-one described as disinformation this exact claim, when it was voiced in June of the same year - just three months earlier - by Ana Losada, spokesperson for an “Asamblea por una Escuela Bilingüe”, in an interview in a digital newspaper notoriously opposed to Catalonia’s independence and right of self-determination: “El castellano en las escuelas catalanas tiene el mismo estatus de la lengua extranjera” (that is, “Spanish in Catalan schools has the same status as a foreign language”) (Fidalgo 2017)[265]. Koponen (2018)[266] reported that “In Spain, Catalonia crisis sparks ‘fake news’ debate”:

> “Russia has denied the claims as “hysteria”, while many Catalans say that the Spanish government has exaggerated the problem.
>
> Some journalists are also skeptical.
>
> Virginia Pérez Alonso, deputy editor-in-chief of the online newspaper *Público*, said that the Spanish central government, led by Prime Minister Mariano Rajoy, sought to portray the recent successes of the Catalan separatist movement as partly the result of “fake news” spread by Russian trolls.
>
> “Some politicians in the conservative side consider this to be true, but there is simply no evidence,” she said, emphasising that the amount of actual “fake news” stories on the issue was insignificant.
>
> “A lot of the mainstream media supports this narrative too, but we are still trying to get to the bottom of this story.”

---

[265] Fidalgo, Sergio (2017). ““El castellano en la escuela catalana tiene estatus de lengua extranjera”“. *ElCatalan.es*, 4 June 2017. https://www.elcatalan.es/castellano-la-escuela-catalana-estatus-lengua-extranjera

[266] Op. cit.

> Pérez said that many false stories and out-of-context pictures were circulated on social media as the events unfolded in October, but that "mistakes were made by both sides", and that the content, which was picked up by some media outlets, was generally not intended to be misleading.
>
> Some observers believe that the Spanish government could be using the "fake news" narrative for its own benefit."

A few months later, on 3 April 2018, *OK Diario* - no fan of Catalonia's quest for independence - published a piece by Alfonso Merlos on "Fake News in Catalonia" (in Spanish, despite the English tiutle). He not only uncritically accepts the official narrative, but goes so far as to say that "la oda a la mentira sigue hasta hoy..." ("the ode to lying continues to this day") (Merlos 2018)[267] and claims:

> "Let's continue with the farce that the defeated independence supporters try to perpetuate, as reported by *OK Diario*, having recently gone so far as to use robots to put around stories about alleged sick elderly folk worried about their health… of martyr Puigdemont." … "the story of the "procés" is a monument to *fake news* in Catalonia, a grotesque operation of disinformation and propaganda which enjoys the support, amongst other agents... of Putin's Russia." … These media "(praise) the numerous actions carried out on the political and social fronts that are today being the cause of numerous cases for offences of sedition and rebellion —in other countries they would be high treason—.".

* 5.6 The Taulé et al. study of tweets

Another study (Taulé et al. 2018)[268] analysed tweets based on corpora of 87,449 tweets in Catalan and 132,699 tweets in Spanish

---

[267] Merlos, Alfonso (2018). 'Fake News' in Catalonia (2018). *OK Diario,* 3 April 2018. https://okdiario.com/opinion/fake-news-in-catalonia-2054071

[268] Mariona Taulé, Francisco Rangel, M. Antònia Martí & Paolo Rosso (2018). *Overview of the Task on Multimodal Stance Detection in Tweets on*

collected from 20 September to the day before the 1 October Referendum. They found no censorship as such (which was not the object of the exercise) but an almost complete divorce in communication between those supporting the opposing views. They found that an overwhelming majority of tweets in Catalan were “in favour”, while there was a split almost down the middle in tweets in Spanish.

Table 3. Distribution of the stance labels for Catalan and Spanish)

	CATALAN			SPANISH		
	TRAINING	TEST	TOTAL	TRAINING	TEST	TOTAL
Favor	4,085	1,021	5,106	1,680	419	2,099
Against	120	29	149	1,785	446	2,231
Neutral	479	119	598	972	243	1,215
TOTAL	4,684	1,169	5,853	4,437	1,108	5,545

However, the community of users followed by users against the Catalan 1 October Referendum was vastly superior:

Catalan #1Oct Referendum, IberEval 2018, Evaluation of Human Language Technologies for Iberian Languages Workshop 2018. p. 149-166. http://ceur-ws.org/Vol-2150/overview-Multistance18.pdf

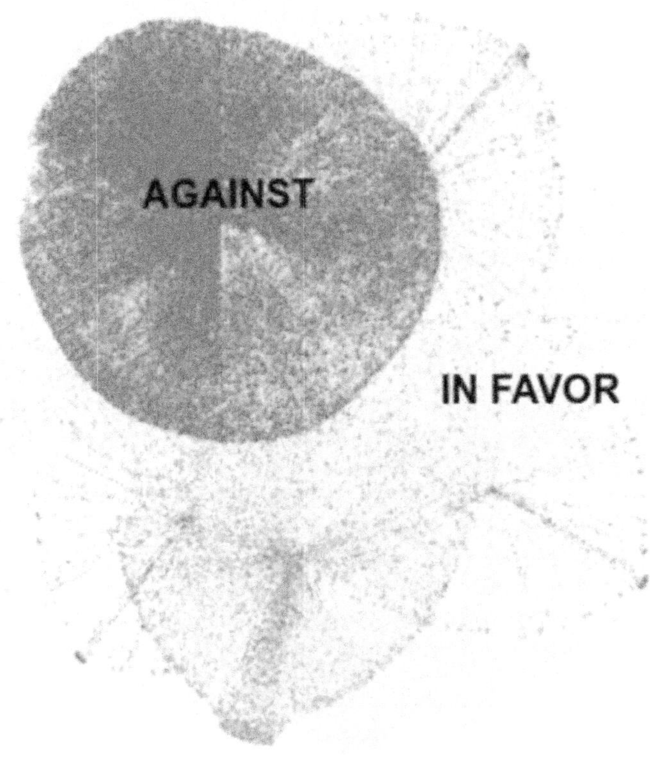

Fig. 3. Stance-based social network communities.

http://ceur-ws.org/Vol-2150/overview-Multistance18.pdf

“In red, representing 71.30% of the total, is the community of users that are followed by users against the Catalan 1 October Referendum. In yellow, with 28.04% of the total, is the community of users that are followed by users in favor of the Referendum. Finally, in blue, with 0.67% of the total, is the community of users that are followed by both users in favor and against the Referendum. We can draw two main conclusions.

> Firstly, the anti-referendum community is much larger (71.30% vs.28.04%), though this might depend on the selected sample. Secondly, the lack of interest in communicating with the other community and understanding the other viewpoint: the blue community is only 0.67% of the total." (Taulé et al. 2018: 164)[269]

* 5.7. Misinformation and violence

Spanish media and academics, partly inspired by *El País*, have not forgiven Julian Assange for the social impact of his public endorsement - which was not of Catalan independence, but of the Catalans' right of self-determination.

In one such paper the authors (Del Fresno & Manfredi Sánchez 2018)[270] say:

> "Misinformation, post-truth and fake news are the consequence of the complex interaction between technological disruption, collective interpersonal communication and sociopolitical action. We analysed the impact of content produced by the hacktivist Julian Assange and his WikiLeaks organization in support of the Catalan independence process in the last quarter of 2017. A total of 1,708,087 unique results were retrieved from multiple streams of Internet data, of which 99.85% is from Twitter with a 93% viralization rate. The 50 most viral tweets were analysed qualitatively to identify the underlying misinformation patterns. The research findings show 1) the extent to which such misinformation favors the internal logic, coherence and survival of the independence worldview, whose main

---

[269] Mariona Taulé et al. (2018). *op cit.*

[270] Del Fresno García, Miguel & Juan Luis Manfredi Sánchez (2018). "Politics, hackers and partisan networking. Misinformation, national utility and free election in the Catalan independence movement". *El Profesional de la Información* ,Vol. 27, Núm. 6 (2018). https://recyt.fecyt.es/index.php/EPI/article/view/64778

value lies in its national utility and 2) misinformation does not use the coercion of lies or falsehoods typical of totalitarian propaganda, but the freedom of citizens to voluntarily engage".

One of the authors made some sage remarks I can endorse, in an article in *El País* (Del Fresno 2018), in which he stretches the bounds of disinformation:

> "Disinformation as a way of thinking in community tends to be justified by the fallacy of the defence of cultural values and individual rights. The problem is not that the truth is the opposite of the lie, but that opinion is elevated to the category of truth. The risk is that opinions cannot support the democratic model because, as political scientist Hannah Arendt wrote, “Freedom of opinion is a farce unless factual information is guaranteed and the facts themselves are not in dispute.”".[271]

How true this is. Just a few months before the referendum, Eduardo Inda, founder and director of *OK Diario*, went so far as to claim (with an opinion disguised as a fact) that

> “I believe that this level of violence was not experienced even in the Basque Country in the hard years. Not even in the Basque Country, because of course, there they could kill a judge or a prosecutor, and they didn’t kill many of them for that matter, either, but...”

… when, much to the frustration of Spanish nationalists, there had been no violence whatever in what from the outset was to be a peaceful, non-violent movement for independence. The indignant uproar was sonorous, and the Catalan Association of Victims of Terrorism actually toyed with the idea of taking the case to the courts.[272]

---

[271] Del Fresno García, Miguel (2018). “Posverdad y desinformación: guía para perplejos”. El País, 16 March.
https://elpais.com/elpais/2018/03/16/opinion/1521221740_078721.html

[272] La Vanguardia (2017) “La asociación catalana de víctimas del terrorismo sopesa denunciar a Eduardo Inda“. La Vanguardia, 17 February 2017.

Coverage of the international reaction to the police brutality against voters on 1 October 2017 was also biased. The above-mentioned letter from Nils Muižnieks, Council of Europe Commissioner for Human Rights, to the then-Prime Minister Mariano Rajoy, on 4 October, got unequal coverage in the Spanish media, as we have seen.[273]

Jordi Xuclà (referred to above when he doubted the existence of alleged campaigns of disinformation in favour of the pro-independence movement in Catalonia), may well have been thinking of the protest by Spanish public TV news reporters, on October 1 2017, the day of the referendum vote. In this regard, Herman (2017) wrote:

> Earlier this month, employees of Spain's government-funded TV news station TVE called for the resignation of their station's director after declaring the state channel's coverage of an October 1 Catalan independence referendum, in which Spanish police attacked unarmed people as they waited to vote, "an embarrassment" and "unbalanced." The TVE protest, which involved much of the newsroom staff, was widely reported in Spain...[274]

---

https://www.lavanguardia.com/politica/20170217/4292680036/eduardo-inda-avt-demanda-violencia-terrorismo-eta-catalunya.html

[273] https://rm.coe.int/letter-to-the-spanish-authorities-concerning-disproportionate-use-of-f/168075ae1a

[274] See also: "The *TVE* News Council (an independent body of journalists that monitors *TVE*'s impartiality), issued a communiqué calling for the immediate resignation of the entire *TVE* news management for "failing in the public service duty entrusted to it by the law as regards the provision of objective, accurate and pluralist reporting in its coverage of the events of 1 October in Catalonia." The communiqué added: "Not only did *TVE* make no special provision for an event of major importance, which would nonetheless have been easy to arrange, but also every effort was made to broadcast a partial vision of what happened."" In RSF (2017) "Catalan referendum: attacks on journalists, biased coverage". 4 October 2017. https://rsf.org/en/news/catalan-referendum-attacks-journalists-biased-coverage

And he may have also thought of the heavy bias of nearly all the Madrid media as regards the Catalan independence process. In Herman's words (2017):

> "Most Spanish coverage of the complex crisis remains heavily spun and buys into the culture of rumours surrounding the Catalan story. That's included coverage by *El País* and ME [sic] Alandete himself. Authoring an October 20 2017 news analysis, "Catalonia: The Gravity of the Situation",[275] Alandete reported that secessionist protesters in Barcelona had stolen "weapons and ammunition" left in a vandalized police car during a large street demonstration on September 20. *[Editor's Note: No one has been charged with stealing weapons, or, for that matter, with leaving them in unlocked vehicles.]*"

At the tail end of the vote, in-depth articles easily convey to readers a particular message: fake news in Catalonia helped the independence cause. "Catalan crisis a 'breeding ground for fake news" reported on 12 October 12 2017, just above a photograph of voters that was anything but a fake. (AFP 2017)[276]

> ""We have never seen this in Spain until now," Clara Jiménez, a journalist in charge of a popular Twitter account called "Maldito Bulo", or "Damned Hoax", which verifies stories that circulate online, told AFP.
>
> She said the flood of fake stories started a few days before the referendum, which was marred by police violence.

---

[275] Alandete, David (2017). «Catalonia: The gravity of the situation". *El País*, 20 October 2017. https://elpais.com/elpais/2017/10/19/inenglish/1508414476_862878.html

He also claimed that "The pro-independence movement has waged a war against the free press".

[276] AFP (2017). "Catalan crisis a 'breeding ground for fake news", *The Local*,12 October 12 2017. https://www.thelocal.es/20171012/catalonia-crisis-a-breeding-ground-for-fake-news.

> The bogus reports, shared widely online, form part of the global phenomenon of "fake news", with Russia in particular being blamed for spreading misinformation in a bid to influence politics."

The *Washington Post* (2017)[277] went as far as to say "How fake news helped shape the Catalan independence vote" on October 1 2017, again quoting Clara Jiménez.

* 5.8. Misinformation on October 1 2017

In the monographic issue of *Quaderns del CAC* (no. 44, Volum XXI) 278 on "Fake news, algoritmes i bombolles informatives" (31.07.2018) an article by Òscar Coromina and Adrián Padilla published an "Anàlisi de les desinformacions del referèndum de l'1 d'octubre detectades per Maldito Bulo".

> "This article takes the events around the referendum for the Independence of Catalonia, which took place on 1 October 2017, as a reference to carry out an analysis on the use of disinformation within a context of political conflict and a highly polarised scenario, as part of a strategic narrative. Based on a proposed analytical methodology, and applying this to the disinformation verified by the fact-checker Maldito Bulo, we have noted that the aim of this disinformation is to discredit the

---

277 Washington Post (2017). "How fake news helped shape the Catalan independence vote", *The Washington Post*, October 19 2017. https://www.washingtonpost.com/news/worldviews/wp/2017/10/19/how-fake-news-helped-shape-the-catalonia-independence-vote/

278 CAC (2018). "Fake news, algoritmes i bombolles informatives", *Quaderns del CAC, 44*, Volume XXI, Juliol de 2018. https://www.cac.cat/documentacio/fake-news-algoritmes-i-bombolles-informatives

The issue includes a book review of "McNair, B. Fake News: Falsehood, Fabrication and Fantasy in Journalism", by Alexandre López Borrull. https://www.cac.cat/sites/default/files/2019-01/Q44_Critica_LopezBorrull_CA.pdf

> people involved, to magnify facts and boost support for the different positions, that the format of this disinformation is a key element regarding its degree of dissemination, and the difficulties faced when determining the precise impact of such disinformation."

They analysed and codified each of the 52 examples of disinformation related to the 1 October 2017 referendum.

> “The codification of the 52 examples of disinformation crosschecked by Maldito Bulo has allowed us to show that 67% of the disinformation (35) formed part of the pro-independence narrative, while 33% (17) belonged to a Unionist narrative.”

However, 16 of the 17 "Unionist" items of disinformation were taken up by the media, whereas this was the case for only two-thirds (23 out of the 35) of the "pro-independence" items.

> “The content of the disinformation analysed allows us to state that most of the disinformation published in the period analysed had very specific objectives: to link independence with violenceto exaggerate the police action of October 1, to accuse the Spanish Government of practising a dirty war, to add fictitious endorsements to both causes and to discredit the leaders of both sides.”

Nevertheless, it adds a caveat:

> "the fact-checker Maldito Bulo may be better equipped to detect some post-truths than others, and this situation may be exacerbated if the media system intervenes to disprove disinformation aligned with a particular narrative, and does so with less intensity as regards the other." (p. 24)

And, in general,

> "In light of the results, all indications are that the pro-independence side is more active as regards the production of disinformation. However, we must not lose sight of the fact that Unionism is much more efficient in

involving the traditional media in propagation and also in denial, a fact that we can relate to the very editorial line of certain media, which leads them to act in alignment with one of the two disputing poles." (p. 24)

* 5.9 The StoryData and other reports

This final conclusion differs from that of StoryData (2019)279, a group of data journalists (Eli Vivas, Sílvia Galilea, Laia Brufau and Carina Bellver), who carefully classified 120 items of fake news recorded by Maldito Bulo for a year, starting at the time of the referendum, and portrayed their results in graphic form.

The «Constitutionalists» or "Unionists" actively spread fake news against the pro-independence movement:

> "[T]he fifty-odd news items that sought to motivate disinformation in favour of the so-called constitutionalist bloc were also concentrated in three ideological battles: October 1, the 21-D elections and the war of symbols over the yellow ribbons. In the case of the referendum, this news also invokes violence, invented in this case, by voters against the police, with photographs or videos of riots that are not from that day. [...]"

The pro-independence camp was active in attacking the «Constitutionalists»:

> "There are also some 40 items of 'fake news' against the constitutionalist ideological bloc. *Ciudadanos* became the most mentioned party with information that, in addition to putting in the headlines things that were not said, also tried to relate the leaders of the orange party with dictatorships such as Francoism or Nazism. In this

---

[279] StoryData (Eli Vivas, Sílvia Galilea, Laia Brufau & Carina Bellver) (2019). "Cinc gràfics interactius per entendre l'impacte de les 'fake news' sobre el procés independentista", *Crític,* 20 March 2019). https://www.elcritic.cat/dades/cinc-grafics-interactius-per-entendre-limpacte-de-les-fake-news-sobre-el-proces-independentista-12210

bloc, the misinformation related to October 1 gained strength, with news of injuries by the police that did not correspond to reality. "

The international scene was also covered:

"The x-ray of the 'fake news' of the *procés* reveals that a significant proportion of the fifteen false news items spread purportedly to reinforce the pro-independence ideological positions tried to generate disinformation related to the external recognition of Catalonia." (Vivas et al. 2019)

Last but not least, a BA dissertation (Delgado 2019)[280] analysed 24 tweets of fake news, selected because they achieved a high number of RTs or were published by someone with a large number of followers. Leaving aside the author's inherent bias (she asks "¿qué derecho tiene Cataluña para autodeterminarse como país?" - "what right has Catalonia to self-determine itself as a country?" - but only quotes one author, who denies it), the selection is interesting.

"We have come across 24 news items in all that were disseminated by hundreds of people and, in other cases, by thousands of people who believed them to be true. Most of the tweets were not rectified by their author, so they continue to circulate on Twitter today. Only 48% of the fake news items were denied by other means or by other users. In this line and in relation to the second hypothesis of the research is the intervention of politics in the dissemination of such false news. After analyzing them, we can observe that they were disseminated not only by anonymous citizens, but also that important journalists and representative figures of the independence

[280] Delgado, Almudena (2019). *El fenómeno de la desinformación en Twitter: Las fake news del 1-O sobre el conflicto catalán*. BA dissertation, Universidad de Sevilla. https://idus.us.es/bitstream/handle/11441/91218/TFG%20ALMUDENA%20DELGADO%20BALONGO%202019.pdf?sequence=1&isAllowed=y

movement in the political panorama made use of them in their official accounts " (Delgado 2019: 76-77).

Let us end this sub-section by pointing out that other Catalan websites give their readers advice on detecting fake news, such as the Fundació Horta Sud (2019) and verificat.cat mentioned in sub-section 2.3 above.[281]

*** 5.10 The October 14th 2019 Supreme Court judgment**

On the very day the judgment was given down, the Observatory of the Penal System and Human Rights (University of Barcelona) issued a "Statement regarding the Supreme Court decision on the Catalan process"[282] which arguably aired the view of not only all those that had voted in the referendum (either way) but of many other Catalans as well:

> "The Observatory of the Penal System and Human Rights of the University of Barcelona wants to express its rejection of the Supreme Court Judgment and its concern about the situation we have been living for some time.
>
> Rejection of a disproportionate sentence that establishes harsh penalties for democratically elected political representatives and also for leaders of Catalan social entities.
>
> Concern because this sentence is committed to a repressive way that severely hinders what is necessary to resolve the existing conflict: political and social dialogue.

---

[281] Fundació Horta Sud (2019). "Com fer front a la Fake News", Fundació Horta Sud. https://fundaciohortasud.org/util-practic-infografia-fake-news/

[282] English: http://www.ub.edu/ospdh/en/statement-regarding-suprem-court-decision-catalan-process

Catalan: http://www.ub.edu/ospdh/ca/comunicat-vers-sentencia-del-proces

Spanish: http://www.ub.edu/ospdh/es/comunicado-en-referencia-la-sentencia-del-proces

We support the social mobilization of rejection of the sentence and express our solidarity with the prisoners and their families."

On 14 October 2019 Craig Murray wrote in his blog:

"The vicious jail sentences handed down today by the fascists (I used the word with care and correctly) of the Spanish Supreme Court to the Catalan political prisoners represent a stark symbol of the nadir of liberalism within the EU. That an attempt to organise a democratic vote for the Catalan people in pursuit of the right of self determination guaranteed in the UN Charter, can lead to such lengthy imprisonment, is a plain abuse of the most basic of human rights."[283]

Murray's reference to "political prisoners" (a term which speaks for itself, but which the official Spanish narrative claims is false), highlights another strategy used by Spain, as revealed empirically by Joe Brew in mid-2018: the more the pro-independence debate centres on the plight of the political prisoners, the less it insists upon putting into place the independent republic declared by the Catalan Parliament under a year earlier.[284] This is something similar to what Juan Luis Cebrián, at the time still President of PRISA, the powerful media group, foresaw: if direct rule was imposed to end Catalonia's move to independence (provided the ballot went that way), "el debate ya no sería cuándo van a lograr la independencia, sino cuándo van a recuperar la autonomía" ("the debate would not be about when indeoendence will be achieved, but

---

[283] Murray, Craig (2019). "Weep for Catalonia, Weep for Liberalism in Europe", blog, 14 October 2018, https://www.craigmurray.org.uk/archives/2019/10/weep-for-catalonia-weep-for-liberalism-in-europe/

[284] Fàbregas, Laura (2018). "Lo que Twitter revela: cuanto más hablan de "presos", menos lo hacen de "independencia. Los principales dirigentes nacionalistas priorizan en la red social la liberación de los encarcelados al objetivo efectivo de la secesión". *Crónica Global*, 6 September 2018. https://cronicaglobal.elespanol.com/politica/twitter-mas-hablan-presos-menos-independencia_164807_102.html

rather about when autonomy will be regained . (Alvarez de Toledo 2017).[285]

The manipulation of the media, deliberate or otherwise, was well exemplified in the coverage of the reactions to the judgment. The confrontation of mainly young people with the police in central Barcelona, with the burning of containers (including grotesque descriptions, e.g. Salvador 2019),[286] received immeasurably greater media attention that the five columns that left Girona, Berga, Vic, Tàrrega and Tarragona, each with thousands of demonstrators, to walk to Barcelona, at least 60 km away, over a period of three days (CCMA 2019,[287] Nació Digital 2019)[288]. On the last day a sixth column converged on Barcelona from Castelldefels (VilaWeb 2019)[289].

Fact-checkers were quick to detect a rapid rise in fake news when Spain's Supreme Court ruling condemning nine political and social leaders to 10 or more years behind bars for an imaginary, undated act of "sedition". *Maldito Bulo* quickly opened a special

---

[285] Álvarez de Toledo, Cayetana (2018). "Juan Luis Cebrián: "Si el yerno del Rey va a ir a la cárcel, ¿por qué no Artur Mas?"", *El Mundo*, 20 February 2017.
https://www.elmundo.es/television/2017/02/20/58aa31cdca4741163a8b45d7.html

[286] Salvador, Antonio (2019). "Ha sido el máximo combate en 30 años de Antidisturbios", *El Independiente*, 23 October 2019.
https://www.elindependiente.com/politica/2019/10/23/ha-sido-el-maximo-combate-en-30-anos-de-antidisturbios/

[287] CCMA (2019). "Les cinc columnes de les Marxes per la Llibertat fan camí cap a Barcelona", *CCMA*, 16 October 2019. https://www.ccma.cat/324/aixi-son-les-marxes-per-la-llibertat-convocades-per-lanc-contra-la-sentencia/noticia/2955813/

[288] Nació Digital (2019). "Les Marxes per la Llibertat: cinc columnes i 100 quilòmetres per la llibertat dels presos", *Nació Digital*, 16 October 2019. Video. https://www.youtube.com/watch?reload=9&v=dtYvzEIb0_4

[289] VilaWeb (2019). "Les Marxes per la Llibertat: cinc columnes i 100 quilòmetres per la llibertat dels presos", *VilaWeb*, 17 October 2019.
https://www.vilaweb.cat/noticies/marxes-llibertat-anc-omnium-resposta-sentencia/

section290 where it gathered 52 hoaxes or pieces of fake news related to the aftermath of the very severe judgment, which basically consisted of the huge marches just mentioned above - which received very little media coverage -, and the burning of containers in central Barcelona, and many instances of repressive policethat over-reacted.

As a backdrop to the latest situation, let us take a quick look at the apparent political intent of the generators of this fake news, as regards the two political camps: pro- and anti-independence. Maldito Bulo recorded 55 such instances. A few were from satirical websites or sources, which when taken out of context were taken by some as being real. A few were deleted or amended as soon as the disseminator was told (often by many people!) the news was fake (e.g., a Vox leader or *El Publico* newspaper). Some are clearly by opponents of the independence process, using videos from other scenarios (Buenos Aires, No. 3; Madrid, No. 5; …).

False information, designed to intoxicate public opinion or, when written by the Spanish civil guard, to influence the courts (Sibina 2020)[291], is not recorded as such by organisations such as Poynter, which were nevertheless active in detecting false news after the judgment (Tardáguila 2019)[292]:

> "Last Monday, when the Spanish Supreme Court sentenced former leaders of the Catalan independence movement to lengthy prison terms, the streets of Barcelona became the stage for violent protests. Inevitably, social media was rife with false information.

---

[290] Maldito Bulo (2019). "Bulos y desinformaciones que circulan tras la sentencia del 'procés'". 15/10/2019. *Maldito Bulo*. 15–25 October 2019. https://maldita.es/malditobulo/2019/10/15/bulos-y-desinformaciones-que-circulan-tras-la-sentencia-del-proces/

[291] Sibina, Marta (2020). "Sobre los bulos de la Guardia Civil: mensaje desde Catalunya". Video (8'01"), Canal Octuvre, No. 23, 26 May 2020. https://www.youtube.com/watch?v=nHoewX9xjxo&feature=youtu.be

[292] Tardáguila, Cristina (2019). "Amid protests and misinformation, fact-checkers are again proving their usefulness". https://www.poynter.org/fact-checking/2019/amid-protests-and-misinformation-fact-checkers-are-again-proving-their-usefulness/

In about 24 hours, Maldita.es[293] and Newtral[294], two fact-checking organizations based in Madrid, caught and managed to debunk at least eight pieces of misleading content that had gone viral.

It was false, for example, that a 5-year-old boy and a man who had a heart attack at El Prat Airport died because protesters wouldn't let an ambulance get to them. It was also false that shares in the Spanish stock market fell as a result of the ruling, and that business owners threatened employees who thought about going on strike.

Spanish fact-checkers also pointed out a series of unproven claims attributed to presidential candidates. The country will have its second election in six months in a few weeks.

What we liked: Maldita.es and Newtral not only worked quickly but also showed they are capable of fact-checking content in different contexts, using different sources: the public health system, the stock market and the presidential campaigns. Maldita even managed to put all its fact checks on one page, which made it easier to read and distribute."

… Catalans [took] to the streets of Barcelona to criticize the Spanish Supreme Court for having sentenced to jail a group of independence leaders.

From the Catalans' point of view, the sentences imposed by the court in Madrid were too harsh (they varied from nine to 13 years in prison) and represented a clear attack on the separatist movement - a good reason to go out and protest.

So far, Spanish fact-checkers have flagged as false a post that claimed a 5-year-old boy had died because the

---

293 https://maldita.es/maldito-bulo/bulos-y-desinformaciones-que-circulan-tras-la-sentencia-del-proces/

294 http://newtral.es/

protesters didn’t let an ambulance get to him and some hoaxes regarding the relationship between the riots and the stock market performance.

Protests in Catalonia are ongoing, and can even interfere with the presidential elections scheduled for Nov. 10. In that part of the world, fact-checkers haven’t had a break.

… What is happening in Barcelona has given fact-checking a new level of exposition. It has made it clear that Maldito Bulo is necessary and that Spain has a misinformation problem,” said Jiménez. “It has also made our team feel more useful because they see that their work is indeed necessary. And, finally, we have also seen journalists who previously questioned the need for a fact-checking platform recognizing our value.” ... "So much exposure, however, demands an extra level of care. Jiménez, for example, has begun to explain in her fact checks which part of an allegedly false claim or video her team has really checked. By doing so, she wants to keep readers from having any doubt about the rating Maldito Bulo applied in a fact check.

...But let’s not forget that street protests and misinformation related to them also represent a great opportunity...”[295]

Two years after the Reporteurs sans Frontères (RsF) complaint, the Council of Europe reported that, “journalists were also threatened, attacked or arrested at demonstrations in Catalonia (Spain)”, and cited three of its Alerts (“Spanish reporter Laila Jiménez assaulted by protesters during Catalonia Independence march”[296], posted 3 October 2019, “Twelve journalists victims of

---

[295] Cristina Tardáguila (2019). Amid protests and misinformation, fact-checkers are again proving their usefulness. https://www.poynter.org/fact-checking/2019/american-newsrooms-2020-efforts-cover-misinformation-but-dont-amplify-it/

[296] See video here, of demonstrators making sure no-one else douses the journalist with liquid: https://www.elplural.com/fuera-de-foco/video-

violence on the sidelines of demonstrations in Catalonia", posted 15 October 2019; and "Violent arrest of reporter Albert Garcia", posted 21 October 2019)[297]. The same report explains that

> "alerts submitted to the Platform in 2019 reported several instances of verbal or physical attacks on PSM and their staff during anti-government protests, notably in France, Serbia and Spain. In several cases [in Spain], TV and radio journalists faced angry crowds who accused them of misreporting or of providing video materials to the police. Employees of Radiotelevisión España and Radio Catalunya [sic] were chased by hostile protesters and had their equipment damaged".

While not endorsing any violent action of any nature, allow me to underline that the level of disinformation in many Spanish media, basically to feed people outside Catalonia time and again with a narrative - the one that suited the Unionists, - close to hate speech, that had exasperated many, many people in Catalonia - and not only independence supporters - increased over a period of several years. Any impartial observer would, I am sure, vouch for the fact that particular Spanish media have been anything but impartial in their treatment of the Catalan conflict (as Mark Herman has pointed out; see above). Xavier Diez has written about "Mentiras fundamentales sobre Cataluña" and notes that his paper "no pretende ser un inventario exhaustivo, pero sí contiene elementos bastante repetidos desde los medios de comunicación y responsables políticos". He adds:

> "Conventional media, as well as a significant proportion of the social networks, have concentrated on stirring up

---

independentistas-agreden-a-una-periodista-en-barcelona-en-la-manifestacion-por-el-1-o_225002102

[297] Safety of Journalists Platform (2020). "HANDS OFF PRESS FREEDOM: ATTACKS ON MEDIA IN EUROPE MUST NOT BECOME A NEW NORMAL". Annual Report by the partner organisations to the Council of Europe Platform to Promote the Protection of Journalism and Safety of Journalists. Council of Europe, p. 23. https://rm.coe.int/annual-report-en-final-23-april-2020/16809e39dd

See also www.coe.int/fom

> hatred against Catalonia by carrying out tasks of blatant information manipulation [...] and, in fact, the topics used do not differ from the resources drawn on by anti-Semites in Central Europe in the years preceding the Second World War." (Diez 2018)[298]

The methods used are often quite subtle. For instance, several media, including *La Vanguardia*[299], and a Spanish website, *The Objective Today*" reproduced a Spanish Agency report about the above-mentioned Council of Europe report and carefully avoided mentioning that many if not most of these cases involved Spanish policemen. Quite the contrary:

> "Of the six Spanish alerts launched in 2019, four are related to attacks or arrests of journalists who were covering pro-independence demonstrations in Catalonia. Two of them were assessed as very serious (the arrest of photographer Albert García and the attacks on journalists at the El Prat airport, "most of them by Mossos d'Esquadra")."[300]

In actual fact, the text at the end in inverted commas does not appear in the Annual Report, nor is a source given by EFE News Agency. Nevertheless, the Spanish media swooped onto it.[301] This must surely be listed as fake news issued by this news agency.

---

[298] Diez, Xavier (2018). "Mentiras fundamentales sobre Cataluña", Diario 16, 19 November 2018. https://diario16.com/mentiras-fundamentales-cataluna/

[299] La Vanguardia (2020). "C.Europa denuncia que crece la intimidación a periodistas para silenciarlos". 29 April 2020. https://www.lavanguardia.com/politica/20200429/48820307478/ceuropa-denuncia-que-crece-la-intimidacion-a-periodistas-para-silenciarlos.html

[300] The Objective Today (2020). "El Consejo de Europa denuncia el crecimiento de la intimidación a periodistas para silenciarlos". 29 April 2020. https://theobjective.com/el-consejo-de-europa-denuncia-el-crecimiento-de-la-intimidacion-a-periodistas-para-silenciarlos/

[301] La Vanguardia (2020). "C.Europa denuncia agresiones a periodistas en manifestaciones Cataluña", *La Vanguardia.* 29 April 2020. https://www.lavanguardia.com/politica/20200429/48821827998/ceuropa-denuncia-agresiones-a-periodistas-en-manifestaciones-cataluna.html

* 5.11 Medals for the police[302]

In moves that can be seen as an attempt to minimise or even deny the oppressive police violence exerted in Catalonia, Spanish policemen have been awarded medals for their service in Catalonia, at least in the disturbances following the October 2019 Supreme court judgment. ("Operación Ícaro").

On 3 February 2020 the Basque Bildu MP Jon Iñarritu asked the Spanish government the following:[303]

> "The National Police Force has decorated 322 officers who took part in 'Operation Icarus', in Catalonia in October of last year.

---

https://www.lasexta.com/noticias/internacional/consejo-europeo-denuncia-crecimiento-intimidacion-periodistas-convertido-campo-batalla_202004295ea9b1b86db51c0001907c5a.html

https://www.canarias7.es/sociedad/tribunales/el-consejo-de-europa-recoge-en-su-informe-el-caso-de-la-reportera-de-rtvc-BI9129650

http://www.rtvc.es/noticias/el-consejo-de-europa-recoge-en-su-informe-el-acoso-a-raquel-guillan-redactora-de-212227.aspx

https://www.diariolibre.com/actualidad/internacional/c-europa-denuncia-que-crece-la-intimidacion-a-periodistas-para-silenciarlos-KO18529416

https://twnews.es/es-news/el-consejo-de-europa-recoge-el-caso-de-la-reportera-canaria

And also across the Atlantic. In Mexico it was syndicated to several dozen local papers, e.g.

https://www.diariodequeretaro.com.mx/mundo/denuncian-creciente-intimidacion-a-periodistas-para-silenciarlos-5164907.html

https://www.elsoldesinaloa.com.mx/mundo/denuncian-creciente-intimidacion-a-periodistas-para-silenciarlos-5164907.html

[302] Professor Henry Ettinghausen (personal communication) points out that this issue is very important. "Couldn't one call it something like the sacralisation of disinformation? i.e., the atrocities meted out by the Police were utterly denied, and, to prove it, here are the medals the Police were awarded..."

[303] http://www.congreso.es/l14p/e0/e_0007878_n_000.pdf

For this reason, I want to know:

1.- What type of decorations were awarded and for what reason to each of them?

2.- What is the merit of each of them?

3.- What rank and to what unit does each of them belong?"

The curt, evasive reply, in March 2020, merely quoted the articles of the 1964 Franco law which were applied to make the awards.[304]

According to *El Español* these medals were awarded by Minister Grande-Marlaska in the same month on October 2019, for it reported on the 24th that the Sindicato Unificado de Policía (SUP) had written to the Minister complaining that not all the police officers sent to Catalonia had been awarded a medal (Araluce 2019)[305]. The same source claimed that "Over 300 officers were injured on facing up to the violent activists, 134 belonging to the National Police." Another source (Cuesta 2020) 306 said that another police organisation, JUPOL, had also complained for the same reason, and claimed that the police had been "sent to control terrorism in Catalonia", to continue fueling the false narrative, and "to control the wave of separatist attacks". According to Salvador (2020)[307], only

[304] http://www.congreso.es/l14p/e1/e_0015749_n_000.pdf

[305] Araluce, Gonzalo (2019). "El Sindicato Unificado de Policía (SUP) plantea la propuesta en una carta remitida al ministro de Interior, Fernando Grande-Marlaska.", *El Español*, 24 October, 2019. https://www.elespanol.com/espana/20191024/condecoracion-policias-nacionales-desplegados-disturbios-cataluna/439206943_0.html

[306] Cuesta, Carlos (2020). "Marlaska irrita a la Policía al no condecorar a todos los agentes enviados a controlar el terrorismo en Cataluña", *OK Diario*, 30 January 2020. https://okdiario.com/espana/marlaska-irrita-policia-no-condecorar-todos-policias-destinados-controlar-ataques-cataluna-5103289

[307] Antonio Salvador (2020). "Interior concederá medallas a 320 policías del operativo en Cataluña por la sentencia del 'procés', *El Independiente*, 24

four of the 320 police officers that were decorated were injured in Operación Ícaro, and these received life-long salary bonuses. These were issued on January 29th, 2020 during the commemoration of the 196th anniversary of the founding of the armed police force.

In his report on the reply, Nicolás Tomás (2020)[308] failed to realise that the parliamentary question related only to the October 2019 repression:

> Far from purging responsibilities, Fernando Grande-Marlaska appreciates the services rendered by the Spanish police in the repression of the 1-O referendum. In response to the EH Bildu MP Jon Iñarritu, the Ministry of the Interior confirms that the Order of Police Merit has been awarded "to different officials in attention to their merits”.

The Agència Catalana de Notícies made the same mistake, while adding that in some cases these medals carry with them lifelong bonuses of up to 20% of their salary. (Diarimes.com 2020)[309]

> Interior Minister Fernando Grande-Marlaska has decided to decorate only certain police officers assigned to Catalonia to control the wave of separatist attacks. Not all the police were sent there for that task. Police unions have

---

January 2020. https://www.elindependiente.com/politica/2020/01/24/interior-concede-medallas-a-320-policias-del-operativo-en-cataluna-tras-la-sentencia-del-proces/

[308] Tomás, Nicolás (2020). “Policías investigados por el 1-O han sido condecorados por Marlaska”, *El Nacional*, 4 May 2020. https://www.elnacional.cat/es/politica/policias-investigados-1o-condecorados-marlaska_499437_102.html

[309] Diarimes.com (2020). “El gobierno español admite haber condecorado policías investigados por uso excesivo de la fuerza el 1-O“, *Agència Catalana de Notícies,* 4 May 2020. https://www.diarimes.com/es/noticias/actualidad/cataluna/2020/05/04/el_gobierno_espanol_admite_haber_condecorado_policias_investigados_por_uso_excesivo_la_fuerza_1_o_81631_3029.html

snapped that one up fast. Jupol judges "the DGP's decision not to decorate all the national policemen who participated in Operation Icarus to be inadmissible." (Cuesta 2020)[310]

Finally, Salvador (2019) recalls that The Spanish police operation ahead of the 2017 Referendum was called "Operación Copérnico"', and explains the meaning of "Operación Ícaro" and "Operación Minerva":

> "'Ícarus': the police operation to cut the wings of violent activists in Catalonia"
>
> The National Police has baptized with the name of 'Ícarus' the operation that has been deployed in Catalonia since the beginning of October [2019] to deal with the disturbances caused by radicals after the Supreme Court passed the sentence that convicted the pro-independence leaders to severe prison sentences.
>
> The National Police Corps has chosen the name of Daedalus's son to refer to the reinforcement operation that has led to more than 1,500 agents being sent to the Catalan community, most of whom are from Police Intervention Unit (UIP) and Prevention and Reaction Unit groups (UPR). Their withdrawal, for now, has no date.
>
> The Mossos d'Esquadra, for their part, have resorted to the name of the Roman goddess of military strategy - Minerva - to name the operational plan that came into effect last September 27 [2019] and which has led them to activate the maximum level of alert." (Salvador 2019)[311]

---

[310] Cuesta, Carles (2020). "Marlaska irrita a la Policía al no condecorar a todos los agentes enviados a controlar el terrorismo en Cataluña", *OK Diario*, 31 January 2020). https://okdiario.com/espana/marlaska-irrita-policia-no-condecorar-todos-policias-destinados-controlar-ataques-cataluna-5103289

[311] Salvador, Antonio (2019). "'Ícaro': el operativo de la Policía para cortar las alas a los radicales violentos en Cataluña", *El Independiente*, 23 October 2019. https://www.elindependiente.com/politica/2019/10/23/icaro-el-

* 5.12 The trial of Trapero, Catalonia's chief of police

Though a trial is not usually treated in a work on disinformation, the case of the chief of the Catalan police, or *Mossos d'Esquadra*, Josep-Lluís Trapero, and three top officials in the Catalan Department of the Interior, is special. Their Minister, Quim Forn, had already been tried, found guilty and sentenced by the Supreme Court to ten and a half years in gaol (Pi 2019)[312].

> "His status as boss of the *Mossos d'Esquadra* during the last phase of the process has completely marked his procedural situation and the accusations against him. In fact, the role of the Catalan police in the events of 1-O [1 October 2017] has always been under suspicion in the case, which is why many of these suspicions fell on Forn." (Pi 2019)

It was to be expected that, despite all the evidence to the contrary, the *Audiencia Nacional* that tried him, in which the presiding judge, Concepción Espejel, was widely feared to be biased in favour of the testimony of the *guardias civiles* whose reports has incriminated them, would issue a flawed judgment. Not least among the reasons was the fact that she is married to a *guardia civil* officer and has received medals from that semi-military corps. [313] The judgment was an acquittal for all four defendants, and was apparently a lesson in clarity, and the public prosecutor decided not to appeal to the Supreme Court. Judge Espejel, who was not the drafter of the

---

operativo-de-la-policia-para-cortar-las-alas-a-los-radicales-violentos-en-cataluna/

[312] Pi, Jaume (2019). "Joaquim Forn, condenado a 10 años y seis meses de prisión por un delito de sedición", *La Vanguardia*, 14 October 2019. https://www.lavanguardia.com/politica/20191014/47880944617/joaquim-forn-setencia-juicio-1o-prision-sedic-tribunal-supremo.html

[313] Parera, Beatriz (2018). "'Caso Alsasua': piden apartar a la jueza Espejel por estar casada con un guardia civil", *ElConfidencial.com,* 02 March 2018. https://www.elconfidencial.com/espana/2018-03-02/acusados-alsasua-jueza-casada-guardia-civil_1529557/

judgment, wrote an extremely lengthy dissenting vote, in the hope that it would be used in the appeal.

The importance of the acquittal is that it contradicts the basic reasons for Minister Forn (who was appointed in July 2017, under three months before the referendum) having been found guilty by the Supreme Court. The facts were the same, the witnesses for the prosecution were in many cases the same, but unlike the Supreme Court, two of the three *Audiencia Nacional* judges had clearly not decided the defendants were guilty before the trial even began.

Chapter 6. Claims of Russian involvement in the Catalan independence process

We shall now see how several organisations have insistently argued (without any convincing evidence) that Russia has interfered in the Catalonia-Spain conflict. Here is the first organisation.

* 6.1 The Institute for Statecraft

Another relevant organisation, concerned with the impact of Russia in Spain, is the Institute for Statecraft, a UK limited company founded in 2006, whose registered headquarters is an abandoned mill in Fife, Scotland, but whose main activity takes place in London[314]. It got into the news for attacking UK Labour leader Jeremy Corbyn online[315]. Soon after that it was hacked, and to this day its website is inactive.

> "A first tranche of documents relating to the Integrity Institute were released on 5 November 2018. The documents lay unnoticed for two weeks until 23 November, when a story on RT brought them to attention. A second tranche of documents was released on 29 November and a third tranche on December 13. The documents were represented as the result of a hack though it is possible that this disguises a leak by an insider."[316]

---

[314] See, for instance, Murray, Craig (2018). "British Security Service Infiltration, the Integrity Initiative and the Institute for Statecraft", Blog, 13 December 2018. https://www.craigmurray.org.uk/?s=Statecraft

and

Elmaazi, Mohamed & Max Blumenthal (2018). "Inside the temple of covert propaganda: The Integrity Initiative and the UK's scandalous information war". *The Gray Zone*, 17 December 2018. https://thegrayzone.com/2018/12/17/inside-the-temple-of-covert-propaganda-the-integrity-initiative-and-the-uks-scandalous-information-war/

[315] https://inews.co.uk/news/politics/foreign-office-investigates-institute-statecraft-attack-jeremy-corbyn-labour-191118/

[316] Paul McKeigue, David Miller, Jake Mason, Piers Robinson (2018). "Briefing note on the Integrity Initiative". Working Group on Syria Propaganda and Media.

On the basis of hacked information and other sources, Wikispooks claims the Institute for Statecraft has received millions of pounds from the UK FCO and commercial organisations, despite the fact that its website stated that "We are totally independent and impartial, not dependent on funding from political or government agencies, industrial interests, or any other source which might call our impartiality into question". Wikispooks uploaded to the net dozens of the Institute's internal documents. Wikispooks contends that

> "A study of the leaked documents underlines not only the permanent war mentality which pervades the group, but also the (generally only implicit) assumption that it is willing and able to exert covert influence over both governments and citizens, an observation strengthened by the number of group members who are either members of intelligence agencies or have backgrounds in psychological warfare".[317]

Among the "senior fellows" of this non-academic organisation (a fact which somehow belies the use of the term "fellow") is Nicolás de Pedro. His appointment took place, it can be gleaned from available website records, sometime between May 25 and December 2018. Sr. De Pedro is listed as a member of the "Temple Place resident team" of the Institute for Statecraft in a document dated 21 December 2018 (McKeigue et al. 2018)[318]. He was previously employed for some years as a chief researcher by CIDOB. The Barcelona Centre for International Documentation (CIDOB), a foundation devoted to the advancement of international studies[319]. Founded in 1973, it is arguably the oldest think tank in

---

21 December 2018. http://syriapropagandamedia.org/working-papers/briefing-note-on-the-integrity-initiative

317 https://wikispooks.com/wiki/Institute_for_Statecraft

318 Paul McKeigue, David Miller, Jake Mason, Piers Robinson /2018). "Briefing note on the Integrity Initiative", Working Group on Syria Propaganda and Media, 21 December 2018. http://syriapropagandamedia.org/working-papers/briefing-note-on-the-integrity-initiative#summary

319 See http://www.cidob.org

Spain. The foundation's board consists of institutional trustees, including several Spanish ministries.[320] This fact did not deter *OK Diario*, a singularly active newspaper in the field of hate speech, as we shall see below, from describing CIDOB as a "pro-independence" organization (14/6/2018).

> "Borja de Lasheras has recently witnessed how his former boss Torreblanca, with the help of the Barcelona Center for International Affairs (CIDOB), another pro-Catalan independence body, has pressured the media to influence the appointment by President Pedro Sánchez of the new Director of National Security, launching a smear campaign against Colonel Pedro Baños."[321]

Connections between the two institutions also include Alan Riley, Senior Fellow, Institute for Statecraft, who co-authored "Brexit: Causes and Consequences" [322] with Francis Ghilès, an Associate Senior Researcher at the CIDOB.

In May 2015, CIDOB published a paper[323] written by Sr. de Pedro: "Responding to Russia's Defiance", in which he offered advice to EU members states in the run-up to the formalisation of the March 2015 Agreement for the complete implementation of the Minsk Protocol on ending Russia's military involvement in Ukraine.

---

[320] Specifically, the Generalitat of Catalonia, Barcelona City Council, Barcelona Provincial Council, Barcelona Metropolitan Area, Spanish Ministry of Foreign Affairs and Cooperation, Spanish Ministry of Defence, Interuniversity Council of Catalonia.

[321] Cerdán, Manuel (2019). La noticia de 'El País' sobre las 'fake news' de dos rusos en Cataluña también era un 'fake', *OK Diario*, 14/06/2018. https://okdiario.com/espana/noticia-pais-sobre-fake-news-dos-rusos-cataluna-tambien-era-fake-2422061

[322] In the Notes Internacionals collection, No. 10/2016. https://www.cidob.org/ca/publicacions/series_de_publicacio/notes_internacionals/n1_159

[323] Nicolás de Pedro (2015). "RESPONDER AL DESAFÍO DE RUSIA". https://www.cidob.org/en/articulos/monografias/el_mundo_en_europa/responding_to_russia_s_defiance

The Institute for Statecraft is one of various institutions, media and organisations interested in Spain. It asked itself in an internal policy paper: "*Why is it so difficult to address the Russia issue in Spain, and what should be done?*"[324]

> “When it comes to Russia, pro-Russian-minded narratives are transversal and often pervading at all levels. The following are among the most recurrent ones: i) “poor Russia” was humiliated by the West in the 90s ii) the West broke the agreements on NATO expansion iii) Russia has a natural right to have a natural area of influence iv) Kosovo -which is particularly sensitive issue for Spain- is the origin of all problems, etc. The debate in Spain tends to be framed in terms of choosing Russia either as a friend/ally or enemy, i.e. a choice between cooperation and conflict. They don’t seem to understand that the real key choice is how to turn Russia into a cooperative neighbor and not an aggressive one.
> […]
> 4) Disinformation and fake news have become a highly politicized issue in Spain. Media-standards are not the best in Spain; information - particularly in public-owned media - tends to be biased and political TV talk-shows (tertulias) dominate the media panorama in the country. First steps of the PP-led Government to address the fake news issue are perceived by many as an attempt to limit the freedom of speech of those critical to the Government."

The reader may ask: why is the issue of Kosovo a “sensitive issue” in Spain? We shall come to that later.

For the moment, let us just add that the Institute for Statecraft showed off its political fire power by its “Integrity Initiative” Spanish cluster being directly responsible for a successful operation to prevent Colonel Baños from being appointed as Director of the

---

[324] https://www.pdf-archive.com/2018/11/28/why-is-it-so-difficult-to-address-the-russia-issue-in-spain/

Spanish government's Departamento de Seguridad Nacional (DSN).[325]

This led Chris Williamson, Labour MP for Derby North, to ask Alan Duncan "what on Earth a government-funded British-based charity was doing interfering in the internal appointments of a fellow European democracy"? According to Williamson, Duncan completely failed to answer.

Furthermore, the Institute started up a special project, "Integrity Initiative", described as a "PsyOp operation, a part of "divide and conquer" strategy designed to split Russia from Western Europe".[326]

We shall endeavour to limit ourselves here, instead, to the issue of fake news and falsehoods.

* 6.2 The UK Parliamentary inquiry on fake news

In Spain "Russian meddling in the referendum in Catalonia in 2017 was best covered by *El Pais*," we are told by Jakob Kalenský[327] in the Disinfo Portal. When the Digital, culture, media and sport Committee of the UK Parliament decided to hold hearings on fake news, on December 19th, 2017, David Alandete from *El País*, Francisco de Borja Lasheras from the *European Council on Foreign Relations* (and author of an easily shot-down report: "Three myths about Catalonia's independence movement" we have mentioned above[328]), and Mira Milosevich-Juaristi from *Elcano Royal Institute*

---

[325] See the tweets by Nacho Torreblanca, "Director the the ECFR office in Madrid, via https://twitter.com/InitIntegrity/status/1004790206795603968?s=20

[326] UK Government, MI6 and "Integrity Initiative" (2020). http://www.softpanorama.org/Skeptics/Political_skeptic/Propaganda/Neo_mccarthyism/integrity_initiative.shtml

[327] Kalenský, Jakuyb (2019) "The US Investigations Highlight Europe's Laxity on Disinformation", Disinfo portal, 29 October 2019, https://disinfoportal.org/the-us-investigations-highlight-europes-laxity-on-disinformation/

[328] Francisco de Borja Lasheras. "Three myths about Catalonia's independence movement". 22 September 2017. European Council on Foreign

(and author of “The ‘combination’: an instrument in Russia’s information war in Catalonia”[329]) were invited to present evidence to this Committee about disinformation on social media during the referendum in Catalonia (shortly before taking part in a seminar in Madrid, organized by the European Council on Foreign Relations, on "Disinformation, authoritarian fellow travelers & post-truth unbound").[330] Note that all three are firmly “Unionist”, and not a single person was invited from any Catalan academic institution.

The minutes of the session have been published.[331] Earlier in the same sitting another guest witness, Samantha Bradshaw, had said:

Relations (ECFR).
https://www.ecfr.eu/article/commentary_three_myths_about_catalonias_independence_movement

In Spanish:
https://www.ecfr.eu/madrid/post/tres_mitos_sobre_el_movimiento_independentista_de_cataluna

In French:
https://www.ecfr.eu/paris/post/trois_mythes_a_propos_du_mouvement_independantiste_en_catalogne

[329] Milosevich-Juaristi, Mila (2017). “La “combinación”, instrumento de la guerra de la información de Rusia en Cataluña”, ARI 86/2017 . 7 November 2017.
http://www.realinstitutoelcano.org/wps/portal/rielcano_es/contenido?WCM_GLOBAL_CONTEXT=/elcano/elcano_es/zonas_es/ari86-2017-milosevichjuaristi-combinacion-instrumento-guerra-informacion-rusia-cataluna

In English: Milosevich-Juaristi, Mila, “The ‘combination’: an instrument in Russia’s information war in Catalonia”, (*Real Instituto Elcano*, November 11th 2017).
http://www.realinstitutoelcano.org/wps/portal/rielcano_en/contenido?WCM_GLOBAL_CONTEXT=/elcano/elcano_in/zonas_in/ARI92-2017-MilosevichJuaristi-Combination-instrument-Russia-information-war-Catalonia

[330] Seminario: Disinformation, authoritarian fellow travelers & post-truth unbound. Madrid, 31 January, 2018.
https://www.ecfr.eu/events/event/seminario_disinformation_authoritarian_fellow_travelers_post_truth_unbound

[331] House of Commons (2017). Digital, Culture, Media and Sport Committee. Oral evidence: Fake News, HC 363. Tuesday 19 Dec 2017. Ordered by the

> "I think ... we are seeing capabilities in this area developing. It is not just Russia; it is a global phenomenon. One of the studies published last summer identified 28 different countries that were developing these kinds of techniques for different purposes. It is not just the Russian Government who are using social media to manipulate public opinion...
>
> "I also think that a lot of planning goes into digital disinformation campaigns; it is not something that you can just turn the bots on and make them work because for them to be very successful takes a lot of time and planning, and a lot of social engineering. ... For events that just sort of happen, such as the Catalonian referendum ... we don't see as much sophistication in terms of the kinds of disinformation campaigns that are happening."

Paul Farrelly MP (who left it on record that he was "no supporter of Catalonian independence") posed the following to David Alandete, as regards his apparent fixation on Russian (and Venezuelan) involvement in and around the time of the Catalan independence referendum:

> "As a journalist, I worked for Reuters, which is the neutral of the neutral—you would hope, unless you are a Russian. The news from Catalonia would never have been, "Catalonia is holding an illegal referendum, and by

---

House of Commons to be published on 19 Dec 2017.
http://data.parliament.uk/writtenevidence/committeeevidence.svc/evidencedocument/digital-culture-media-and-sport-committee/fake-news/oral/74926.html

See also Interim Report (29 July 2018), Ref. HC 363:
https://publications.parliament.uk/pa/cm201719/cmselect/cmcumeds/363/363.pdf

See also Final Report (18 February 2019), Ref. HC 1791:
https://publications.parliament.uk/pa/cm201719/cmselect/cmcumeds/1791/1791.pdf

> the way a few people are getting kicked by the police". That would not be the news. The actions of the Spanish Government gave them the opportunity to spread fake news and exaggerate. All this fake news may not have affected those people who had already voted in the referendum, but it certainly may have affected the image of Spain outside Spain, and possibly the image of Spain to some people in Spain, and how sophisticatedly the Spanish Government might react to such circumstances in future. The Spanish Government gave them the core of news; would you not agree?"

During the same session, Dr. Bradshaw's opinion was countered by that of Mira Milosevich-Juaristi, a senior research fellow at the Elcano Royal Institute and a university lecturer.

> "My hypothesis is that it is impossible to realise such a complex operation with different instruments without the support of a Government agency. Of course, I do not have material to justify that—it is a hypothesis."

During the hearing Paul Farrelly complained that in a widely-quoted paper by Javier Lesaca, on the subject of alleged Russian interference in the Catalan independence process:

> "unlike a scientific paper, there is no control, no comparator. Sputnik and the Russians were identified; they were the fourth largest of the 5 million that were sending their messages all around. But they were behind *El Diario*, the BBC and *El País*. So I would have liked to have seen, particularly, a comparator paper about what analysis of the BBC content and the way the BBC content was shared around the world".

Francisco de Borja Lasheras went to far as to claim that 900 Catalan voters were NOT treated by the medical services, which is what had been reported and substantiated even at that time (we shall return to this below):

> "You mentioned the BBC, but there is an ongoing discussion — I am not a journalist, but I work with journalists — about the fulfilment of journalistic

standards and the use of quotes without attribution. There was talk of 900 people injured in Catalonia, but that never happened."

Later in the same session, he was asked by Ian C. Lucas MP:

"[T]here are all sorts of people - there are people who attack me on social media who have connections in different places, but it is a serious allegation to say that the Russian Government is seeking to interfere with the referendum in Catalonia. We are interested in the evidence. That is what I want to know and I have had an answer. Do you think that the Russian Government is seeking to interfere with the outcome of the referendum in Catalonia?"

Francisco de Borja Lasheras' reply really reveals the value of his testimony: "Like I said, we have no specific evidence."

*** 6.3 The McGrath report**

Their evidence, and particularly on the role of Julian Assange and Wikileaks in the Catalonia-Spain conflict, was later studied by M. C. McGrath, the founding director of Transparency Toolkit, a US-based NGO, in the form of written testimony submitted to the Commission inquiry. [332] In his document he scrutinized their testimony, along with other publications about Russian interference in Catalonia, such as

(i) the *El País* story "Russian meddling machine sets sights on Catalonia"[333],

---

[332] Written evidence submitted by M C McGrath. http://data.parliament.uk/writtenevidence/committeeevidence.svc/evidencedocument/digital-culture-media-and-sport-committee/fake-news/written/80989.html

[333] David Alandete (2017). "Russian meddling machine sets sights on Catalonia. The global network that acted in favor of Donald Trump and Brexit turns attention to Spain", *El País,* 28 September 2017. https://elpais.com/elpais/2017/09/26/inenglish/1506413477_994601.html

(ii) the research report by Ben , “#ElectionWatch: Russia and Referendums in Catalonia?” from *Atlantic Council's Digital Forensic Research Lab*[334],

(iii) the report mentioned above, “The ‘combination’: an instrument in Russia’s information war in Catalonia”, by Mira Milosevich-Juaristi, in which she refers, as a given fact, to "Russia’s information war in Catalonia during and in the wake of its illegal referendum"[335] published by her institution, the *Real Instituto Elcano* , and

(iv) articles about the findings of Javier Lesaca's unpublished report.

McGrath discovered numerous instances of misinterpretation of data sources, use of inaccurate information, lack of attention to detail, and poor research methodology. As a result of these errors, he "suggested" that the conclusions drawn in these reports and presented in the December 19 Committee session are exceptionally misleading. Specifically, his review identified six key problems in existing reports:

It is a translation of the original article, published four days earlier: “La maquinaria de injerencias rusa penetra la crisis catalana. La red global que actuó con Trump y el Brexit se dedica ahora a España”, 25 September 2017. https://elpais.com/politica/2017/09/22/actualidad/1506101626_670033.html

[334] Nimmo, Ben, “#ElectionWatch: Russia and Referendums in Catalonia? Assessing claims of Russian propaganda in Spain”, (Digital Forensic Research Lab, September 28th 2017) https://medium.com/DFRLab/electionwatch-russia-and-referendums-in-catalonia-192743efcd76

After voting day Nimmo was quoted as saying that he did not think Russian media had “specific orders by the Kremlin about how to cover Catalonia.” https://www.france24.com/en/20171012-fake-news-fuels-catalonia-crisis-tension

[335] (op. cit.)

“The ‘combination’ (*kombinaciya*) is an operation which integrates diverse instruments (cyber warfare, cyber-intelligence, disinformation, propaganda and collaboration with players hostile to the values of liberal democracy) in Russia’s information war in Catalonia during and in the wake of its illegal referendum.”

(1). Failure to accurately use digital analytics tools;

(2). Dubious research methodology;

(3). One-sided analysis that ignores botnets disseminating anti-Catalan independence messages;

(4). Exaggeration of the influence of bots and trolls;

(5). Careless analysis of data from questionable sources; and

(6). Overstating the influence of Assange on *RT* and *Sputnik.*

There is not enough space here to go into McGrath's findings in greater detail. Suffice it to quote one final finding:

> ... This @marilena_madrid tweet [from the anti-independence side] was retweeted over 15,000 times, but 'liked' only 99 times. Researchers working on Twitter bot detection have discovered that bots often have low likes-to-tweets ratios, often below 0.1 [12]. In contrast to Julian Assange's tweets, which receive 1.14 'likes' per retweet on average, this tweet from @marilena_madrid has a 'likes' per retweet ratio of only 0.0062.

As McGrath points out, in his scathing, detailed demolition of *El País*, its "articles about the social media response to the situation in Catalonia are widely cited by Elcano and other groups in Spain".

McGrath's paper was well summarised by Gisela (2018) in April.[336], and was covered as a news piece by CCMA[337].

---

336 Rodríguez, Gisela (2018). "Report to UK Parliament on "exceptionally misleading" claims Russia promoted Catalan independence", *El Nacional*, Friday, 20 April 2018. https://www.elnacional.cat/en/news/report-uk-parliament-russia-catalan-independence_260421_102.html

337 CCMA (2018). "Un informe per al Parlament britànic desmunta la tesi de la ingerència russa en el procés", *CCMA*, 20 April 2018. https://www.ccma.cat/324/un-informe-del-parlament-britanic-desmunta-la-tesi-de-la-ingerencia-russa-en-el-proces/noticia/2851189/

It is important to add that McGrath is not on his own: Marc Herman, in *Columbia Journalism Review*, noted that “suspicion of *El País* has left much of Spain and Spanish readers without a place to read even modestly neutral coverage of the complex Catalan crisis"[338].

An equally scathing attack, aimed at David Alandete, by Thomas Harrington, after giving one particular quotation, said ironically that "the brilliant journalist at Spain’s leading newspaper was not content to stop with this morsel of infantile thinking".[339]

*** 6.4 Report on Soros and Catalonia**

Alandete was also attacked, in this case as being under the spell of George Soros, in Chapter 4 of an 80-page e-book by Juan A. Castro and Aurora Ferré.[340] Their approach is to attempt to dismiss all claims of Kremlin interference in the Catalan independence process, and to shoot down anyone claiming the opposite. The book was published in Madrid on 18 February 2019, the saint’s day, we are informed, of San Eladio de Toledo. The authors are kind enough, in an annex, to highlight those of the 197 non-violent tactics listed by Gene Sharp that they claim to have been attested to in Catalonia. Ten months before this, the authors of this then-unpublished book were interviewed and provided information for an article in Confilegal.com (Rodriguez & Berbell 2018)[341].

---

[338] Herman, Marc (2017)“Spain’s most famous paper stumbles amid Catalonia independence crisis”, *Columbia Journalism Review,* 27 October 2017. https://www.cjr.org/business_of_news/catalonia-independence-el-pais-spain.php

[339] Harrington. Thomas (2017). “Largest Newspaper in Spain Blames Russia and Antiwar.com for Catalonia Pro-Independence News”. *Antiwar blog*. 23 September 2017. https://www.antiwar.com/blog/2017/09/23/largest-newspaper-in-spain-blames-russia-and-antiwar-com-for-catalonia-pro-independence-news/

[340] Castro, Juan A. & Aurora Ferré (2020). *Soros rompiendo España.* https://tubrujuladigital.com/upload-files/9093srejadc.pdf

[341] Rodriguez, Yolanda, & Carlos Berbell 2018). “Fue el financiero Soros y no Rusia quien influyó en el conflicto de Cataluña. De acuerdo con un informe de inteligencia privado al que ha tenido acceso Confilegal“,

The article contains a link to an intricate chart[342] (illegible in the e-book) linking up George Soros and his foundations with a wealth of people and organizations all round the world, and also in Catalonia and Spain. As an illustration, let us look at the links that claim that Carles Puigdemont is funded by George Soros both through Jonathan Soros and J S Capital, and through the American Enterprise Institute. A search for news linking Sr. Puigdemont and JS Capital reveals a blog entry, citing another one. Under the headline in this blog entry, "Puigdemont holds a secret meeting with the son of George Soros in Ghent", the text turns out to be a pure speculation (or at the very least, no evidence is provided to substantiate the claim):

> "Specifically, Puigdemont is expected to hold a crucial and desperate meeting with Jonathan Soros, chief executive of JS Capital Management, in the Flemish city of Ghent, with the aim of obtaining funds to try to continue the already defeated secessionist *procés*" […] "... According to Spanish intelligence, during his stay in Belgium and more specifically in the Flanders region, Puigdemont plans to meet with one of the sons of George Soros, the greatest promoter and financier of the crazy Catalan separatist bid." (Redadler 2017[343])

Confilegal, 27 April 2018. https://confilegal.com/20180427-fue-el-financiero-soros-y-no-rusia-quien-influyo-en-el-conflicto-de-cataluna/

[342] https://confilegal.com/wp-content/uploads/2018/04/SorosCAT_grafo.pdf

[343] The URL given is https://redadler.wordpress.com/2017/10/30/puigdemont-se-reune-en-secreto-con-un-hijo-de-george-soros-en-gante/ but the blog is apparently private. It was cited in an blog entry by Eladio Fernández, on 4 November 2017: "El viaje de Puigdemont y su equipo a Bruselas ha sido para ser formados en estrategia por ´JS Capital de Jonathan Soros (hijo de George Soros). Los Soros dirigen la deriva independiente catalana para Daniel Rothschild". https://eladiofernandez.wordpress.com/2017/11/04/el-viaje-de-puigdemont-y-su-equipo-a-bruselas-ha-sido-para-ser-formados-en-estrategia-por-js-capital-de-jonathan-soros-hijo-de-george-soros-los-soros-dirigen-la-deriva-independiente-c/

The actual source was another blog entry, dated four days earlier, on 31 October 2017, in "Astillas de realidad", a blog viscerally opposed to Catalonias's independence: "Pero, ... ¿realmente han proclamado la república

This, a hypothetical future meeting, is sufficient (unless the chart has been drawn by the Spanish secret service (CNI), which is of course possible) for the first alleged association. This appears to be a classic example of fake news.

How about the second? Is the American Enterprise Institute , a Conservative think tank, funding Carles Puigdemont? Again, a Google search reveals the following:

> To highlight the conservative nature of Puigdemont's agenda, the President of the Catalan Generalitat held a meeting with Arthur C. Brooks. Brooks chairs the American Enterprise Institute , the largest conservative think tank in the United States. Brooks knows the Catalan reality well: he is married to Ester Munt, sister of the actress Sílvia Munt. And yes, he speaks Catalan." (Vilallonga 2017)[344]

Does that merit the second claim that Soros is funding Puigdemont? Hardly. But the director of the Institute presumably got into Spain's bad books (and his Institute into the chart) by offering his view that "An independent Catalonia could be an example of vitality and economic dynamism (Barnils 2017)[345].

---

catalana?", https://astillasderealidad.blogspot.com/2017/10/pero-realmente-han-proclamado-la.html

344 Vilallonga, Borja (2017). "Puigdemont a Amèrica: a la cerca d'aliats per al referèndum», *El Temps*, 2 April 2017. https://www.eltemps.cat/article/1174/puigdemont-a-america-a-la-cerca-daliats-per-al-referendum

«Puigdemont has been to America. The official five-day visit to the United States has begun to resemble an official visit by a head of state. Smothered by the Spanish government, the Catalan diplomacy prepared a tight agenda with politicians, press and strategic contacts in order to inform about the referendum on self-determination and the right of the Catalans. Behind it, the perpetual search to know what Catalonia can offer the world.»

345 Arthur C. Brooks: "'An independent Catalonia could be an example of vitality and economic dynamism'", *VilaWeb*, 2 May 2017. https://www.vilaweb.cat/noticies/arthur-c-brooks-an-independent-catalonia-could-be-an-example-of-vitality-and-economic-dynamism/

> "No matter how much autonomy is had, for instance by the Basque Country, it is nothing like the autonomy of Texas. Texas has much more. and the United States are much more federal systems, but here in Spain the system is super centralist."

In another interview,[346] he offered a more forthright view of a hypothetical independent Catalonia:

> "The President of the American Enterprise Institute (AEI), Arthur Brooks, said in an interview with the ACN that an independent Catalonia in the European Union "could, in a strange and paradoxical way, have a greater benefit than Europe could imagine." [...] "… Catalonia, with its business culture, could become "an example" for other countries and help "resurrect" a Europe that is "suffering"."

If these two alleged channels of funding are based merely on what has been reported in the media, the whole chart comes into doubt, as regards its validity.

In an interview, the exiled President of Catalonia**,** Rt. Hon. Carles Puigdemont, described in *Komsomolskaya Pravda* as *the "peaceful rebel" from the Iberian Peninsula*, claims that the alleged 'hand of the Kremlin' interfering in Catalonia is itself fake news.[347] Indeed, if its word is anything to go by, on October 1 2017, the Russian Embassy in Spain stated clearly: "The position of Russia as regards Catalan separatism: All procedures must be based on the

---

[346] El Nacional (2017). "Un think tank de EE.UU sostiene que una Catalunya independiente "resucitaría" la UE". *El Nacional,* 20 May 2017. https://www.elnacional.cat/es/politica/catalunya-independiente-resucitar-ue_159600_102.html

[347] 'Puigdemont: "'The hand of the Kremlin' interfering in Catalonia is fake news". Edward Chesnokov. *Elnacional.cat.* 23 January 2019. https://www.elnacional.cat/en/news/carles-puigdemont-interview-russian-newspaper_346896_102.html

rules laid down by the Spanish constitution"[348]. That has obviously not sufficed to put an end to contrary claims.

* 6.5 Hiding the causes of the independence movement

With an insistence that borders on obsessive obstinacy, opponents of Catalonia's independence - declared by a Catalan Parliament resolution on October 27 2017, but not yet implemented because it was immediately aborted by the Spanish government - have continued to convey the impression that the Catalan people have no intrinsic reason for wanting to be a sovereign nation. As Thomas S. Harrington neatly - and sarcastically - put it,

> "what other reason could the Catalans, whom centralists like Alandete have always treated with mocking condescension despite their demonstrably higher levels of civic democracy and culture, have any reason to break up their perfect marriage?". (Harrington 2017)[349]

The Spanish establishment (which goes well beyond the government and the opposition) attributes the undeniable existence of a clear majority of Catalan-born people (of whatever extraction) in favour of independence to political manipulation, media control, ideological indoctrination - which they happily, frivolously attribute to the strategies used by the Nazis in general and to the teachings of Herr Goebbels in particular - and last but not least, to the interference of external forces.

There has undoubtedly been a great deal of interest on the part of Spain to establish a Russian connection to the Catalan independence process. As we have seen, the Madrid daily *El País* was quick to jump on this hobby-horse, on the basis of what we shall soon see has been regarded as flimsy evidence, but which suited the

---

[348] "La postura de Rusia ante el separatismo catalán: Todo proceso debe basarse en las normas constitucionales españolas", *Blog «Tribulaciones Metapolíticas»*, 1 October 2017. https://adversariometapolitico.wordpress.com/2017/10/01/la-postura-de-rusia-ante-el-separatismo-catalan-todo-proceso-debe-basarse-en-las-normas-constitucionales-espanolas/

[349] Op. cit.

Spanish government down to the ground in its attempt to neutralise international doubts about the appropriateness of its political, legal and police efforts to quell the Catalan independence movement (e.g. Díez & Mateo 2017).[350]

We may agree to some extent, in general terms, with conspiracy-minded authors sensitive to disinformation, such as J. J. Patrick, author of "Alternative War" who in an article published on October 2 2017 (Patrick 2017a)[351], titled "EU Under Fire: The Catalan Bear Trap" wrote:

> "You are being used to spread disinformation. You are being emotionally tweaked to react in a predictable fashion. You are being used to spread infection as far as it will go. You are being used to further interests which are contrary to your own.
>
> You are being used to the pave the way for the next event, and the next event, and the next…"
>
> Read more at:
> https://www.byline.com/column/67/article/1855

El País is his main source to claim, in the same article, that

> "Malign intentions were trained on the Catalan referendum from the outset. Hands we now recognise have been all over it. Snowden, Assange, RT, Sputnik. Every single one of them suddenly appeared in the sphere of commentary and from this point the situation began to transform at pace."

---

[350] Díez, Anabel & Juan José Mateo (2017). "El Gobierno constata la intervención en Cataluña de 'hackers' procedentes de Rusia y Venezuela. El Ejecutivo afrontará la cuestión el lunes en el Consejo de ministros de Exteriores de la UE." *El País*, 11 NOV 2017. https://elpais.com/politica/2017/11/10/actualidad/1510313190_375883.html

[351] J. J. Patrick (2017a). "EU Under Fire: The Catalan Bear Trap", *Byline*, 2 October 2017. https://byline.com/2017/10/02/eu-under-fire-the-catalan-bear-trap/

In this particular case, it was an article by David Alandete published on September 25th 2017, shortly before the referendum on self-determination. Other articles by the same author, days before that, gave the news Agency "Europa Press" its dramatic news piece "Russia interferes in Catalan separatism by publishing information with an anticonstitutional bias" ("Rusia se entromete en el independentismo catalán publicando información con sesgo anticonstitucional").[352]

His article, however, is a backdrop to another piece published a month later, on October 23rd 2017 (Patrick 2017b),[353] just four days before the declaration of independence:

> "… What you need to understand first is that this disinformation campaign by Assange is aimed not primarily at Spain internally, but at the international audience. And his centrality is key in understanding this.
>
> "We already know disinformation surrounding Catalonia is a Kremlin-Led operation, aimed at further destabilising the EU and, by proxy, NATO. And this is further confirmed by this new analysis…
>
> "The domestic data shows a much more natural state of affairs in the social media discussions, confirming that what we are seeing from outside is a more focused disinformation campaign. Activity designed to drive a foreign narrative, provoking seperatism [sic] elsewhere."

Patrick had previously looked into foreign involvement in the Catalan referendum, in relation to the LEAVE.EU Brexit activities. He addressed one of its leaders:

---

[352] Europa Press (2017). "Rusia se entromete en el independentismo catalán publicando información con sesgo anticonstitucional", *Europa Press*, 23 September 2017. https://www.europapress.es/nacional/noticia-rusia-entromete-independentismo-catalan-publicando-informacion-sesgo-anticonstitucional-20170923131551.html

[353] J.J. Patrick (2017b) "Julian Assange: The Key To Russia's Disinformation Machine", *Byline*, 23 October 2017, : https://www.byline.com/column/67/article/1903

"In Wigmore's words they [LEAVE.EU] are: "*Part of Goddard Gunster - splitting California for starters and a dozen referendums.*"

This is intriguing news, and though I asked Andy directly if they were involved in Catalonia, the Kurdish independence referendum, or others, he hasn't yet replied.

Catalonia, *we now know*,[354] has been a target of Russian interference. First came the deployment of Russian asset Julian Assange, acting as a disruptive force true to the distinct pattern in all previous Russian activity. And, latterly, more direct engagement has become clear, as publicised yesterday by the EU STRATCOM team - who are part of Europe's defences against Russian disinformation war."[355]

*** 6.6 The EU disinformation website, and Catalonia**

We mentioned above the European Union's disinformation website, https://euvsdisinfo.eu. What does it have to say about Catalonia? A search yields 14 items consisting of, or including, claims of disinformation related to Catalonia[356].

In its zeal to track down Russian disinformation, this website is occasionally - in the view of this author - hypersensitive. In one of the 14 examples (No. 8 in the chart below), directly involving Catalonia, it claims to "disprove" that "The Europeans invented the theory of global separatism. What is now happening in Catalonia is not an exception. The same is happening in Italy. The same will

---

[354] My italics. His source: David Alandete's article, published four days earlier in El País: "La maquinaria de injerencias rusa penetra la crisis catalana", El País, 22 September 2017. https://elpais.com/politica/2017/09/22/actualidad/1506101626_670033.html

[355] Patrick, J. J. (2017). "Russian Linked Leave. EU Figures Targeting Elections Worldwide", *Byline.com*, 26 Sept. 2017: https://www.byline.com/column/67/article/1842

[356] https://euvsdisinfo.eu/disinformation-cases/?text=catalonia&disinfo_issue=&date=

happen in Belgium. And then it will go on [in Europe]".[357] This is clearly an updated version of Kissinger's domino theory. EUvsDisinfo incorrectly claims that "no evidence is given" of this hypothesis, which was at the time, nevertheless, common parlance in discussions on the EU's position, voiced by academics and also by top officials... including the then Commission President Jean-Claude Juncker himself, just days before the broadcast of the affirmation denounced by EUvsDisinfo! The list of sources referring to the fear of a "domino effect" is indeed long. Here is a short selection:

- Levrat, Nicolas; Antunes, Sandrina; Tusseau, Guillaume; Williams, Paul (2017). "*Catalonia's Legitimate Right To Decide. Paths to Self-Determination*". 31 August 2017. Generalitat de Catalunya. 161 pages. http://exteriors.gencat.cat/web/.content/00_ACTUALITAT/notes_context/FULL-REPORT-Catalonias-legitimate-right-to-decide.pdf

- Catherine Hardy (2017): "EU fears a Catalan "domino effect"". *Euronews*, 11 September 2017. https://www.euronews.com/2017/09/11/eu-fears-a-catalan-domino-effect

- Ryan Heath and David M. Herszenhorn (2017). "Josep Borrell warns of Catalan 'domino effect'. The veteran Spanish Socialist politician — himself a Catalan — says that the independence argument is based on a myth", *Politico*, 21 September 2017. https://www.politico.eu/article/catalonia-referendum-independence-josep-borrell-warns-of-domino-effect/

- Hannah Strange (2017). "Juncker says Catalonian independence could cause domino effect across Europe", *Daily Telegraph*, 13 October 2017.

---

[357] EUvsDisinfo (2017). "Disinfo: The Europeans invented the theory of global separatism". 23 October 2017. https://euvsdisinfo.eu/report/the-europeans-are-spreading-separatism-on-their-continent-now-therefore-on-the-very-eve-of-the-parade-of-referendums-on-independence-russia-got-a-chance-to-separate-gradually-europe-from-the-us-h/

https://www.telegraph.co.uk/news/2017/10/13/juncker-says-catalonian-independence-could-cause-domino-effect/

- David Coburn MEP (2017). "Jean-Claude Juncker and other top-level EU policymakers stated they are not in favour of independence for Catalonia, because this would cause 'a domino effect'". Question for written answer E-006866-17 to the Commission, 7 November 2017. https://www.europarl.europa.eu/doceo/document/E-8-2017-006866_EN.html

- Real Instituto Elcano (2019). "The independence conflict in Catalonia". *Real Instituto Elcano.* (updated version 2019). http://www.realinstitutoelcano.org/wps/wcm/connect/d8496562-e096-44a1-81da-b871c91ccf62/Catalonia-dossier-elcano-october-2019.pdf

> "Institutions and other Member States also want to avoid two types of risk: a) The possibility of a domino effect in other regions, such as Flanders, northern Italy, Corsica and minorities in Hungary, which could destabilise Member States or result in a proliferation of states that renders the current model unworkable." p. 39.

The conclusion is clear: the inclusion of the Russian article in EUvsDisinfo as an example of "disinformation" is totally unwarranted and might itself be classified as an example of "disinformation".

Here is the list of the ten references to Catalonia (four make very oblique references to Catalonia and have been omitted):

	Date	Title	Outlets	Country
1	05.11.2019	Catalan protests are staged by the US and Soros to punish Spain for its relations with Cuba	Stoletie	Cuba, US, Spain

		https://euvsdisinfo.eu/report/catalonian-events-are-staged-by-the-us-to-punish-spain-for-its-relations-with-cuba/		
2	18.10.2019	By supporting Euromaidan, the EU promoted similar protests in the EU https://euvsdisinfo.eu/report/by-supporting-ukrainian-euromaidan-the-eu-fell-in-its-own-trap-and-now-crumbling-because-of-catalonia/	Sonar2050	Kosovo, Ukraine, US, Spain
3	18.10.2019	Catalan leaders have recognized Crimea https://euvsdisinfo.eu/report/catalan-leaders-have-recognized-crimea/	Vremya Pokhazhet @ Pervyi Kanal [45:56 - 46:06]	Ukraine, Spain
4	04.07.2019	New head of European diplomacy, Josep Borrell, refuses to fight separatism in the EU https://euvsdisinfo.eu/report/borrell-refuses-fight-separatism-eu/	Sputnik Spanish	Spain
5	29.01.2019	Macron distributes fake news on Russian meddling in referendums https://euvsdisinfo.eu/report/macron-distributes-fake-news-on-russian-meddling-to-referendums/	RT France	UK, Russia, France, Spain
6	26.01.2019	Western Leaders Welcome the Beginning of a Bloody Civil War in Venezuela	Russkaya Vesna	Venezuela

		https://euvsdisinfo.eu/report/western-leaders-welcome-the-beginning-of-a-bloody-civil-war-in-venezuela/		
7	27.10.2017	Global powers prepare ground for war in Europe https://euvsdisinfo.eu/report/global-powers-prepare-ground-for-war-in-europe/	Politexpert, oane.ws	Ukraine, Spain
8	23.10.2017	The Europeans invented the theory of global separatism https://euvsdisinfo.eu/report/the-europeans-are-spreading-separatism-on-their-continent-now-therefore-on-the-very-eve-of-the-parade-of-referendums-on-independence-russia-got-a-chance-to-separate-gradually-europe-from-the-us-h/	Vremya pokazhet @Pervyi kanal, 6:42	Italy, Belgium
9	11.10.2017	The EU's ruling elite intend to take the bloc down https://euvsdisinfo.eu/report/flanders-can-separate-from-belgium/	Global Research	Belgium
10	08.10.2017	The logical answer from Europe to the Catalan referendum would have been: Recognize the independence of Catalonia and bomb Madrid https://euvsdisinfo.eu/report/the-logical-answer-from-europe-to-the-catalonia-	Voskresnoe Vremya @Channel 1	Kosovo, Spain

		referendum-would-have-been-recognize-the-independence-of-catalonia-and-bomb-madrid/		

The DisInfo Portal regards as biblical fact the Russian involvement in the social media in and around the October 1 referendum in 2017:

> "Pro-Kremlin accounts promoted Catalonian independence on social media, but on a smaller scale than was the case in the US.

On Russian state-controlled TV, the Catalonian referendum was accompanied with alarmist claims that Europe might "break up into small states"; that the world will "collapse"; that there was "a whiff of civil war"; that the Spanish authorities' policies towards Catalonia were "suicidal"; that "Spain stands at the beginning of a real civil, not even conflict, but war" and that this was a result of "European liberal ideology."[358]

In the same vein, a paper by an anonymous author: "Framing Russian meddling in the Catalan question", is dated October 2017[359]. It draws heavily on the *El País* line. It says that the "prevailing interpretation" among "external observers" is that "Russia has activated its propaganda apparatus to contribute to destabilizing Spain as this fits its overall narrative about a dysfunctional, weakening and almost collapsing EU". The other hypothesis it plays with is that " pro-independence activists bought Assange's support".

The square Assange hypothesis ("Assange has been actively involved and at times playing a highly-visible role") is then

---

[358] EUvsDisinfo (2018). "Russian Election Meddling in the US and Beyond", EUvsDisinfo, 24 September 2018. https://euvsdisinfo.eu/russian-election-meddling-in-the-us-and-beyond/

Immediately reproduced on the Disinfo Portal, here: https://disinfoportal.org/russian-election-meddling-in-the-us-and-beyond/

[359] https://www.stopfake.org/content/uploads/2017/12/Framing-Russian-meddling-in-the-Catalan-question.compressed.pdf

fruitlessly bashed into the round hole of fact. The paper reproduces a tweet by Assange (9 September 2017) discouraging the use of tanks by Spain, then adds "One day and a half later the Vice-President (regional Government) thanked him", but the thanks were clearly, visibly, for a separate tweet showing a picture of the massive September 11 demonstration in Barcelona. Further down, as might be expected, *El País* is quoted: “According to *El País*, Russian bots increased by 2,000% the impact of the Catalan question on Twitter”, and “Mainstream Russian media also stepped enthusiastically into the issue.” Lower down, though, it is forced to admit that “The DFRLab [Atlantic Council's Digital Forensic Research Lab] considers that some attributions and Kremlin links taken for granted by *El País* articles are still unclear.”

A Russian-based website, *Geopolitica*.ru, recorded that prime minister Rajoy was also forced to admit to the *COPE* radio station that he had no evidence of Russian government interference in the independence process.

> “...the alleged "interference" of the Russian government in the separatist coup in Catalonia, does not convince even the President of the Spanish government, who has not been carried away by the "intelligence" of some of its ministers. The Prime Minister, Mariano Rajoy, said he had no record that the Russian government is behind the alleged disinformation campaign on social media regarding the Catalan conflict.” [...] "I have no information that tells me that the Russian government is behind this", said the Spanish prime minister during an interview on Cadena COPE radio.”[360]

Just months later, an anonymous author dared to ask himself or herself: "Why is it so difficult to address the Russia issue in Spain, and what should be done?" in a 2018 document apparently hacked

---

[360] Geopolitica (2017). Rajoy desmiente el cuento de la “injerencia rusa” en Cataluña: Reconoce que no tiene “ningún dato”. Geopolitica.ru, 16 November 2017. https://www.geopolitica.ru/es/article/rajoy-desmiente-el-cuento-de-la-injerencia-rusa-en-cataluna-reconoce-que-no-tiene-ningun

from the same "Integrity Initiative" website.[361] In answer to his or her own question, the author suggests three priorities:

> "**Increasing the knowledge about today's Russia**: a better understanding of Putin's agenda, goals and regime's nature would contribute to raise awareness.
>
> **Expand and solidify the network of likeminded individuals**: despite the complaints of the Russian Embassy in Madrid, there are few individuals working on this issue in Spain. The more engaged they are among them the better in terms of impact and results. The political context is not particularly propitious for them. Links with European colleagues help reinforce their legitimacy in front of Spanish audiences.
>
> **More people and voices from more sectors are badly needed**: for instance, on the one hand it was positive that *El País* reported extensively about the Russian meddling in Catalonia. But on the other, it was negative that almost only *El País* reported about it. In the end it seemed like a fight between *El País* and *RT* in Spanish. ..."

In June 2018 readers of *OK Diario* (as I have said, an unabashed disseminator, thanks to its founder and director, Eduardo Inda, of fake news about Catalonia were offered a double fake, that is, a false fake. Not known for portraying a balanced view of the Catalan independence question, it published a piece on *El País* "La noticia de 'El País' sobre las 'fake news' de dos rusos en Cataluña también era un 'fake'" ("the *El País* news about the "fake news" about two Russians in Catalonia was itself a fake").362 The paper

---

[361] Integrity Initiative (2018). "Why is it so difficult to address the Russia issue in Spain, and what should be done?" hacked from Integrity Initiative" website, 15 April 2018.
https://wikispooks.com/wiki/Document:Why_is_it_so_difficult_to_address_the_Russia_issue_in_Spain

[362] Cerdán, Manuel"La noticia de 'El País' sobre las 'fake news' de dos rusos en Cataluña también era un 'fake'", *OK Diario*, (14/06/2018 02:32).

first notes that the new director of what it aims to regard as its arch-rival, Soledad Gallego-Díaz, among other measures, had decided to sack José Ignacio Torreblanca as head of the Opnion section, *OK Diario* claims one of the reasons for sacking him was that he supported George Soros's international lobbying (he had been director of the ECFR363, the European Council on Foreign Relations, in Spain, from 2007 to June 2016, we are told). Incidentally, we shall also look into the views on Catalonia of the then-deputy director of *El País*, David Alandete, who was especially concerned with Russian interference in Spain.

OK Diario tries to persuade its readers that the ECFR is an international organization with its seat in Berlin, funded by George Soros. As early as 11 October 2017 *OK Diario* claimed Soros "has become one of the unconditional collaborators with Catalan separatism", and was supporting the independence movement through his foundation, though the examples he gives, for activities in 2015 and 2016, suggest quite the contrary: that the Catalan government, or pro-independence parties, actually PAID for the services of Soros' organisations.364 Less than a year later he was not charging for his services, according to the same newspaper, but actually funding the independence movement: *OK Diario* claims that

---

https://okdiario.com/espana/noticia-pais-sobre-fake-news-dos-rusos-cataluna-tambien-era-fake-2422061

[363] «About half of ECFR's funding comes from foundations, one third from governments and the rest from corporations and individuals. Open Society Foundations is the main donor to ECFR, funding with its grants one third (£2,345,566 in 2017) of ECFR's total income: 7,278,122 in 2017). Other donors include major organizations mainly from Europe and the Western world such as the foundation Stiftung Mercator [DE] (£710,753 or ~10% total funding in 2017), European and the Japanese governments, NATO, leading corporations such as Daimler AG and Microsoft as well as wealthy individuals.» https://en.wikipedia.org/wiki/European_Council_on_Foreign_Relations#Funding

[364] Manuel Cerdán (2017), "Soros, el gurú de la especulación, apoya al independentismo a través de su fundación", *OK Diario*, 11 October 2017. https://okdiario.com/investigacion/soros-guru-especulacion-apoya-independentismo-traves-fundacion-1406004

Jordi Vaquer, the director of Open Society Europe “financia a los movimientos secesionistas catalanes con dinero de Soros” (“funds the Catalan secessionist movements with Soros’ money”). In the same 2018 article, as stated above in sub-section 6.1, *OK Diario* went so far as to make the preposterous claim that “la función última de CIDOB es la de hacer de pregonero internacional del proceso separatista” (“CIDOB's ultimate function is to act as an international herald for the separatist process“). I have given details about CIDOB, the Barcelona Centre for International Documentation, above.

As we have seen, *El País* has come under fire for its position on Russia. In one case (*Sputnik News*. 2017[365]) one of the "accused" media has defended itself, and this of course reduces the value of its criticism.

We have seen above that McGrath was especially scathing in his analysis of the El País / Elcano contribution to the Committee. (2018)[366]. In the event, the Intelligence and Security Committee of [the UK] Parliament published its Report on Russia in July 2020,367 and understandably given the extremely poor value of the Spanish testimonies, it makes no mention of Spain or Catalonia. We have also seen Thomas Harrington’s scathing criticism of *El País* in general, and David Alandete in particular:[368]

---

365 “'El País' de la posverdad: cómo el medio español tergiversa las palabras de Putin y el trabajo de Sputnik y RT“. *Sputnik News*, 14 November 2017. http://www.derechos.org/nizkor/espana/doc/cat2239.html

366 http://data.parliament.uk/writtenevidence/committeeevidence.svc/evidencedocument/digital-culture-media-and-sport-committee/fake-news/written/80989.html

367 https://docs.google.com/a/independent.gov.uk/viewer?a=v&pid=sites&srcid=aW5kZXBlbmRlbnQuZ292LnVrfGlzY3xneDo1Y2RhMGEyN2Y3NjM0OWFl

368 Harrington, Thomas (2017). «Largest Newspaper in Spain Blames Russia and Antiwar.com for Catalonia Pro-Independence News», AntiWar.com website, 23 September 2017. https://www.antiwar.com/blog/2017/09/23/largest-newspaper-in-spain-blames-russia-and-antiwar-com-for-catalonia-pro-independence-news/

> "Providing still more graphic proof of its pathetic and truly cringeworthy descent from the status of a great liberal paper to that of a shameless corporatist rag dominated by baseless Atlanticist talking points, Madrid's El País has recently suggested that behind the current drive for a vote on independence in Catalonia there there can be found the diabolical hand of Putin's Russia." (Harrington 2017)

But *El País* was not alone. *StopFake.org* seemed to jump into the pool soon afterwards, on 26 September, taking for granted the "de la guerra de información realizada por el gobierno de Rusia" ("information war carried out by the Russian government"), with an article that can give searchers of disinformation plenty to work on.

> According to data offered by Audiense, a social analysis platform, Assange got almost 940.000 mentions on Twitter in September alone, the vast majority with hashtags on independence: *#Catalonia, #1oct, #Catalonianreferendum, #1O, #Rajoy.*[369]

On reading this article one reaches the conclusion that Spain really resents Assange or Snowden's opinions getting such wide coverage. However, it is in actual fact merely a reproduction (with permission!) of an article written by David Alandete himself in El País [370] , and uncritically swallowed hook line and sinker by StopFake. To describe as "fake news" this personal opinion "If today is a guide on Oct 1 Europe will birth a new 7.5m nation or civil war.

---

[369] Alandete, David (2017). «La maquinaria de injerencias rusa penetra la crisis catalana», reproduced on Stopfake.org website, 26 September 2017. https://www.stopfake.org/es/la-maquinaria-de-injerencias-rusa-penetra-la-crisis-catalana/

[370] Alandete, David (2017). "La maquinaria de injerencias rusa penetra la crisis catalana. La red global que actuó con Trump y el Brexit se dedica ahora a España". *El País*, 22 September 2017. https://elpais.com/politica/2017/09/22/actualidad/1506101626_670033.html

Front page news English media hide"[371] is in my view a discredit to stopfake.org.

Stopfake.org further discredits itself by claiming, at the end of this sentence, that

> "As of August 28, it has published 42 news items on the crisis in Catalonia, some with incorrect headlines such as "The EU will respect Catalan independence, but it will have to go through a correct joining process".

In the end, trying to unravel any real interference by Russia in this process, one finds oneself caught in the cross-fire of the arch-enemies of Vladimir Putin (and his satellite media), and of the arch-enemies of George Soros. In November 2019, just to give a taste of the dilemma, we were advised by " protests are staged by the US and Soros to punish Spain for its relations with Cuba" in Stoletie[372]. This is one of the 14 news items singled out by the EUvsDisinfo website since September 2016, when Isvestia first wrote a piece about Catalonia and Crimea, in itself a recurrent issue.

So, all in all, what is the answer to Ellis Palmer's question (Palmer 2017): Did Russian 'fake news' stir things up? https://www.bbc.com/news/world-europe-41981539

He seems to take sides in saying "that Carles Puigdemont and some allies are in Belgium, *in self-imposed exile"*.[373] He mentions

---

[371] https://twitter.com/DefendAssange/status/907306176244797441

Tweet recovered via "Assange, molt actiu a la xarxa durant la manifestació de l'11 de setembre", CCMA, 11 September 2017. https://www.ccma.cat/324/assange-molt-actiu-a-la-xarxa-per-l1-o/noticia/2808141/

[372] "Catalan protests are staged by the US and Soros to punish Spain for its relations with Cuba". *Stoletie,* 5 November 2019. https://euvsdisinfo.eu/report/catalonian-events-are-staged-by-the-us-to-punish-spain-for-its-relations-with-cuba/

[373] My italics.

all the accusations we have seen above, and adds a dissenting voice (ahead of the McGrath revelations).

> “Klaus-Jurgen Nagel, an expert on nationalism at Pompeu Fabra University in Barcelona, disagreed. Nagel said the Russian role had been "exaggerated by those who want to show that the only friends that the separatists have left have dubious democratic pedigrees, such as Russia, Venezuela and Cuba".

The view of Francesc Pallarés, a political science professor at the same Catalan university, is significant. He "told the BBC that Russian reporting in Catalonia was part of wider rivalry between Russia and the West."

> "Russian media offer a perspective on Catalonia, based on their own geopolitical interests. These can be contrary to Western interests," Mr Pallarés said.
>
> "We are in an 'information war' based on the selection and presentation of information in both the West and Russia to create opinion favourable to the dominant interests."

This latter statement is the key to the whole affair: all sides have been feeding on disinformation about Catalonia’s independence process, and I have been giving plenty of evidence not only that Spain’s ruling elite has been far worse in its use of fake news, smear campaigns and manipulation than has, say, Russia, but that it has been and still is far more prevalent, being endlessly repeated and quoted, with only a handful of dissenting Spaniards who see through the strategy (without necessarily being in favour of Catalonia’s independence), such as Suso de Toro, Jesús Pérez Royo... and the star critic of Spain’s strategy, John Carlin (see above). Moreover, it has scarcely been broached in the academic literature. What is needed is probably less "Fact-checking Russian news on Catalonia" and more, far more, "Fact-checking Spanish news on Catalonia".

* 6.7 The Disinfo Portal and alleged Russian disinformation on Catalonia

A search for "Catalonia" on the **Disinfo Portal** (apart from the 2018 Polyakova & Meserole article we have referred to above) yields the following six articles, of which only one is devoted to Catalonia as such:

1. The Only Thing Catalonia and Crimea Have in Common Is the Letter C[374]

A Bloomberg piece in October titled “Why Catalonia Will Fail Where Crimea Succeeded” by Russian writer Leonid Bershidsky is an example of moral equivalence run amok. He compares two completely unrelated events - referenda in Crimea and Catalonia.

Diane Francis writes:

> "Clearly, the only linkage between Crimea and Catalonia may be the invisible hand of the Kremlin and its confederates who broke up Ukraine and are interested in destabilizing and atomizing Spain and other western nations."

2. The US Investigations Highlight Europe’s Laxity on Disinformation[375]

> “This article is a part of a special series for #StratComDC 2019.
>
> On October 8, the United States Senate Intelligence Committee released its updated report on Russian interference into the 2016 US presidential election.

Readers of this article by Jakub Kalenský are assured that "Russian meddling in the referendum in Catalonia in 2017 was best covered by *El Pais...*"

---

[374] https://disinfoportal.org/the-only-thing-catalonia-and-crimea-have-in-common-is-the-letter-c/

[375] https://disinfoportal.org/the-us-investigations-highlight-europes-laxity-on-disinformation/

3. #EUelections2019: Spanish Weaknesses Against Kremlin Disinformation[376]

29 April 2019

David Alandete (by that time the US correspondent for the Spanish newspaper ABC)

"The Russian government scored a goal during their visit to Madrid last November. Foreign minister Sergei Lavrov somehow convinced his host to sign a mutual agreement to jointly fight disinformation. Several months have gone by and the agreement has been largely forgotten..."

"After popular Russian media personalities scorned the previous cabinet for its rebuke of Moscow's interference in Catalonia, its replacement [PSOE] stopped short of publicly identifying any aggressors in the situation"...

"In 2017, Spain suffered a major hostile information operation. Kremlin media targeted the Catalan independence crisis, publishing false stories, misleading maps, and fabricated data. With the aid of Wikileaks, Julian Assange, and Edward Snowden, the Kremlin's media outlets portrayed Spain as a fascist and abusive state, unable to guarantee democratic freedoms and inclined to use violence and repression to stifle dissent. The conservative government at the time failed to react decisively, allowing the Kremlin to distort what was happening in Spain for both domestic and international audiences."

4. How the Kremlin Exploits a Crisis[377]

Jakub Kalenský

---

[376] By David Alandete, 19 April 2019. https://disinfoportal.org/euelections2019-spanish-weaknesses-against-russian-information-warfare/

[377] https://disinfoportal.org/how-the-kremlin-exploits-a-crisis/

1 February 2019

"Such operations regularly appear following every event that creates strong emotions on both sides of the barricade. As was the case when Russia's media reported about the referendum in Catalonia, the Kremlin-controlled troll factory attempted to polarize the debate, notably the issue of racial and minority rights in the United States, and when Moscow amplifies stories or invents outright false narratives about the divisive issue of the migration crisis in Europe."

5. Russian Election Meddling in the US and Beyond[378]

"By EU vs Disinfo

24 September 2018.

Pro-Kremlin accounts promoted Catalonian independence on social media, but on a smaller scale than was the case in the US.

On Russian state-controlled TV, the Catalonian referendum was accompanied with alarmist claims that Europe might "break up into small states"; that the world will "collapse"; that there was "a whiff of civil war"; that the Spanish authorities' policies towards Catalonia were "suicidal"; that "Spain stands at the beginning of a real civil, not even conflict, but war" and that this was a result of "European liberal ideology"."

6. Reluctant Russophobes: The Underwhelming International Response to Putin's Hybrid War[379]

Peter Dickinson

3 April 2018.

---

[378] https://disinfoportal.org/russian-election-meddling-in-the-us-and-beyond/

[379] https://disinfoportal.org/reluctant-russophobes-the-underwhelming-international-response-to-putins-hybrid-war/

> This article was originally published in UkraineAlert by the Atlantic Council. Peter Dickinson is, we are informed, a nonresident fellow at the Atlantic Council and publisher of Business Ukraine and *Lviv Today* magazine.
>
> "Since the start of the Kremlin campaign in Ukraine, Russia has buzzed US warships, hacked the Bundestag, *fanned the flames of separatism in Catalonia*, and plotted coups in the Balkans—all the while protesting its innocence and accusing its victims of rampant Russophobia."

* 6.8 Russian spies and Catalonia

Further ammunition for the "Reds under the (Catalan) bed" was supplied by *Bellingcat* (Moritz Rakuszitzky 2019). [380]

> "Bellingcat can now reveal the true identity and background of this GRU officer, who operated internationally under the cover persona of Sergey Vyacheslavovich Fedotov. In fact, this person is Denis Vyacheslavovich Sergeev, a high-ranking GRU officer and a graduate of Russia's Military Diplomatic Academy....
>
> In 2010, Denis Sergeev received his alter ego, "Sergey Vyacheslavovich Fedotov". A new, valid passport was issued under this name, by the same "770001" passport desk in Moscow that issued cover passports to Mishkin, Chepiga other GRU operatives, and "VIP" citizens....
>
> Using four different airline booking, PNR, and border-crossing databases, Bellingcat has collated and analysed

[380] Moritz Rakuszitzky (2019). "Third Suspect in Skripal Poisoning Identified as Denis Sergeev, High-Ranking GRU Officer". *Bellingcat.com*, February 14, 2019. https://www.bellingcat.com/news/uk-and-europe/2019/02/14/third-suspect-in-skripal-poisoning-identified-as-denis-sergeev-high-ranking-gru-officer/

> travel records for the persona "Sergey Fedotov" for the period of 2012-2018. He used two different (consecutive) passports during this period-both of which were issued by the same 770001 passport desk and had numbers from batches that we have identified to include other GRU undercover officers….
>
> On 5 November 2016, Fedotov flew to Barcelona, and left back to Moscow from Zurich six days later. He returned to Barcelona one more time: on 29 September 2017, two days before the Catalunya independence referendum. Once again, by coincidence or otherwise, Fedotov remained in Spain during the October 1 vote, and flew back via Geneva to Moscow on 9 October 2017."

The locations from which General (as the paper calls him) Sergeev allegedly made phone calls in Barcelona during the 19 hours he was there on 29-30 September were reported by *El País* last December (Sahuquillo 2019).[381]

All these allegations were either triggered court investigations or else leaked information from these same investigations. López-Fonseca & Pérez (2019) have written:[382]

> "Spain's High Court, the Audiencia Nacional, has opened an investigation into the alleged activities of a group linked with the Russian intelligence service during the 2017 Catalan breakaway bid, three sources have confirmed to EL PAÍS. The sealed investigation, opened

---

[381] María R. Sahuquillo (2019). "Las 19 horas en Barcelona de Fedótov. El móvil utilizado por el militar ruso delata dónde estuvo en la capital catalana cuando viajó en septiembre de 2017", *El País*, 27 December 2019. https://elpais.com/politica/2019/12/26/actualidad/1577390217_522414.html

[382] López-Fonseca, Óscar & Fernando J. Pérez (2019). "Spain's High Court opens investigation into Russian spying unit in Catalonia. Judge Manuel García-Castellón is probing whether an elite military group known as Unit 29155 carried out actions aimed at destabilizing the region during the separatist push", *El País*, 21 November 2019. https://english.elpais.com/elpais/2019/11/21/inenglish/1574324886_989244.html

> by Judge Manuel García-Castellón, has been assigned to the General Information Office of the National Police, which specializes in counter-terrorism. The case centers on an elite military group called Unit 29155, which intelligence services from several countries have linked to alleged attempts to destabilize Europe."
>
> The High Court is investigating an alleged intervention of Unit 29155 that is related to the separatist drive in Catalonia, a legal source and two police sources have confirmed to *El País*. These sources have defined the investigations as "confidential," and the judge has kept the preliminary proceedings under seal.

These allegations were added to another investigation on Russia being carried out by the "Audiencia Nacional" court in Madrid:

> "The National Court (Audiencia Nacional) is investigating the presence in Spain of a Russian spy who was in Catalonia the days before the illegal October 1 referendum. It was Sergey Fedotov, a high-ranking officer in the Russian military service department...
>
> The investigation is part of a broader case that is looking into the activities of Russian espionage in Spain aimed at politically destabilizing the country and promoting the independence of Catalonia. The case is in the hands of the Central Investigating Court No. 6 headed by Manuel García-Castellón, and the Public Prosecutor's Office, and both the Security Forces and the intelligence services have participated in it.
>
> The most visible part of this alleged Russian spying would be in pro-independence activity on the social network…." (Marraco & Sanz 2019)[383]

---

[383] Marraco, Manel & Luís Ángel Sanz (2019). "La Audiencia Nacional sigue el rastro de un espía ruso que estuvo en Cataluña justo antes del 1-O", *El Mundo*, 21 November 2019,

The Audiencia Nacional court is mentioned again in another article in *El Mundo,* (Marraco et al., 2019)[384]:

> “The investigation of the National High Court on Russian espionage in Catalonia includes the activities of a Russian citizen and a Ukrainian who on October 4 were arrested in La Jonquera (Girona) when they were traveling on the AP-7 towards France. On searching the vehicle, an expensive Mercedes registered in Belarus, the Fiscal section of the Guardia Civil found inside a briefcase a Russian-made M-75 grenade "in perfect condition”.

This article also referred to alleged meetings mentioned above, between Víctor Terradellas and Prof. Serguei Marko.

El País named three Russian intelligence officers, or "spies" - Denis Sergeev, Alexey Kalinin and Mikhail Opryshko - in its report, and added that

> "Spanish diplomatic sources admitted yesterday that the Spanish government's suspicions about the existence of Russian interference come from afar. "Starting in the spring of 2018, and after the Skripal case, the British and American intelligence services provided information on various destabilization actions by Russians on western soil, which in the case of Spain were focused on Catalonia," they point out." (López-Fonseca & Sahuquillo 2019).[385]

---

https://www.elmundo.es/espana/2019/11/21/5dd66bb721efa0e9708b45e1.html

[384] Marraco, M., A. Martialay, F. Lázaro & X. Colás (2019). “La Audiencia Nacional investiga a dos espías rusos detenidos en Cataluña llevando una granada”, *El Mundo,* 23 November 2019.
https://www.elmundo.es/espana/2019/11/23/5dd84d14fdddff2c898b45ec.html

[385] López-Fonseca, Óscar & María R. Sahuquillo (2019). “Three suspected Russian spies travelled to Barcelona in 2016 and 2017. According to information obtained by El País, members of the elite military group, Unit 29155, made a total of four trips to the Catalan capital”. *El País*, 27

December 2019.
https://english.elpais.com/elpais/2019/12/27/inenglish/1577438583_199403.html

Chapter 7. The Covid-19 pandemic, democratic values, and disinformation

According to Rothkopf (2003)[386], who coined the term, an "infodemic" is

> "a few facts, mixed with fear, speculation and rumor, amplified and relayed swiftly worldwide by modern information technologies, have affected national and international economies, politics and even security in ways that are utterly disproportionate with the root realities." ... "Infodemics are emerging as one of the most virulent phenomena known to man, able to transit continents instantly. In virtually every respect they behave just like any other disease, with an epidemiology all their own, identifiable symptoms, well-known carriers, even straightforward cures. Yet to date many in power seem unable to contain them or unwilling to acknowledge their existence."

The WHO used the term "infodemic" in February 2020 to refer to the Coronavirus pandemic.[387] It explains that eating garlic, living in hot and humid countries, drinking alcohol, cold weather and snow, taking a hot bath, 5G mobile networks... are all fake news.[388]

In the words of Ben Zimmer (2020)389, "with social media whipping up a global panic surrounding the coronavirus, we just

---

[386] Rothkopf, David J. (2003). "When the Buzz Bites Back", The Washington Post, Sunday, May 11, 2003. http://www1.udel.edu/globalagenda/2004/student/readings/infodemic.html

[387] WHO (2020). "Novel Coronavirus (2019-nCoV) Situation Report - 13", World Health Organization, 2 February 2020. https://www.who.int/docs/default-source/coronaviruse/situation-reports/20200202-sitrep-13-ncov-v3.pdf

[388] COVID-19 Myth busters, WHO website. https://www.who.int/emergencies/diseases/novel-coronavirus-2019/advice-for-public/myth-busters

[389] Zimmer, Ben "'Infodemic': When Unreliable Information Spreads Far and Wide. The shorthand term was coined during the SARS outbreak and is back

might be facing the biggest infodemic of all", and Carl Barney adds that alongside that,...

> "The current "infodemic" about COVID-19 has infected federal, state, and local governments, who are taking draconian actions that are crippling the economy and severely disrupting the lives of people around the world". 390

Beyond the communication aspects, the effects of the virus not only threaten the economy. The democratic values put in quarantine by many governments' measures to cope with the pandemic have been compellingly explained by Bjørnskov and Voigt (2020)[391] in "The State of Emergency Virus":

> "...Considering that more than half of the world's democracies have declared a state of emergency, the rule of law will be subject to a number of dangers in the following months.
>
> Until today, almost 100 countries on all continents have declared a state of emergency. And this is only counting emergencies declared on the national level, implying that federal countries like Australia and Canada could be

---

for the new coronavirus". *Wall Street Journal*, March 5, 2020. https://www.wsj.com/articles/infodemic-when-unreliable-information-spreads-far-and-wide-11583430244

[390] Wall Street Journal article, "Infodemic: When Unreliable Information Spreads Far and Wide" by Ben Zimmer. https://www.wsj.com/articles/infodemic-when-unreliable-information-spreads-far-and-wide-11583430244 . Referred to here: Carl Barney (2020) "COVID-19 and Other Viruses". Blog entry, 20 March 2020. https://carlbarney.com/2020/03/20/covid-19-and-other-viruses/ :

"Earlier this month in the *Wall Street Journal*, Rothkopf observed that "there were strong similarities between the way a disease spread through a population and the way an idea would 'go viral' on the Net.""

[391] Bjørnskov, Christian & Stefan Voigt (2020). "The State of Emergency Virus", *Verfassungsblog on Matters Constitutional*, 19 April 2020. https://verfassungsblog.de/the-state-of-emergency-virus/

added to the list, as the authority to declare emergencies in these countries often rests with regions.

A state of emergency regularly implies that the government has the right to derogate from some basic rights - such as the freedom to assemble, to move freely, to practice one's religion, the right to privacy and so on. And governments are making ample use of their additional powers, just think of the various tracking measures imposed by many governments. A state of emergency also implies that the other two branches of government are weakened. ...

Given all the evidence regarding the dangers of a state of emergency, it is difficult to comprehend how the World Health Organization could encourage countries to declare a state of emergency. If not, the separation of powers that has characterized the developed world since 1945 may be yet another victim of the crisis...."

Similar fears have been voiced by the Institut Ostrom Catalunya (València & Medina 2020)[392]:

"We are faced by an arbitrary and disproportionate limitation of fundamental rights in Spain, aggravated by an State of Alarm that in effective prevents the use of the vast majority of elements to protect citizens against the State as regards their fundamental rights.

An exercise in comparative politics, moreover, shows that there is indeed an alternative way, which shows full respect for the rights and liberties of citizens and which is also efficient in controlling the epidemic. If we assume that the basis of the democratic state is freedom, exercised and practical, we find that we are situated at a turning point; against the trend of centuries, the limitations and suspensions in force need to be done

---

392 València, Roger & Roger Medina (2020). *Els drets fonamentals davant l'estat d'alarma. Institut Ostrom, 3 May 2020.* https://institutostrom.org/2020/05/03/drets-fonamentals-estat-alarma/

away with as soon as the situation of emergency has passed."

A recent study by Lührmann (2020)[393] has analysed measures taken by 129 countries throughout the world to cope with the pandemic, to assess the risk of democratic declines in each of them.

> Our research shows that government responses to the coronavirus pandemic may accelerate these anti-democratic trends. To track the risk of decline in democracy during the pandemic, we constructed the Pandemic Backsliding Risk Index using data compiled by nearly 30 scholars in early April
>
> - 48 countries have a high risk of democratic declines during the Covid-19 pandemic and 34 countries are at medium risk.
> - The Pandemic Backsliding Risk Index tracks government responses to Covid-19 and uses V-Dem data to factor in the general risk of democratic declines.
> - 47 countries are not at risk of pandemic backsliding demonstrating that responding to the pandemic is possible without jeopardizing democratic standards.

Spain and Switzerland are the only countries in Western Europe that are not in the Low Risk category.

The International Foundation for Electoral Systems, based in the USA, has recently homed in on the possible effects of the pandemic on democratic elections.[394]

---

[393] Anna Lührmann; Amanda B. Edgell & Seraphine F. Maerz (2020). "*Pandemic Backsliding: Does Covid-19 Put Democracy at Risk?*", POLICY BRIEF No. #23, 2020. V-DEM INSTITUTE. http://homepage.ntu.edu.tw/~hanstung/Home_files/pb_23.pdf

[394] https://www.ifes.org/covid-19

> The COVID-19 pandemic threatens public health, economies and democracies. International Foundation for Electoral Systems (IFES) experts are working around the globe to deliver critical analysis and innovative solutions for our partners during this time of uncertainty. This page serves as a hub for essential information to safeguard democratic rights, elections and rule of law along with transparent, accountable and effective governance while also protecting the health of our families and communities. IFES encourages all people who desire free, democratic societies to stay vigilant, informed and compassionate during this crisis.

It has focussed, up to now, on four separate issues:

1. Global Impact of COVID-19 on Elections
2. Covid-19 Corruption: Key Risks to Democratic Institutions
3. Democratic Stakeholders Adapting in MENA
4. How to Protect Gender Equality in Elections During COVID-19

In Spain, Andrea Mármol hit the nail on the head with her comment (Mármol 2020)[395] that the Spanish Cabinet, consisting of PSOE and Podemos, is trying to foist off legitimate criticisms of its management of the crisis as disinformation."

> "...It so happens that today the usual lies are called hoaxes with the particularity of being disseminated at breakneck speed and outside the "official sources" that the last CIS survey referred to, surely in strict reference to the information provided by the Government. The PSOE and Podemos cabinet intends to brand as disinformation the legitimate criticism of its handling of the crisis. So much so that, as the Chief of Staff of the Civil Guard pointed out yesterday, the institution works

---

[395] Andrea Mármol (2020). "No hay lugar para lo nuestro", *TheObjective.com*, 20 April 2020. https://theobjective.com/elsubjetivo/no-hay-lugar-para-lo-nuestro/

"with the aim of minimizing this climate of criticism" (Mármol 2020)

The present Prime Minister himself seems to have indulged in some false information, claiming Spain was fifth in a tests rating no-one has tracked down (MacLean & Pérez 2020).[396] The relevant CNN tweet got no fewer than 24,300 RTs... @kim_soler pointed this out, and showed that in the last 350 CNN tweets, only two have got close to 5,000 RTs, that is, barely a fifth of this one. Yet has this blunder hit the Spanish media?, asks the tweeter.

Throughout the world there has been an explosion of fake news about the coronavirus, its causes, its potential effects - not merely in the health and economic fields - and its remedies. The European Parliament has taken a stance on this (perhaps unwittingly using Otte's 2010397 expression: the virus of disinformation).398

> Today 2 April, on International Fact-checking Day, Parliament is contributing to raising awareness of the dangers of disinformation, not only for citizens' health, but also for democracy.
>
> Whereas many battle day and night to save lives from the coronavirus, health organisations and fact-checkers have uncovered another dark side of the pandemic - organisations and individuals exploiting the crisis for

---

[396] Scott MacLean & Laura Pérez Maestro (2020). Spanish prime minister fails to prove existence of international coronavirus testing rankings he cited", CNN, 9 May 2020. https://edition.cnn.com/2020/05/09/world/spain-prime-minister-sanchez-johns-hopkins-coronavirus-testing-ranking/index.html

https://twitter.com/CNN/status/1259214331323002880?s=20

[397] Otte, Max (2010). *El crash de la información: los mecanismos de la desinformación cotidiana*. Barcelona: Ariel. https://revistas.ucm.es/index.php/HICS/article/download/59843/456445654692

[398] "Fact-checking Day: Fighting the virus of disinformation on Covid-19". 2 April 2020. https://www.europarl.europa.eu/news/en/press-room/20200401IPR76306/fact-checking-day-fighting-the-virus-of-disinformation-on-covid-19

political or commercial manipulation, instead of supporting those saving lives...

A recent article by Miguel Ramos (2020)399 focusses particularly on the dissemination of disinformation, in the context of the pandemic, by neo-Fascist organizations and media …

> "In the midst of the coronavirus crisis, hoaxes have taken on a prominent role. They have sneaked into parliamentary debates, into government press conferences and even into the mouths of representatives of the State Security Forces, who have warned of the damage they cause in an exceptional situation where uncertainty and fear are fertile terrain for the awakening of all kinds of emotions.
>
> Various media outlets and more than one social media analyst have done a great job identifying and dismantling not only hoaxes, but also **their main spreaders** and the **automated bot plots** that help their expansion. Characters who have spent years defecating all kinds of lies on their social networks, in their media and from their lecterns with the sole objective of stoking hatred, fear and anxiety in the population. Fascism has always drawn on these ingredients. And today, with the internet and the media that have lost not only all notion of ethics but also all their scruples, the have found a vein that these days is proving even more worrying."

El País also noted the increase in fake news on Covid-19, and began speaking of an "infodemic".[400] It claimed the Spanish

---

[399] Miguel Ramos (2020). "Ultraderecha. El derecho a mentir y a difundir el odio. Quizá sea el momento de empezar a penalizar a las marcas o empresas que con su publicidad patrocinan páginas de odio o desinformación", *ctxt Revista Contexto*, 13/04/2020.
https://ctxt.es/es/20200401/Firmas/31907/extrema-derecha-bulos-redes-sociales-miquel-ramos.htm

[400] "La pandemia se convierte en 'infodemia'. La crisis del coronavirus dispara la difusión de bulos. El Gobierno identifica más de un millar". *El*

Government was the target of many of these “attacks”, and that it has identified over a thousand examples of disinformation directly or indirectly related with the illness. Apparently over 200 are of a strictly health-related nature. The ultra-right-wing party Vox has been reported to the prosecutors for its part in disseminating such fake news.

The concern about this issue is shared round the world. For instance, Sewanee, “The University of the South”, in Tennessee, set up a website on "Misinformation and Covid-19"[401]:

> “This guide provides reliable sources for information on Covid-19, along with discussions of how misinformation is affecting conversations about Covid-19, and tools for evaluating information found on the virus and the surrounding situation.”

It also gives guidance on how to fight an infodemic.

As early as 15 February 2020 NPR (National Public Radio, USA) drew attention to the infodemic issue:

> “The disease caused by coronavirus has killed more than 1,500 people and has spread beyond China. But the World Health Organization says there's another threat spreading faster - false information. They've called the spread of misinformation about the disease an infodemic (ph). And we wanted to learn more about how coronavirus misinformation is spreading online…” (NPR 2020)[402]

Several months later the European External Action Service Strategic Communications and Information Analysis Division wrote an "EEAS SPECIAL REPORT UPDATE: Short Assessment of

---

País, 19 APR 2020, https://elpais.com/espana/2020-04-18/la-pandemia-se-convierte-en-infodemia.html

401 http://library.sewanee.edu/c.php?g=1010468&p=7320329

402 NPR (2020). Troll Watch: Misinformation Around The CoronaVirus. NPR, 15 February 2020. https://www.npr.org/2020/02/15/806365997/troll-watch-misinformation-around-the-coronavirus

Narratives and Disinformation around the COVID-19/Coronavirus Pandemic" on 24 April 2020. (EEAS 2020)[403]. It claims that

> "Despite their potentially grave impact on public health, official and state-backed sources from various governments, including Russia and - to a lesser extent - China, have continued to widely target conspiracy narratives and disinformation both at public audiences in the EU and the wider neighbourhood."

One report explains how “Facebook, Twitter, YouTube, and TikTok are all battling misinformation related to the novel coronavirus" (Ghaffery & Heilweil 2020)[404]. Although the headline only mentions Facebook, this article describes how various social media platforms are responding to Covid-19 misinformation. Of particular interest is the report “How Facebook can Flatten the Curve of the Coronavirus Infodemic”[405]. The study indicates that Facebook is rife with bogus cures and conspiracy theories that remain on the platform long enough to put millions of people at risk.

The newly founded *Observatorio Europeo sobre la Desinformación,*ObEDes seems to confound its own purpose as soon as it broaches the subject of the coronavirus. In one of its own postings it makes a highly questionable claim: that an academic paper on which it reports (Davis et al 2020406) says that “fake news”

---

[403] European External Action Service (EEAS) (2020). “EEAS SPECIAL REPORT UPDATE: Short Assessment of Narratives and Disinformation around the COVID-19/Coronavirus Pandemic”. EEAS Strategic Communications and Information Analysis Division, 24 April 2020. https://euvsdisinfo.eu/eeas-special-report-update-2-22-april/

[404] Ghaffary, Shirin & Rebecca Heilweil (2020). “Facebook doubles down on removing coronavirus conspiracy theories”. *Vox*, 4 March 2020: https://www.vox.com/recode/2020/1/31/21115589/coronavirus-wuhan-china-myths-hoaxes-facebook-social-media-tiktok-twitter-wechat

[405] Avaaz (2020). “How Facebook can Flatten the Curve of the Coronavirus Infodemic”. Avaaz website, April 15, 2020: https://secure.avaaz.org/campaign/en/facebook_coronavirus_misinformation/ PDF: https://avaazimages.avaaz.org/facebook_coronavirus_misinformation.pdf

[406] Davis, Jessica; Nicola Perra; Qian Zhang; Yamir Moreno & Alessandro Vespignani (2020). Phase Transitions in Information Spreading on Structured

is propagated the same way as viruses, but more quickly and reaching far more people.407 No mention is made of the term “virus” in either the abstract or the supplement.

On the other hand, there has been an up-surge across Europe of instances of fake news attached to the Covid-19 pandemic. These include false, and sometimes dangerous, remedies for the sick.

Some dwell on the link between disinformation and the coronavirus pandemic, using (perhaps unwittingly) Max Otte’s 2010 metaphor: "Desinformació, el virus més nociu" ("Disinformation is the most harmful virus"; Domene 2020[408])

> «Until now, viruses caused damage to health due to their viral effect. [...] we said that everyone can be a receiver and sender of messages, it has complicated the state of being informed. [...] a few million poor people to make the world a more viable place. ... There is also the theory that all this has been done to give credibility to...» (Domene 2020)

Populations, *Nature Physics,* No. 16, pp. 590–596, 2 March 2020. https://www.nature.com/articles/s41567-020-0810-3

“Our findings highlight the importance of the underlying population structure in understanding social contagion phenomena and have the potential to define new intervention strategies aimed at hindering or facilitating the diffusion of information in socio-technical systems.” (Supplement: https://static-content.springer.com/esm/art%3A10.1038%2Fs41567-020-0810-3/MediaObjects/41567_2020_810_MOESM1_ESM.pdf)

See also: “Transmisión de la desinformación a través de los bulos sobre COVID”. ObEDes, 21 April 2020. https://www.observatorioeuropeodes.org/post/transmisi%C3%B3n-de-la-desinformaci%C3%B3n-a-trav%C3%A9s-de-los-bulos-sobre-covid

[407] ‘Las “fake news“ se propagan igual que los virus pero de forma más rápida y alcanzando a muchas más personas’.

[408] Domene, Manel (2020). “Desinformació, el virus més nociu”, Report.cat, 18 de març 2020. https://www.report.cat/desinformacio-el-virus-mes-nociu-coronavirus/

Other initiatives have been developed to counter this phenomenon, such as this one announced by the enigmatic "Observatorio Europeo de análisis y prevención de la desinformación", ObEDes, that we referred to early in this book:

> **Fact Checking and critical thinking to fight Fake News**
>
> The *Revista científica sobre Estilos de Aprendizaje* ("Journal of Learning Styles") in cooperation with the European Observatory on Disinformation Analysis and Prevention has extended the call for proposals on the impact of Disinformation and Fake News on society, politics, culture and the economy during the Covid-19 crisis .409

The EU's concern about disinformation and the pandemic has also been disseminated in Catalan:

> "The coronavirus outbreak has led to the spread of fake news and disinformation that hamper efforts to contain the pandemic [...] Crisis for its political or commercial manipulations, instead of supporting those who save lives [...] Evidence of European solidarity can easily be found"[410]

During one of the press conferences on the Spanish government's strategy to cope with the pandemic, the head of the

---

[409] https://www.observatorioeuropeodes.org/post/la-verificaci%C3%B3n-de-hechos-fact-checking-y-el-pensamiento-cr%C3%ADtico-para-luchar-contra-las-fake-news

There is also a special issue of *Revista sobre Estilos de Aprendizaje*, Vol. 13, on «Transformación e innovación educativa durante la crisis del COVID-19. Estilos y modelos de enseñanza y aprendizaje», http://revistaestilosdeaprendizaje.com/issue/view/258

[410] Parlament Europeu (2020). "Verificació de dades: lluita contra la desinformació en temps del Covid-19". Press Office, 2 April 2020. https://www.europarl.europa.eu/spain/barcelona/ca/premsa/verificaci%C3%B3-de-dades-lluita-contra-la-desinformaci%C3%B3-en-temps-del-covid-19

Guardia Civil Chief of Staff, General José Manuel Santiago, actually admitted their information services were working to "to minimize all that climate contrary to the management of the crisis by the [Spanish government]' and to 'avoid the social stress that all these falsehoods seek' ("minimitzar tot aquell clima contrari a la gestió de la crisi per part del govern [espanyol]' i per a 'evitar l'estrès social que persegueixen totes aquestes falsedats'") (VilaWeb 2020)411.

Another richly documented source has analysed the use of terms by the Spanish authorities during the Covid-19 pandemic (Morales 2020).[412]

> "This analysis has allowed us to lexicometrically explore part of the Spanish regulations derived from the management of Covid-19. The tools of analysis and interpretation provided by discourse analysis has allowed us to see how the anomalous statistical use of words such as authority, national, order or force give a strong coercive component to the norm and, in some cases, the identified linguistic uses are closer to other types (such as political or military) of discourse.
>
> Josep Ramoneda warns that, after crisis situations such as Covid-19, in which governments bring in emergency measures, "leaves an authoritarian imprint, even if rights are restored, and other things are lost forever."
>
> Finally, we would like to publish a new entry later to compare the vocabulary of these royal decrees with that of laws passed in other nearby countries (such as France, Italy or the United Kingdom) to identify similarities and

---

[411] VilaWeb (2020). "Un correu intern de la Guàrdia Civil confirma les ordres de perseguir publicacions contràries al govern espanyol", *VilaWeb*, 21 April 2020. https://www.vilaweb.cat/noticies/guardia-civil-ordres-perseguri-publicacions-govern-espanyol/

[412] Morales, Albert (2020). La lluita (discursiva i legislativa) contra la COVID-19 (I), *Blog de la Revista de Llengua i Dret*, 21/5/2020. https://eapc-rld.blog.gencat.cat/2020/05/21/la-lluita-discursiva-i-legislativa-contra-la-covid-19-i-albert-morales/

divergences in terms of the drafting of emergency laws in the context of Covid-19."

There is a fascinating and useful list of resources on fact-checking, in an article written by Myriam Redondo (2020).[413] Plataforma en Defensa de la Libertad de Expresión also saw the need to bring out a list of useful resources (PDLO 2020).[414]

And in Spain, an on-going collection of items of fake news related to the Coronavirus amounted to 491 by May 4th (Maldito Bulo 2020)[415]:

> "Fake news about Coronavirus is another epidemic. Infodemic. We've verified 491 items and cases of disinformation about Covid-19. We need your help to stop them and we can only do it together. Disinformation about the coronavirus outbreak (Covid-19) that aim to create more fear or seek to take advantage of the situation of alarm...."

---

[413] Redondo, Myriam (2020). "Recursos contra la desinformación para una cuarentena (coronavirus y más)", *Globograma.es*, 18/03/2020. http://www.globograma.es/recursos-bulos-verificacion-desinformacion-coronavirus/

[414] PDLO (2020). "*Recursos para identificar bulos y campañas de desinformación*". Plataforma en Defensa de la Libertad de Expresión (PDLO) website, 10 April 2020. http://libertadinformacion.cc/recursos-para-identificar-bulos-y-campanas-de-desinformacion/

[415] "El coronavirus y sus bulos: 491 mentiras, alertas falsas y desinformaciones sobre COVID-19", Maldito Bulo, 4 May 2020). https://maldita.es/malditobulo/2020/05/04/coronavirus-bulos-pandemia-prevenir-virus/

Chapter 8. The Covid-19 pandemic: a new excuse to hammer the Catalan independence process

In Catalonia, as elsewhere, many voices have been very critical of the way Spain has handled the pandemic. Lamarca (2020) comments on several of them:

> "'*The Guardian'* and *'NYT'* single out Spain for its mismanagement of the health crisis pointing to the lifestyle of the people of Madrid, the "clumsy and slow" response of the Government and the scandal regarding old people's homes. In short, two articles in two prestigious newspapers that make Spain blush for its management of the health crisis. For its part, a report commissioned by the Institute of Certified Management Accountants of Australia has described the management of the health crisis of the Government of Spain as the worst in the world considering elements such as data quality or institutional transparency, sometimes influenced by populism. Even the US news agency Bloomberg, has said that the Spain's tragedy was all too predictable, denouncing that Spain ignored the health crisis that had previously unfolded in Italy and China and [saying] that it should have implemented "more drastic" blockade measures." […]
>
> "Spain ignored the warnings of the WHO and the EU to hoard medical equipment against the coronavirus. The government did not see the need to make additional (preventive) purchases of material to "ensure that workers are protected", as recommended in a report dated 3 February" [...]
>
> "Nor did Spain see the need to close land, air, sea and rail borders in the face of increasing numbers of people coming from Italy and around the world, where the pandemic had already left its mark." [...]
>
> "I still can't explain today […] why Spain did not confine, isolate or close the hotspots with most active cases, such

as Madrid or Catalonia. China did so with Wuhan and Italy with Lombardy" [...]

"Spain has carried out a patriotic, nationalist and centralist management of the pandemic. They have put nationalism ahead of health emergency. Initially they said that "the virus knew nothing about borders", thus denying the proposal of total confinement for Catalonia, but now they propose to de-escalate the measures taking into account the realities of each territory.

"Another example of this inherent nationalism in Spain's management of the pandemic is the presence of police, military and law enforcement forces in all the press conferences that have taken place so far. The fact which has had the most impact on me is that no other country has made that decision. It is very significant that Spain is the only country in which State Security Forces have been present at press conferences."[416]

Significantly, however, the author makes no appeal for independence. It is a criticism, full stop.

This, then, is the most recent phase in the use of disinformation, which as we shall see is related to Catalonia. We shall see whether the coronavirus issue has generated fake news for either of the two political camps: pro- and anti-independence. During the coronavirus crisis, both Newtral and Maldito Bulo have been active in tracking down, sourcing and explaining fake news and disinformation. In late October 2019417, Poynter, incidentally, had issued a notice praising

---

[416] Lamarca, Xavier (2020). Dels aplaudiments a les cassolades?". *Connectats24h* website, 1 May 2020. https://connectats24h.cat/dels-aplaudiments-a-les-cassolades/

[417] https://www.poynter.org/fact-checking/2019/amid-protests-and-misinformation-fact-checkers-are-again-proving-their-usefulness/

In its "Fact check of the week", Poynter wrote of incidents reported also above, in Chapter 5.10:

"Last Monday, when the Spanish Supreme Court sentenced former leaders of the Catalan independence movement to lengthy prison

the work of Newt lal and Maldito Bulo, stating that "Amid protests and misinformation, fact-checkers are again proving their usefulness" (Tardáguila 2019)418, after the harsh Supreme Court ruling against 9 political and social leaders of the independence movement. On 18 March 2020, Poynter wrote: "FALSE: The Army is requisitioning coronavirus protection material in Catalonia. Explanation: The Defense ministry denies the claim".419

Since the coronavirus outbreak, Poynter had by 7 May 2020 singled out just five instances related to Catalonia420. Three were false claims about contingency plans in the education system421,

---

terms, the streets of Barcelona became the stage for violent protests. Inevitably, social media was rife with false information.

In about 24 hours, Maldita.es and Newtral, two fact-checking organizations based in Madrid, caught and managed to debunk at least eight pieces of misleading content that had gone viral.

It was false, for example, that a 5-year-old boy and a man who had a heart attack at El Prat Airport died because protesters wouldn't let an ambulance get to them. It was also false that shares in the Spanish stock market fell as a result of the ruling, and that business owners threatened employees who thought about going on strike." October 17 2019.

https://www.poynter.org/fact-checking/2019/american-newsrooms-2020-efforts-cover-misinformation-but-dont-amplify-it/

[418] Tardáguila, Cristina (2019). «Amid protests and misinformation, fact-checkers are again proving their usefulness"», Poynter, 24 October 2019. https://www.poynter.org/fact-checking/2019/amid-protests-and-misinformation-fact-checkers-are-again-proving-their-usefulness/

[419] Poynter (2018). "False: The Army is requisitioning coronavirus protection material in Catalonia", *Poynter* website, 18 March 2018. https://www.poynter.org/?ifcn_misinformation=the-army-is-requisitioning-coronavirus-protection-material-in-catalonia

https://www.newtral.es/defensa-niega-requisando-material-proteccion-coronavirus-cataluna/20200318/

[420] Note, however, that none is more recent than March 18. In the view of this author, the gap may well be due to the massive worldwide accumulation of disinformation about the coronavirus crisis.

[421] (3) 14 March 2020: https://www.poynter.org/?ifcn_misinformation=catalonia-valencia-and-

which to my mind can hardly be associated with the independence movement. A fourth false claim was about ambulance workers allegedly infected with coronavirus[422], and the last was indeed issued from the pro-independence camp: the author "had been informed" that the army was requisitioning coronavirus protection material purchased by Catalonia.[423] The Ministry of Defence hotly denied this … but since then such requisitioning has purportedly taken place, following Government instructions, albeit by uniformed customs officials (e.g. the Siemens case was widely reported).

Inside Catalonia attention is being devoted to disinformation related to the virus. The Catalan police have information on their website, on phishing and other illegal activities related to the

---

aragon-cancel-classes-in-schools-colleges-and-universities-because-of-coronavirus-outbrea

https://www.newtral.es/cataluna-creditos-convalidados-coronavirus/20200314/

(2) 12 March 2020. https://www.poynter.org/?ifcn_misinformation=catalonia-valencia-and-aragon-cancel-classes-in-schools-colleges-and-universities-because-of-coronavirus-outbreak

https://maldita.es/malditobulo/2020/03/12/el-pais-se-cancelan-todas-las-clases-cataluna-comunidad-valenciana-aragon-coronavirus/

(1) 26 February 2020: https://maldita.es/malditobulo/2020/02/26/suspendido-clases-actividades-escolares-cataluna-2-marzo-riesgo-contagio-coronavirus/

https://www.poynter.org/?ifcn_misinformation=school-has-been-suspended-in-catalonia-until-march-2

[422] 11 March 2020: https://www.newtral.es/tecnicos-ambulancias-cataluna-coronavirus-bulo/20200311/

https://www.poynter.org/?ifcn_misinformation=seven-ambulance-workers-infected-with-coronavirus-in-catalonia

[423] 18 March 2020: https://www.newtral.es/defensa-niega-requisando-material-proteccion-coronavirus-cataluna/20200318/

https://www.poynter.org/?ifcn_misinformation=the-army-is-requisitioning-coronavirus-protection-material-in-catalonia

pandemic, as well as false rumours.424 Media.cat has also been active, in this case by keeping a close eye on controversial measures by the Spanish government to fight "disinformation" as regards the coronavirus pandemic. 425 Curiously enough, months before the pandemic, the website of the (2019)[426], devoted to health issues, published an interesting paper on how disinformation spreads on the internet and in social networks.

On 2 April, International Fact-Checking Day, the European Parliament's Barcelona office issued a statement (Parlament Europeu 2020)[427] on its website about fact-checking and disinformation related to the Covid-19 pandemic.

> "According to a report by EUvsDisinfo, the European External Action Service's (EEAS) anti-disinformation working group, some of the fake claims come from actors close to the US alternative right "alt-right", China and

---

[424] Estafes relacionades amb el Coronavirus / Falsos rumors relacionats amb el Coronavirus. Mossos website. 10 May 2020. https://mossos.gencat.cat/ca/temes/Internet-xarxes-socials-i-aplicacions/Falsosrumors_Estafes/index.html

[425] "Polèmica per les mesures del govern i institucions de l'estat espanyol contra la 'desinformació'". Media.cat, 21 April 2020. https://www.media.cat/2020/04/21/polemica-per-les-mesures-del-govern-i-institucions-de-lestat-espanyol-contra-la-desinformacio/

[426] "Així s'expandeix la desinformació sanitària per Internet i xarxes socials" per Esther Samper. 09/09/2019. https://diarisanitat.cat/aixi-sexpandeix-la-desinformacio-sanitaria-per-internet-i-xarxes-socials/

"When undertaking a search using the browser we stumble across both proven and reliable health information and scams, erroneous news and health rumours… A news item titled "Dandelion Weed Can Boost Your Immune System And Cure Cancer" was shared, commented on and liked more than 1.4 million times on Facebook … 'Doctor Google' is not a safe place to look for information".

[427] Parlament Europeu (2020). "Verificació de dades: lluita contra la desinformació en temps del Covid-19. El brot del coronavirus ha donat lloc a una propagació de notícies falses i desinformació que dificulten els esforços per contenir la pandèmia." Parlament Europeu, Oficina a Barcelona. https://www.europarl.europa.eu/spain/barcelona/ca/premsa/verificació-de-dades-lluita-contra-la-desinformació-en-temps-del-covid-19

Russia. In these cases, the goal is political: to harm the European Union or to create a political change."

A Catalan Government foundation, "Fundació TIC Salut Social", set up to promote the use of ICT in health issues, published a webpage (2020) 428 on "mobile appliances as a channel for disinformation" in which it suggests six verification procedures, the acronym of which is "PIRATA".

> "We propose the PIRATA method to check up on any information
>
> - **P**rotection of data: Check whether the consulted web or App have a data protection policy, what data is gathered and why they do so.
> - **I**nformation updated: Check if the date of the last content update you are consulting is given. Often old contents are used to illustrate current situations.
> - **R**esponsibility: It's important to have access to the person responsible for the contents or the App itself, and information on the team of people involved.
> - **A**uthorship: It must give references about the author of the contents. Once identified, look for them on the internet (on official pages) to contrast their experience on the subject.
> - **T**ransparency: the sources of funding and aims of the web must appear. The web of an

[428] Fundació TIC Salut Social (2020). "Els dispositius mòbils com a canal de desinformació". https://ticsalutsocial.cat/actualitat/els-dispositius-mobils-com-a-canal-de-desinformacio/

NGO is not the same as one belonging to a private enterprise.

- Accessibility: Suitable language and ease with which one may access the resources are important features so as to avoid being cheated."

We can conclude that the pro-independence camp has not been at all active in the Coronavirus pandemic, as far as disinformation is concerned.

* 8.1 The Perpignan rally (29th February 2020)

How about the anti-independence camp? Well, they worked on their obsession about the impact of the pro-independence Perpignan demonstration on Saturday 29 February, when President Puigdemont set foot in Catalonia - albeit Northern Catalonia, in France - for the first time since travelling to Brussels after direct rule was imposed and the political leaders were charged and imprisoned (the social leaders, Jordi Cuixart and Jordi Sànchez had already been arrested after heeding a court summons). The anti-independence camp claimed that given the Covid-19 outbreak it had been foolhardy not to postpone the rally (which brought together about 100,000 people from all over Catalonia). A blog, CatCovidTransparencia.blogspot.com, issued a Manifesto on March 31, and then a fairly long report on 7 May in Spanish[429], English[430] and French[431] (and not, significantly in this author's view, in Catalan) in which it argues that

"In the following 15 chapters, we demonstrate that:

---

429 https://catcovidtransparencia.blogspot.com/2020/05/manifestacion-cero-de-cataluna.html

430 https://catcovidtransparencia.blogspot.com/2020/05/ground-zero-demonstration-of-catalonia.html

431 https://catcovidtransparencia.blogspot.com/2020/05/manifestacion-zero-de-catalogne.html

- a synchronised explosion of deaths happened on March 17th in ALL Catalonia.
- this synchronisation of ALL Catalonia, from March 17 to 27th, created a world record of death grow (isc) in 10 days.
- that this exceptional synchronisation comes from a massive precise contagion in the 29-F Demonstration."

The authors, to be fair, do at least say that "In ALL this analysis, every time we point to a negligence, intentional omission or responsibility of [the Government of Catalonia] and health managers and advisers, we make it very clear that it is an hypothesis."

In their Manifesto,[432] the authors thank a digital newspaper - that in the opinion of this author has been a scourge of the independence movement for years, including not a few items of fake news and manipulation - e-Notícies and its founder-editor Xavier Rius - for disseminating their work:

- 31/03, 16,500 viewings: **Conexión Perpiñán.** https://sociedad.e-noticies.es/conexion-perpinan-130070.html
- 01/04, Youtube, 20,800 viewings: **La conexión Perpiñán.** https://www.youtube.com/watch?v=oBUkARt5JhU
- 03/04, 8,500 viewings: **¿El mitin de Perpiñán actuó de brote gigante?** https://sociedad.e-noticies.es/el-mitin-de-perpinan-actuo-de-brote-gigante-130157.html

432 https://catcovidtransparencia.blogspot.com/2020/03/catcovidtransparencia-manifiesto.html

See also "*Ground Zero demonstration of Catalonia*". 7 May 2020. https://catcovidtransparencia.blogspot.com/2020/05/ground-zero-demonstration-of-catalonia.html

Their basic hypothesis falls flat when one compares the statistics for Catalonia and Madrid (which had no huge public event on February 29). Note that the report fails to refer to the number of cases, which is surely as important in explaining the increase in the number of deaths[433].

a. Cases (cumulative totals)

Date	**Madrid**	**Barcelona** (sic)
29/2/2020	7	5
1/3/2020	10	6
2/3/2020	29	15
3/3/2020	49	15
4/3/2020	70	15
5/3/2020	70	15
6/3/2020	137	24
7/3/2020	174	24
8/3/2020	202	49
9/3/2020	469	75
10/3/2020	782	124
11/3/2020	1024	156
12/3/2020	1388	260
13/3/2020	1990	316

[433] The reader should bear in mind that Spain's Covid-19 statistics are not reliable – as probably happens elsewhere - and are not collected in every "autonomous community" using the same criteria.

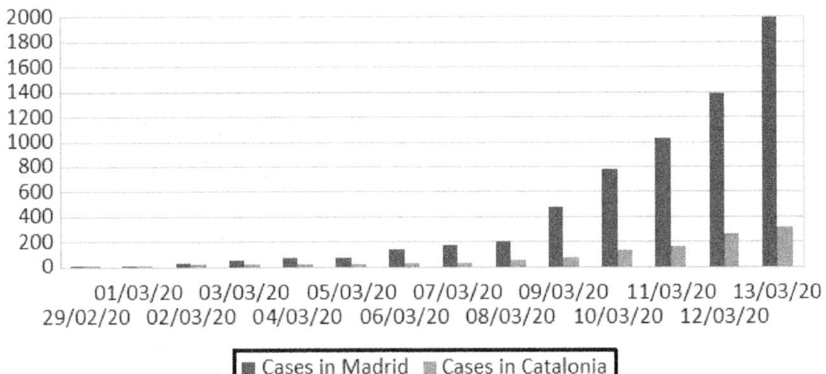

The graph of this data suggests that all eyes should be on what happened, and why, in Madrid, rather than on Catalonia. Note, moreover, that on March 8, when in Madrid there were already 202 confirmed cases, Vox filled the in a rally with 9,000 supporters having, early the same day, issued a communiqué "so that the more vulnerable can follow the Vistalegre event from their homes" because of the pandemic (Aduriz 2020)[434]. Note also that later on the same day there were International Women's Day rallies throughout Spain, including Barcelona (in Catalonia, 49 confirmed cases) and Madrid (where 120,000 attended the rally, 202 confirmed cases)(Güell 2020)[435]. This has led to the issue being taken to courts by the Spanish opposition, and yet again there are serious

[434] Aduriz, Iñigo (2020). "Vox no logra llenar Vistalegre el 8M en un acto para presentarse como "la única alternativa" al PP", *El Diario*, 8 March 2020. https://www.eldiario.es/politica/Vox-Vistalegre-presentarse-alternativa-PP_0_1003699814.html

[435] Güell, Oriol (2020). "Las marchas del 8-M se celebraron en contra del criterio de la agencia europea. El Centro para el Control y Prevención de Enfermedades llama a "evitar actos multitudinarios innecesarios" en países en los que se registren contagios locales", *El País*, 13 March 2020, https://elpais.com/sociedad/2020-03-12/las-marchas-del-8-m-se-celebraron-en-contra-del-criterio-de-la-agencia-europea.html

criticisms of the Guardia Civil reports substantiating the accusations, as happened after the events of 20-21 September 2017 and the 1 October 2017 referendum (Castro & Pinheiro 2020[436]; Sáenz de Ugarte 2020[437]).

In between February 29 and March 8 2020 the EU's European Centre for Disease Prevention and Control issued, on 2 March, one of its "Rapid Risk Assessments" in which it recommended that "Individual social distancing measures (e.g. avoiding shaking hands and kissing, such as avoiding crowded transports and unnecessary mass gatherings) should be followed during all the scenarios as a preventive measure" (ECDC 2020, p. 12).[438] The Spanish government did not heed (perhaps it did not dare heed) these recommendations which, in any case, were issued several days after the Perpignan rally.

b. Deaths (cumulative totals)

Date	Madrid	Barcelona
6/3/2020	1	1
7/3/2020	2	1
8/3/2020	5	1
9/3/2020	16	2
10/3/2020	21	3
11/3/2020	31	3
12/3/2020	56	4

---

436 Castro, Irene & Pinheiro, Marcos (2020). "La Guardia Civil manipuló la declaración de un testigo para inculpar al Gobierno por la manifestación del 8M", *El Diario*, 26 May 2020. https://www.eldiario.es/politica/Vox-Vistalegre-presentarse-alternativa-PP_0_1003699814.html

437 Sáenz de Ugarte, Iñigo (2020). "Los bulos tienen las patas tan largas que acaban apareciendo en un informe de la Guardia Civil", *El Diario*, 26 May 2020. https://www.eldiario.es/politica/coronavirus-Guardia-Civil-bulos_0_1031347628.html

438 ECDC (2020. "Outbreak of novel coronavirus disease 2019 (COVID-19): increased transmission globally –fifth update. 2 March 2020". European Centre for Disease Control. https://www.ecdc.europa.eu/sites/default/files/documents/RRA-outbreak-novel-coronavirus-disease-2019-increase-transmission-globally-COVID-19.pdf

13/3/2020	81	6
14/3/2020	86	6
15/3/2020	213	8
16/3/2020	213	12
17/3/2020	355	18
18/3/2020	390	41
19/3/2020	498	55
20/3/2020	628	82
21/3/2020	804	122
22/3/2020	1021	191
23/3/2020	1263	245
24/3/2020	1535	282
25/3/2020	1825	516
26/3/2020	2090	672
27/3/2020	2412	880

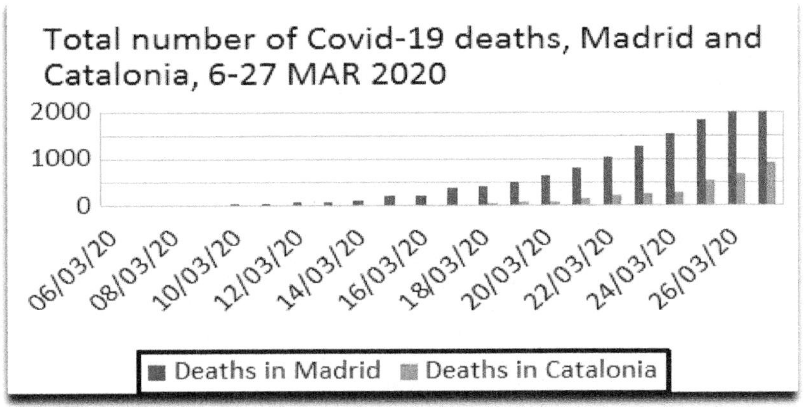

As before, these statistics (despite gaps in the series) are alarming as regards Madrid, which takes off sooner, and at a far faster rate, than Catalonia.

In conclusion, rather than the Perpignan rally (which, moreover, was allowed by the French authorities), it is surely the events in Madrid that should be looked into: especially, the Vox rally in the Vistalegre stadium and the International Women's Day rally, both on March 8th, following which several politicians contracted the disease.

That does not mean to say the Catalan Government, the Generalitat, has been happy about the way the Spanish government - after declaring a state of alarm and thus (temporarily) removing the regional governments' power to react locally (like the German Länder or the Swiss cantons) - has been handling the pandemic.

e.g.

- La República (2020) : Minister Vergés speaks out against the Spanish government: «We shan't wait sitting down»[439]

Yet vicious attacks have been made in the media and in the social media, against anyone in Catalonia questioning the Spanish government's strategy to cope with the pandemic. Dr. Oriol Mitjà, in particular, an epidemiologist who leads a team of advisors for the Catalan government, has been in the eye of the storm (Gutiérrez 2020, Buesa 2020).[440] Even the financial support for his research offered by the *Assemblea Nacional Catalana* (alongside many other donors) is regarded as revealing and deserving of a headline (2020).[441] *Crónica Global* described him as "the separatist virologist" and "the

---

[439] La República (2020) «[VÍDEO] La contundència de la consellera Vergés contra el Gobierno: "No esperarem asseguts", *La República*, 24 April 2020. https://www.larepublica.cat/noticies/la-contundencia-de-la-consellera-verges-contra-el-gobierno-no-esperarem-asseguts/

[440] Alex Gutiérrez (2020). "El pim-pam-pum mediàtic a l'epidemiòleg Oriol Mitjà. 'El Periódico' publica una dura crítica al doctor i nega que les UCI s'hagin col·lapsat". *Ara Balears,* 9 April 2020. https://www.arabalears.cat/firmes/alex_gutierrez/pim-pam-pum-mediatic-epidemioleg-Oriol-Mitja_0_2432156907.html

Jokin Buesa (2020). "La mesquina campanya d'El País contra Oriol Mitjà se li gira en contra i recula", *El Nacional*, 12 June 2020. https://www.elnacional.cat/enblau/ca/televisio/oriol-mitja-campanya-el-pais-titular-recula_513033_102.html

[441] Anguera de Sojo, Iva (2020). "El independentismo financia al médico Oriol Mitjà, con el dinero recaudado para el procés". *El Independiente*, 26 March 2020. https://www.elindependiente.com/politica/2020/03/26/el-independentismo-financia-al-medico-oriol-mitja-con-el-dinero-recaudado-para-el-proces/

doctor-hero of the "indys"" (Jorro 2020[a], 2020b)[442], Pena (2020)[443]. As reported in the latter article, social media pressure made El País hastily change the initial headline, "Oriol Mitjà's test with hydroxychloroquine to prevent Covid-19 fails..." tweeted at 9.22 a.m., to a scientifically correct (and valuable!) "Hydroxychloroquine fails as a method to prevent Covid-19..." by 9.34 a.m. *ABC*, on the other hand, kept the headline (Armora 2020).[444] Mitjà, even early on, did not remain silent in the face of this onslaught (e.g. Mitjà 2020).[445]

Former French Prime Minister, Barcelona-born and current local councillor Manuel Valls, the day after being condemned by the European Court of Human Rights for his policy, as Interior Minister, of expelling Romanian citizens on the grounds of being gypsies (VilaWeb 2020)[446], accused the Catalan government of being

[442] Ignasi Jorro (2020a). "Oriol Mitjà, el médico-héroe de los 'indepes' que la pifió con el coronavirus". *Crónica Global.* 17 March 2020. https://cronicaglobal.elespanol.com/vida/oriol-mitja-coronavirus_328584_102.html

Ignasi Jorro (2020b). "El Govern ficha a Oriol Mitjà como asesor". 6 April 2020. *Crónica Global.* https://cronicaglobal.elespanol.com/politica/oriol-mitja-asesor-cataluna_335469_102.html

[443] Josep Pena (2020). "Oriol Mitjà: Un enemic del poble". *El Punt Avui.* 8 April 2020. https://cronicaglobal.elespanol.com/vida/oriol-mitja-coronavirus_328584_102.html

[444] Armora, E. (2020). "Fracasa el ensayo de Oriol Mitjà: la hidroxicloroquina no previene el coronavirus", *ABC*, 20 June 2020. https://www.abc.es/espana/catalunya/abci-fracasa-ensayo-oriol-mitja-hidroxicloroquina-no-previene-coronavirus-202006121016_noticia.html

[445] Mitjà, Oriol (2020). Twitter, 23 May 2020. https://twitter.com/oriolmitja/status/1264092087882002433?s=20

[446] VilaWeb (2020). "El TEDH condemna França pel desallotjament de romanesos d'ètnia gitana promoguda per Manuel Valls. Quan era ministre d'Interior, Valls va promoure l'expulsió de gitanos del territori francès", VilaWeb, 16 May 2020. https://www.vilaweb.cat/noticies/tedh-condemna-franca-desallotjament-gitanos-valls/

fanatical and hate-ridden in its management of the Covid-19 pandemic (EFE 2020)[447]:

> "The former French prime minister and spokesman for *Barcelona pel Canvi*, Manuel Valls, has condemned that "in the first part" of the COVID-19 crisis in Catalonia the pro-independence cabinet took the opportunity to "impose its narrative "as regards this situation, "sometimes with fanaticism and hatred".
>
> In an interview with the Efe Agency, the former French Prime Minister regretted that it had shifted from a "Spain steals from us" slogan to "Spain kills us" and that, in his opinion, public and private media subsidized by the Catalan government had been used to leak that secessionist "propaganda" into the context of the health crisis."

Rubio Jordán (2018)[448] studied the coverage of the Catalan process on the front pages of six newspapers: four based in Madrid - *La Razón, ABC, El Mundo* and *El País* - and two in Barcelona - *La Vanguardia*, and *El Periódico de Catalunya.* The latter newspaper is amazingly described as "de corte nacionalista y defensor del proceso catalán" ("od Nationalist leanings and a defender of the Catalan process"). The author's brief explanation of the rise of the Catalan independent movement fails to mention the detonator: the 2010 Constitutional court judgment on the 2006 Statute of Autonomy,

---

[447] EFE (2020). "Manuel Valls: El independentismo ha gestionado la crisis con fanatismo y odio", EFE, 16 May 2020. https://www.efe.com/efe/espana/politica/manuel-valls-el-independentismo-ha-gestionado-la-crisis-con-fanatismo-y-odio/10002-4247934

[448] Rubio Jordán, Ana Virginia (2018). "33. El referéndum catalán del 1-O y la Declaración de Independencia de Cataluña en los medios: análisis comparado del tratamiento informativo en las portadas de la prensa española", in Luis Mañas Viniegra, Sendy Meléndez Chávez, Estrella Martínez Rodrigo (eds.). *La comunicación ante el ciudadano*, Barcelona: Gedisa. pp. 435-446.

See also, in the same issue, Laura Teruel Rodríguez, "El objetivo político de la desinformación en la esfera internacional: la propagación de las "noticias falsas" a través de las redes sociales", pp. 463-476.

further reducing the credibility of the article. Rubio firmly offers the following unsubstantiated explanation: "The economic risk has forced them to formally commit themselves against the secessionist *procés* and to seek other clearly commercial objectives over and above ideological ones". Other Catalan newspapers such as *Regió 7, Ara, El Punt Avui* o *Segre* would have given a far more plural impression. She repeats a recurring falsehood: in actual fact it was the Parliament and not the President that had to declare independence, so President Puigdemont's October 11 speech was not an (immediately withdrawn) declaration of independence.

Finally, she happily and uncritically quotes a highly questionable affirmation by García Arvelo (2016):

> "Today more than ever and in a way that we had never seen before, there is a pro-independence current that is shaking a large part of the social environment of Catalonia and that everything that implies Spain, whatever is Spanish, is the object of expressions of displeasure and rejection" (García Arvelo, 2016[449], p. 1504)."

San José (2018)[450] did the same in a much more limited study: only two Spanish and two Catalan newspapers.

There have been at least clear indications by people who think the Catalans will further their cause thanks to the pandemic. One is Josep Borrell, whom we have encountered earlier in this paper. He again tried to link the Catalan independence movement with "populisms", reacting on the same day that President Torra and spokesperson Meritxell Budó had claimed their government would

---

[449] García Arvelo, J. L. (2016). "Nacionalismos e independentismo: breve historia y alguna reflexión desde el mensaje televisivo", in *La pantalla insomne,* 2ª edición, p. 1494-1507. Tenerife: Universidad de La Laguna.

[450] San José Herrero, Óscar (2018). "La lucha por la independencia en el 'Procés' de Cataluña: un análisis del tratamiento informativo en la prensa de referencia". Universidad de Valladolid (BA dissertation). http://uvadoc.uva.es/bitstream/handle/10324/33108/TFG_F_2018_135.pdf

have coped better with the pandemic and fewer lives would have been lost:[451]

> “The high representative for EU Foreign Policy, Josep Borrell, has warned of the "temptation to build walls" saying that nationalisms and populisms are going to find space in this pandemic to "sell their thesis", and has given as an example the statement by the Catalan President, Quim Torra, that Catalonia would have managed the crisis better “if it were independent”. The Catalan Minister of the Presidency and spokesperson for the Government has also expressed herself to the same effect today”.

*** 8.2 De Pedro and disinformation in Catalonia**

Another flank of the offensive is a paper by Nicolás de Pedro, "senior fellow" at the Institute for Statecraft mentioned earlier. He had a lavishly presented 17-page paper published in early April 2020 by an organisation this author had not heard of: the *Instituto de Seguridad y Cultura*, which “promotes the prevention of violent extremism and investigation on Security and Defence”. Its twitter account was opened in February 2017 and it was officially founded in mid-2017. The title of the paper is "*Crisis del Coronavirus: La Desinformación del Separatismo Catalán como Desafío Estratégico para España*" (“Coronavirus crisis: Catalan separatist disinformation as a strategic challenge for Spain”).452 Its references consist of 13

---

[451] La Vanguardia (2020). “Borrell advierte que la pandemia puede impulsar el nacionalismo y señala a Torra“. *La Vanguardia*, 20 April 2020. https://www.lavanguardia.com/politica/20200420/48640496711/josep-borrell-advierte-pandemia-coronavirus-impulsar-nacionalismo-quim-torra.html

[452] de Pedro, Nicolás /(2020). Cr*isis del Coronavirus: La Desinformación del Separatismo Catalán como Desafío Estratégico para España.* Instituto de Seguridad y Cultura. https://seguridadycultura.org/wp-content/uploads/2020/04/ISC_Desinfo-CAT_AFF.pdf

tweets. There is no mention to a single official document, not even quotes from newspapers or extracts from interviews. Just 13 tweets.

Seven of these illustrate the points he wishes to put across in the first section: "Why Disinformation is a Strategic Threat for Democracies") (pages 6-11) and the other six illustrate the second section: "Disinformation and internacionalization of the Catalan Separatist Process" (pages 12-16).

This paper was manna from heaven for the Unionist camp: it was immediately and generously covered by Europa Press[453], Vox Populi[454], Confilegal[455], *Economía Digital*[456]...; and, to be fair, it was also mentioned in Catalan media such as *El Món*[457].

His main claims are (and I apologize to any reader who may disagree with my having found it preferable not to reduce this text):

---

[453] Europa Press (2020). "Un informe desvela la estrategia de desinformación del separatismo catalán utilizando la crisis del coronavirus" https://www.europapress.es/nacional/noticia-informe-desvela-estrategia-desinformacion-separatismo-catalan-utilizando-crisis-coronavirus-20200402130148.html (April 2 2020)

[454] Voz Populi (2020). "El Instituto de Seguridad y Cultura denuncia la instrumentalización del coronavirus por parte del independentismo", https://www.vozpopuli.com/elliberal/politica/Instituto-Seguridad-Cultura-instrumentalizacion-independentismo_0_1342367054.html (April 6 2020)

[455] Confilegal (2020). "'El separatismo catalán está aprovechando la situación actual para promover un discurso de odio a España', advierte el investigador Nicolás de Pedro", https://confilegal.com/20200406-el-separatismo-catalan-esta-aprovechando-la-situacion-actual-para-promover-un-discurso-de-odio-a-espana-advierte-el-investigador-nicolas-de-pedro/ (April 6),

[456] Economía Digital (2020). "Las 'fake news' de Torra (y su entorno) para aprovechar la pandemia", https://www.economiadigital.es/politica-y-sociedad/coronavirus-las-fake-news-de-torra-y-su-entorno-para-aprovechar-la-pandemia_20050032_102.html (April 2 2020)

[457] El Món (2020). "Una consultora d'intel·ligència espanyola relaciona coronavirus amb el "separatisme català"", https://www.elmon.cat/politica/consultora-intelligencia-espanyola-relaciona-coronavirus-separatisme-catala_2118903102.html (April 2 2020)

“In Catalonia we are witnessing an unprecedented phenomenon of institutional disobedience from within and without the very democratic state to which Catalonia belongs and is fighting against. The Process has had a lot of simulation, imposture and ambiguity, but if one thing has been confirmed in the last five years, it is that fake news generates real effects.

Since the democratic transition, Catalan nationalism has promoted a process of nation-building with an all-encompassing vocation. Forty years later, as a result, there is an overwhelming political and cultural hegemony of nationalism in the whole of the Catalan institutional, media, educational and cultural fabric. Hence, the division - at least with respect to the question of independence - and political fragmentation that the successive electoral results in Catalonia reflect remain invisible in the public and communicative space.

"The repeated denial of this division by nationalism, the insistence on slogans such as that of “one people”, the desire to monopolize public spaces with yellow ribbons or the patrimonialization of the Catalan concept and identity admits several readings.

This hegemony feeds on promoting and subsidizing the like and by progressively expelling the dissident.

The public media such as TV3 or *Catalunya Ràdio* play a central role in the articulation of this uncontested nationalist narrative, infused with grievance and permanent victimhood in relation to a Spain always characterized as authoritarian, uncouth, aggressive and hostile. And it is not just about informational or analytical spaces. It is a narrative that permeates the spaces of their own production and is evident in successful comedy shows such as Polònia or APM. To avoid misunderstandings, it is not a crude imposition of directives from above, but the natural and normalized result of this nationalist discursive hegemony.

From the point of view of information and communication, the consolidation of tight communities favours polarization and is a vulnerability that - as happened in October 2017 and has been happening since then - can be exploited by foreign actors. Russian interference is still largely a story to be written, but it is probably only a matter of time before the details about it and any subsequent cover-up operation come to light.

What admits legitimate diverse interpretations is the motivation, impact achieved and specific objectives that the Kremlin and its interposed actors were pursuing with this campaign. There is an ongoing investigation in the National Court on the activities in Barcelona of agents of the GRU, Russian military intelligence, during those decisive days. Regarding the latter, it should be pointed out in a preliminary way that the rank and profile of the main agent identified suggest that the Kremlin considered different scenarios and possible outcomes of the Catalan crisis at that time.

What is relevant, it should be emphasized, is the cumulative and sedimentary effect of this disinformation in terms of delegitimization of Spanish democracy (objective of independence), but also of the whole of the EU itself (objective of the Kremlin campaigns).

Torra's interview on the BBC continues with the effort to appeal for outside intervention. The aim is to move from an internal conflict between Catalans to a question between Catalonia and Spain conceived as two separate entities and which require international mediation due to the alleged democratic deficits of the Spanish State. Obviously, in the midst of a pandemic, the practical impact that can be expected from this interview or from the letters sent by Torra to the members of the European Council is, quite simply, zero.

The effectiveness of Spanish diplomacy to date should neither invite us to lower our guard nor underestimate the relevance of international public opinion, where the pro-independence narrative has penetrated strongly.

What seems certain is that the issue will not be resolved with fact-checking. When Torra said on the BBC on March 19 that the Madrid government is preventing the confinement in Catalonia - despite speaking from his confinement himself since the screen appears superimposed "Spain has been in near total lockdown since Saturday" [15 March] - it's not that reality is not known, it's simply that it doesn't matter.[458]

---

[458] Real Decreto-ley 9/2020, de 27 de marzo, por el que se adoptan medidas complementarias, en el ámbito laboral, para paliar los efectos derivados del COVID-19. https://www.boe.es/buscar/act.php?id=BOE-A-2020-4152

Sánchez anuncia la paralización de la actividad económica no esencial hasta el 9 de abril. https://www.eldiario.es/politica/Sanchez-paralizacion-actividad-economica-esencial_0_1010699341.html

"Sánchez, que hasta ahora se había negado a paralizar por completo la actividad, como le solicitaban algunos gobiernos autonómicos y grupos políticos, porque defendía que España había tomado ya las medidas más "drásticas" de los países del entorno, ha explicado que el Gobierno toma una decisión "tan contundente y tan dura" por la cercanía de la Semana Santa." "...esa medida, que entrará en vigor desde el lunes hasta el próximo 9 de abril..."

"Torra celebra la paralización de la actividad económica y pide al Gobierno "no dejar en fuera de juego" a los trabajadores"

Casos Espanya 13/3/2020, 21 h: 4,209

https://www.isciii.es/QueHacemos/Servicios/VigilanciaSaludPublicaRENAVE/EnfermedadesTransmisibles/Documents/INFORMES/Informes%20COVID-19/Informe%20COVID-19.%20N%C2%BA%209_13marzo2020_ISCIII.pdf

Casos Espanya 29/3/2020, 21 h: 85,195
https://www.isciii.es/QueHacemos/Servicios/VigilanciaSaludPublicaRENAVE/EnfermedadesTransmisibles/Documents/INFORMES/Informes%20COVID-19/Informe%20n%C2%BA%2018.%20Situaci%C3%B3n%20de%20COVID-19%20en%20Espa%C3%B1a%20a%2030%20marzo%20de%202020.pdf

> To verify this, it is enough to visit Twitter these days and note, on the one hand, the consensus generated between respected and respectable activists and academics with a nationalist sensitivity regarding the ongoing "recentralization" or the "hidden 155" as the only response of the State to the coronavirus. And, on the other hand, to verify with what depth a Spanish-phobic hate discourse has penetrated a not inconsiderable segment of this independence movement impervious to any other narrative, now fed with the theory that the coronavirus "comes from and is the fault of Madrid", of a State that does not care about the "death of Catalans" or that, simply, with "independence, there would be fewer deaths".
>
> The sending of letters by a para-state institution [sic!] such as the Catalan National Assembly (ANC) to the consuls assigned to Barcelona, blaming "the people of Madrid for the spread of the coronavirus" and accusing the Guardia Civil of "withholding and requisitioning" medical supplies sent to Igualada - one of the main focuses of the pandemic in Catalonia - shows how the Generalitat is trying to fix in the nationalist consciousness an insidious narrative with a conspiratorial tone that can poison civic coexistence, while trying to spread it internationally.

De Pedro seemingly has not the slightest idea of the status ("paraestatal"!) or spelling (he writes "Asamblea") for that matter of the Assemblea Nacional Catalana[459], which is an NGO. Nevertheless,

---

Oriol Solé Altimira (2020). "Torra applauds the paralysation of economic activity and asks the Government "not to leave workers in the lurch", *El Diario*, 28 March 2020. https://www.eldiario.es/catalunya/politica/Torra-paralizacion-actividad-Gobierno-trabajdores_0_1010699413.html

[459] Let us recall that the *Assemblea* has been under fire for several years now. e.g.

"Judge Ismael Moreno of the National Court is investigating the Catalan National Assembly (ANC) on charges of rebellion and sedition for "promoting" and "calling for" motions by Catalan local councils in support of the independence resolution of the Catalan Parliament, annulled by the Constitutional Court", *EFE / Diario Información*, 3 February 2016.

his claim that it might "to poison civic coexistence" does at least reveal that he does not believe that has yet happened. He ends with an unanswered question:

> "In fact, if the setting for the described dynamics is not changed, what must be queried is if time and demography play in the favour of Spain or of the independence movement."

De Pedro bursts with righteous indignation at the comparison of recent Spanish government measures with the application of Article 155 at the end of October 2017. The fact is, though, that the tweet he chooses to illustrate his point "155, 155 digital, 155 coronavirus" is by Catalan minister Jordi Puigneró,[460] Minister of Digital Policy and Public Administration, whose plans to extend digital democracy, including blockchain technology, were deliberately foiled by a recentralizing Royal Decree-Law hastily published by the Spanish government, in Spanish, Catalan, Galician and Basque. (Jefatura del Estado 2019)[461].

---

https://www.diarioinformacion.com/nacional/2016/02/03/investigan-anc-delitos-rebelion-sedicion/1723625.html.

"On the same day that it was reported that the National Court was investigating the ANC for rebellion or sedition, the pro-independence organization responded with a legal report that denies the basis of the accusation. The Assemblea considers that the Penal Code does not consider secession to be a State crime if there is no violence, riots and disorders", *La Vanguardia*, 4 February 2016.
https://www.lavanguardia.com/politica/20160204/301908302403/anc-asamblea-joan-anton-font-audiencia-nacional-rebelion-sedicion.html

Two years earlier, in an editorial in its Seville edition on 14 MAR 2014, *ABC* had called for it to be immediately outlawed: "Disolver la Asamblea [sic] Nacional Catalana ya". https://www.abc.es/cordoba/20140314/sevp-disolver-asamblea-nacional-catalana-20140314.html

[460] https://twitter.com/jordiPuignero/status/1238934510106038272?s=20

[461] Jefatura del Estado (2019). Real Decreto-ley 14/2019, de 31 de octubre, por el que se adoptan medidas urgentes por razones de seguridad pública en materia de administración digital, contratación del sector público y telecomunicaciones. *BOE*, 5 November 2019.
https://www.boe.es/diario_boe/txt.php?id=BOE-A-2019-15790

El Español (2019a)[462] revealed this deliberate intention:

> "This is what the decree with which the Government seeks to prevent the Catalan digital administration looks like. It lays down measures to turn the DNI (identity card) into the only document with enough weight for accreditation to be unique and exclusive."
>
> "According to the Government, this royal decree will greatly improve the capacity of the State to react to projects that go against the general interest such as Identicat..."

And a couple of months later the same newspaper (Flores, Chema 2019)[463] again referred to "Royal decree-law 14/2019 that Sánchez passed last November to put a halt to a possible Catalan digital republic" ("El Real Decreto-ley 14/2019 que Sánchez sacó adelante el pasado noviembre para frenar una posible república digital catalana...").

> "The spokesperson for JxCat [Junts per Catalunya] in the Spanish Parliament, Laura Borràs, [464] speaks of the "abusive digital decree" and that the State has implemented a "digital *coup d'état* with a decree that is introduced in an irregular fashion without parliamentary approval and which enables communication intervention to be carried out…"

---

[462] El Español (2019). "Así es el decreto con el que el Gobierno quiere evitar la Administración digital catalana", *El Español,* 6 November 2019. https://www.elespanol.com/espana/20191106/decreto-gobierno-quiere-evitar-administracion-digital-catalana/442455993_0.html

[463] Flores, Chema (2019). "El PNV pacta con Sánchez modificar el '155 digital' y da alas a la 'República digital catalana'", *El Español,* 30 December 2019. https://www.elespanol.com/omicrono/20191230/pnv-sanchez-modificar-155-digital-republica-catalana/455954797_0.html

[464] See also her straightforward explanation of why independence is wanted in Catalonia: https://twitter.com/Erramun2014/status/1257423601218846722?s=20

> The mayoress of Barcelona, Ada Colau, considers that Pedro Sánchez's government wanting to intervene the social networks if they threaten public order is "a serious attack on fundamental rights and liberties". …"

Next in line to comment on the decree was the Real Instituto Elcano (let us remind ourselves: it is "the think tank of international and strategic studies, carried out from a Spanish, European and global perspective" ("el *think-tank* de estudios internacionales y estratégicos, realizados desde una perspectiva española, europea y global"); the Hon. President of its Board of Governors is the King in person; and among its collaborating organizations we find Google, Microsoft, Deloitte and Everis (all of which to my knowledge are committed to truthful reporting). This institute also openly ratifies the end-purpose of the decree-law:

> "We are faced with the adoption of a regulation or measure that brings on a process of destruction of the Constitution, in Smith's terminology, that some Catalan political forces have been trying to carry out since 2014 and that reached the maximum level of challenge to legality in the referendum of October 1 and the unsuccessful declaration of independence of October 10, 2017. Faced with this situation, and given the possibility that this Process will continue to use the enormous possibilities that cyberspace provides, the State decided to act by bringing in the following norms that modify six laws, one of them organic" (Moret 2020).[465]

---

[465] Moret Millás, Vicente (2020). "El Real Decreto-Ley 14/2019: una nueva regulación del ciberespacio en clave nacional". Real Instituto Elcano, 14 January 2020, ARI 4/2020. http://www.realinstitutoelcano.org/wps/portal/rielcano_es/contenido?WCM_GLOBAL_CONTEXT=/elcano/elcano_es/zonas_es/ciberseguridad/ari4-2020-moret-real-decreto-ley-14-2019-nueva-regulacion-ciberespacio-en-clave-nacional

Amnesty International (2020)[466] and *Article 19* also hammered this decree.

So inasmuch as the decree-law, decided unilaterally, encroached on the autonomy of the Catalan government and Parliament, it is hardly surprising that it was compared with Article 155, the article in the Spanish Constitution designed to oblige defiant autonomous communities (regions) to comply with central government instructions, which was used with highly questionable legitimacy to quell Catalonia's October 27 2017 declaration of independence, depose the Catalan government, establish direct rule and immediately call an election (a prerogative of the President of Catalonia). Again, it is surely understandable that a State of Alarm that, among other things, unilaterally recentralized the health systems of Spain, would be likewise compared with Article 155.

Sandrine Morel, a *Le Monde* journalist who in the past has not been sympathetic to the Catalan independence movement (a trait shared by the vast majority of Madrid-based foreign correspondents), however peaceful, non-violent and democratic it is, gave her support (wittingly or otherwise) to De Pedro's thesis, in a recent *Le Monde* piece. Blissfully unaware of the distribution of power between central government and the "autonomous" governments in this field, she associates coping with the coronavirus as if it were a pro-independence strategy.[467]

> "On Thursday April 16, the President of the Catalan government, the radical independentist Quim Torra (JxCat) clearly let it be known that Catalonia would have better managed the health crisis had it been independent, as did "the small states". On April 14, it was the President

---

466 "El Real Decreto Digital propicia la censura previa y el secuestro de contenidos en Internet por parte del gobierno", 11 February 2020. https://www.es.amnesty.org/en-que-estamos/noticias/noticia/articulo/el-real-decreto-digital-propicia-la-censura-previa-y-el-secuestro-de-contenidos-en-internet-por-part/

467 Sandrine Morel (2020). En Catalogne, une lutte contre le coronavirus… et " l'Etat espagnol ". *Le Monde*, 18 avril 2020. https://www.lemonde.fr/international/article/2020/04/18/en-catalogne-une-lutte-contre-le-coronavirus-et-l-espagne_6037015_3210.html

> of ERC, Oriol Junqueras, who, from the prison where the pro-independence leaders convicted of sedition are serving their sentences, defended this idea." …
>
> "The Spanish state, he explained in the newspaper *La Vanguardia,* is slow to react, centralist, nationalist, militarist, oligopolistic and hopelessly inefficient", and as a consequence, it "is not useful for the citizens of Catalonia"…
>
> **"The slow Catalan reaction to the epidemic**
>
> Less affected than Madrid, Catalonia is nonetheless one of the main focuses of the epidemic in Spain. And the rebel region has not been distinguished by more efficient management than the others".

Support for this view comes from none other than the High Representative of the EU for Foreign Policy, Josep Borrell, who "warns" that the pandemic could give an impulse to "nationalism", and he singles out President Quim Torra (who, incidentally, was subjected to a personal and family inferno ever since his adversaries chose to completely distort, out of context, a 2011 article of his; and as already explained, was ousted from his post by the Supreme Court) (La Vanguardia 2020)[468].

With remarkable aplomb and not a little cynicism (his own country has one of the very worst track records in the world, in per capita terms, in dealing with the pandemic), Borrell was quoted as saying that "the response in countries with greater democratic quality has been better", that "more mature democracies have responded better and will make themselves better", and that "there will be a battle of narratives about which system is most capable of responding to situations of this kind". In this latter case he is right. Four days earlier President Torra had put his case in a press conference,

---

[468] "Josep Borrell advierte que la pandemia puede impulsar el nacionalismo y señala a Torra", *La Vanguardia, 20 April 2020.* https://www.lavanguardia.com/politica/20200420/48640496711/josep-borrell-advierte-pandemia-coronavirus-impulsar-nacionalismo-quim-torra.html

described by one fervently Unionist paper, *Libertad Digital*, as a "new attempt to seek confrontation with the Spanish government".

Yet President Torra based his view ("He points out that the «truly» federal states or smaller countries have coped better with the coronavirus pandemic» (Señala que los países federales "de verdad" o los países pequeños han manejado mejor la pandemia del coronavirus")(Manchón 2020)[469] not only on the stark facts, but also on the long-standing view of the prestigious German think-tank Konrad Adenauer Stiftung.

> "Torra ... has claimed that the priority of his government has been to save lives, yet he has defended that a smaller country could have managed better. He assured that the Konrad Adenauer Stiftung concluded that decentralized crisis management in large countries is the best option, as well as that small countries have reacted "more skillfully and quickly"." (Europa Press)[470]

While not mentioning to which particular article or report he was referring, it is certainly the case that Hofmeister & Friedek 2020)[471] were seemingly scandalised, a few days earlier, by the fact that

---

[469] Manchón, Manuel (2020). "Torra busca otro choque con el Gobierno a propósito de las cifras de muertos". *Crónica Global*, 16 April 2020. https://cronicaglobal.elespanol.com/politica/torra-busca-choque-gobierno_338691_102.html

[470] Europa Press (2020). "Torra dice que un país más pequeño habría respondido mejor que España o Francia", *Europa Press*, 24 April 2020. https://www.europapress.es/nacional/noticia-torra-pide-comuns-presionar-gobierno-desconfinamiento-propio-20200424122442.html

See also: Heraldo de Aragón (2020). "Quim Torra asegura que un país más pequeño habría respondido mejor que España o Francia al coronavirus". *Heraldo de Aragón*, 24 April 2020. https://www.heraldo.es/noticias/nacional/2020/04/24/coronavirus-torra-dice-que-un-pais-mas-pequeno-habria-respondido-mejor-que-espana-o-francia-1371362.html

[471] Hofmeister, Wilheml & Martin Friedek (2020). "Das Coronavirus erschüttert Spanien", 30 March 2020. Konrad Adenauer Stiftung,

> "On March 25, just under two weeks after the alarm was declared, Health Minister Salvador Illa surprisingly announced that a major order had been agreed with Chinese companies to the tune of €432 million for the purchase of 550 million masks, 955 ventilators and 5.5 million rapid tests to be delivered successively over the following eight weeks. In view of the negative dynamic development of the number of cases, one wonders to what extent this delivery period of the material will really be helpful."

Both *Bloomberg* (Giugliano 2020)[472] and the *New York Times* (Minder 2020)[473] have slammed the Spanish government for its "dithering" and not reacting in time. *The Guardian* asked "How did Spain get its coronavirus response so wrong?" (Tremlett 2020)[474]. It goes without saying that any criticism of the handling of the case goes hand-in-hand with the belief that faster and more stringent initial measures would have saved lives. But for Catalan leaders to say this out loud has inflamed many Spanish politicians and media. Catalan government spokesperson, Sra. Meritxell Budó, has often made it clear that the government priority is to save lives, rather than

---

https://www.kas.de/de/laenderberichte/detail/-/content/das-coronavirus-erschuettert-spanien

The article has been summarised here: Lluís Bou (2020). "Coronavirus |German report strongly criticises Pedro Sánchez's crisis management", 1 April 2020. https://www.elnacional.cat/en/politics/coronavirus-germany-merkel-report-critical-pedro-sanchez_487845_102.html

[472] Ferdinando Giugliano (2020) "Spain's Tragedy Was All Too Predictable. The prime minister dithered before imposing lockdown measures that could have saved thousands of lives", Bloomberg, 6 April 2020. https://www.bloomberg.com/opinion/articles/2020-04-06/how-spain-tragically-bungled-its-coronavirus-response

[473] Raphael Minder (2020). "Spain's Coronavirus Crisis Accelerated as Warnings Went Unheeded", *New York Times*, 7 April 2020, https://www.nytimes.com/2020/04/07/world/europe/spain-coronavirus.html

[474] Giles Tremlett (2020). "How did Spain get its coronavirus response so wrong?", *The Guardian*, 26 March 2020, https://www.theguardian.com/world/2020/mar/26/spain-coronavirus-response-analysis

the economy (Al Dia 2020)[475]. President Torra has said the same. (La República 2020)[476].

But when she stated clearly that an independent Catalonia would have taken more drastic measures, much sooner (see also Sesé 2020 for a similar comment made nearly three weeks earlier)[477], the reaction was rapid.

> "Meritxell Budó ... in statements in an interview on Radio 4 has asserted that in an independent Catalunya "there would probably not be so many deaths or so many contagions". Budó has argued that the Generalitat would have decreed the total lock-down fifteen days sooner, and in her opinion, "if we had acted earlier, things would be different"". (El Punt Avui 2020)[478]

The Spanish government spokesperson, Sra. Maria Jesús Montero, insisted in her response that "the virus [Covid-19] knows nothing about frontiers and ideologies: it is a global pandemic that affects all countries" (*El Punt Avui* 2020). But the truth is that on each

---

[475] Al Dia (2020). "Coronavirus.- Budó avantposa la salut a l'economia: "Entre vides i economia, aquest Govern escull vides"", *Al Dia*, 23 March 2020. https://www.aldia.cat/catalunya/noticia-coronavirus-budo-avantposa-salut-leconomia-vides-economia-aquest-govern-escull-vides-20200323141508.html

[476] La República (2020). "Torra, al PPC: "Lliçons ni una. M'he dedicat a salvar vides des que va començar la pandèmia"". *La República*, 24 April 2020. https://www.larepublica.cat/minut-a-minut/torra-al-ppc-llicons-ni-una-mhe-dedicat-a-salvar-vides-des-que-va-comencar-la-pandemia/

[477] Sesé, Gerard (2020) "5 raons per les quals la Covid-19 ha de fer pujar l'independentisme. Amb la pandèmia, els indecisos ja no tenen arguments i es demostra que Catalunya surt molt perjudicada seguint dins d'Espanya", *La República*, 01/04/2020. https://www.larepublica.cat/opinio/tribuna/5-raons-per-les-quals-la-covid-19-ha-de-fer-pujar-lindependentisme/

[478] El Punt Avui (2020). "Montero, a Budó: "El virus no entén de fronteres ni d'ideologies. El comentari està fora de lloc"", *El Punt Avui*, 20 April 2020. http://www.elpuntavui.cat/politica/article/17-politica/1777392-montero-a-budo-el-virus-no-enten-de-fronteres-ni-d-ideologies-el-comentari-esta-fora-de-lloc.html

side of frontiers different strategies have proved more or less successful: Portugal is a good (successful) case in point.

Two days later, Joan Canadell, the pro-independence head of the Barcelona Chamber of Commerce, seconded Sra. Budó's view (Nació Digital 2020).[479] And he was not the last to voice the same opinion, much to the exasperation of Joaquín Luna (2020)[480]:

> "One after another, the President of Catalunya, the spokesperson of the Generalitat, MP Borràs at the Congress or the Speaker have said this week that the Republic would save lives. All they had to add was that the Republic would resuscitate the dead"[...]" One of the people responsible for the report of the Konrad Adenauer Foundation, Wilhelm Hofmeister, its director in Spain, is the very authority who on February 18, 2019, described Catalan independence as "first and foremost a fatal ideological poison"."

Not surprisingly, perhaps, the Guardia Civil prepared to deal with possible social reactions, including sabotage and riots, to the economic crisis the pandemic has wrought in Spain (Lozano & Rendueles 2020)[481]:

---

[479] Nació Digital (2020). "Canadell: "Espanya és atur i mort, Catalunya és vida i futur". El president de la Cambra carrega durament contra l'Estat i afirma que una Catalunya independent "hauria salvat milers de vides"", *Nació Digital*, 22 April 2020. https://www.naciodigital.cat/noticia/200967/canadell/espanya/es/atur/mort/catalunya/es/vida/futur

[480] Joaquín Luna (2020). "La república els ressuscitarà", *La Vanguardia*, 26 April 2020. https://www.lavanguardia.com/opinion/20200426/48721679963/la-republica-els-ressuscitara.html

[481] Lozano, Vanesa & Rendueles, Luis (2020). "La Guardia Civil alerta de posibles "disturbios" y "sabotajes" durante la desescalada", *El Periódico de Catalunya*, 13/05/2020. https://www.elperiodico.com/es/sociedad/20200513/guardia-civil-coronavirus-disturbios-sabotajes-7958982

“"Order 21/20 Delta Papa, signed by Lieutenant General Santafé, Chief of the Operations Command, is entitled 'Action by the Guardia Civil within the framework of the Transition Plan towards a new normality.' It also contemplates the possible appearance in this transition phase of protests for political or of a "separatist nature", alluding to Catalonia.”

This allegedly leaked order (“a document that bears the ‘confidential’ seal and to which *El Periódico* has had access” (“un documento que lleva el sello de 'confidencial' y al que ha tenido acceso El Periódico”) was published in *El Periódico de Catalunya*, whose credibility in the eyes of many has not recovered from the forged CIA document it published some days after the August 2017 terrorist incidents in Barcelona and Cambrils, in a desperate attempt to smear the Catalan police despite their having rapidly hunted down the surviving culprits (Nació Digital 2017).[482]

---

[482] Nació Digital (2017). “Les lliçons d'anglès de Sala-i-Martín al director d'“El Periódico” pel document de la CIA. El rotatiu publica la suposada nota que advertia els Mossos d'Esquadra d'un atemptat imminent a Barcelona“, *Nació Digital,* 31 August 2017.
https://www.naciodigital.cat/noticia/137352/llicons/angles/sala-i-martin/al/director/periodico/document/cia

The newspaper, presumably fed the fakes by the Spanish (secret) police, stuck to its guns:

“Los Mossos intentaron destruir la alerta de EEUU sobre la Rambla. La Policía les incautó en una incineradora el original en inglés desvelado por EL PERIÓDICO, que Forn y Trapero tacharon de “montaje””, *El Periódico de Catalunya,* 21 January 2018.
https://www.elperiodico.com/es/politica/20180121/mossos-intentaron-destruir-alerta-eeuu-rambla-6567677

“Historia de un acoso y un silencio. Los nacionalistas intentaron desacreditar a EL PERIÓDICO para proteger al Govern. Las organizaciones periodísticas, con una elocuente ausencia, apoyaron al diario”, *El Periódico de Catalunya*, 21 January 2018. https://www.elperiodico.com/es/politica/20180121/el-aviso-de-la-cia-sobre-la-rambla-historia-de-un-acoso-y-un-silencio-6566608

See also: “Mossos va rebre un avís sobre atemptats a la Rambla, però no era de la CIA. El Govern ho va considerar de “baixa credibilitat” després de contrastar-ho amb l'Estat”, Diari de Tarragona, 31 August 2017, 17:15 h.

"The Minister of the Interior of the Generalitat, Joaquim Forn, and the chief of the Mossos d'Esquadra, Josep Lluís Trapero, have denied this Thursday that they received a note from the CIA about a possible attack on La Rambla [483] in Barcelona, although they received a warning on May 25 of a possible attack in the summer on this avenue from other sources - without specifying them - and that it had "low credibility".

In a press conference at the Ministry of the Interior, Forn said that the department of the Generalitat communicated this warning to the State and that it "did not give veracity to the threat", in addition to which it was not discussed later in the anti-terrorism risk assessment tables, either on the 25th itself or on June 8.

Forn added that the State also subsequently ruled out that this warning and all other receipts were related to the attacks of 17 and 18 August in Barcelona and Cambrils (Tarragona)..."

The director of the FOIA Information Management Division of the US National Counter-terrorism Center (NCTC), Sally A. Nicholson (not the person mentioned in the article, incidentally), said in a letter dated 8 September 2017 and signed by Sally A. Nicholson, Chief FOIA, Information Management Division, [484] that no communications had been sent to the Catalan police (the "Mossos") on May 25 or to the CITCO on August 21, as claimed by *El Periódico de Catalunya* (Camps 2020):

---

https://www.diaridetarragona.com/catalunya/Mossos-va-rebre-un-avis-sobre-atemptats-a-la-Rambla-per-no-era-de-la-CIA-20170831-0041.html

[483] Note that the bombings, planned by the Ripoll imam and his terrorist cell, never took place – because the house in Alcanar where the bombs were being assembled blew up), and the apparent targets did not include La Rambla or Cambrils, where the terrorists, in the event, improvised their actions and ran over people with their vehicle.

[484] Camps, Carlota (2020). "La intel·ligència dels EUA no troba la suposada nota de la CIA als Mossos", *El Nacional,* 21 September 2017. https://www.elnacional.cat/ca/societat/nota-cia-mossos_193689_102.html

"This responds to your request dated 5 September 2017 (Encloswe), received in the Information Management Division of the office of the Director of National Intelligence on 6 September 2017. Pursuant to the FOIA, 5 U.S.C. §552, as amended, you requested information on the communication between NCTC and Spanish CITCO agency, as well as communication between NCTC and the Catalan police.

Your request was processed under the FOIA, 5 U.S.C. §552, as amended. After a thorough search in our records and databases, we were unable to locate any records responsive to your request."

Público (Bayo & López 2017)[485] double-checked with specialists the veracity of the alleged CIA message and this letter, and reached a resounding conclusion just nine days before the referendum, including a significant final answer with which we start to close this chapter:

"The reply signed by Nicholson leaves no doubts: there was no direct official warning from the US Intelligence to the Mossos, nor is the message in "Spanglish" which as filtered to support this first fakehood authentic. However, who and why made this forgery on an issue in which there were numerous victims of terrorism in limbo?"

I myself received a reply from the Spanish Ministry of the Interior in late 2020, saying that this was sensitive information protected from being revealed to citizens and to the media by law. Given that the *El Periódico* article was widely read, and no legal action is known to have been taken against it for revealing official secrets, one can easily conclude that the *El Periódico*'s alleged CIA notes were indeed a fabrication, though it doggedly stuck to its guns

---

[485] Bayo, Carlos Enrique & López, Patricia (2017). "La Intel·ligència dels EUA desmenteix la "nota" als Mossos de l'amenaça a la Rambla", Público, 22 September 2017. https://www.publico.es/public/nota-cia-terrorisme-intel-ligencia-dels-eua-desmenteix-nota-als-mossos-l-amenaca-rambla.html

after Spanish police swooped onto documents being taken by the Catalan police to be incinerated, following another apparent leak. [486]

El Público, on 15-19 July 2019, revealed the results of its own investigations, which strongly suggested the Spanish secret police, the CNI, were at the very least negligent in monitoring its informant, Abdelbaki es Satty - whom they had helped become the imam of Ripoll - in his highly suspicious activities, with a group of young Jihadists, just six weeks before the planned referendum on independence. Five months later (4 December 2019[487]) Jon Iñarritu MP wrote to the Spanish Government to ask if it was aware of these findings, and what measures it would take to clear up all the outstanding issues. In its reply, (23 December 2019)[488] the Spanish Government denied any knowledge of the content of the investigations and fobbed off the issue by claiming it would be fully covered in the judicial investigation. We have since witnessed that the presiding judge has made sure the trial was limited to just the activities of the three survivors, and it is widely feared that the truth will not come out from this trial about the alleged CIA connection and mismanagement of its informant. So yet again justice will probably neither be done nor be seen to be done.

---

[486] "El Periódico (2018). "Los Mossos intentaron destruir la alerta de EEUU sobre la Rambla", *El Periódico de Catalunya,* 21 January 2018. https://www.elperiodico.com/es/politica/20180121/mossos-intentaron-destruir-alerta-eeuu-rambla-6567677

[487] http://www.congreso.es/l14p/e0/e_0003438_n_000.pdf

[488] http://www.congreso.es/l14p/e0/e_0008479_n_000.pdf

Chapter 9. Conclusion

1. We have found compelling evidence of a Unionist narrative, spear-headed by the Spanish Ministry for Foreign Affairs, the Real Instituto Elcano [489], the *El País* newspaper, and particular individuals in the CIDOB, the Institute for Statecraft and the European Council on Foreign Relations, to portray a significant involvement of the Russians in the Catalonia-Spain conflict.

2. We have found no compelling evidence that Russian interference in the Catalan referendum made any significant impact on the outcome of the self-determination referendum, described as "illegal" by the Rajoy administration as early as 13 Nov 2013[490] and 13 MAR 2013[491] by the Ciudadanos party leader Albert Rivera, despite both the November 2014 non-binding poll and the October 2017 referendum being covered by their respective Catalan Parliament laws.

3. We have found no evidence of direct Russian involvement in the Catalan independence process, despite intense efforts to that effect.

4. We have found no evidence that in the social media the opinions of Julian Assange and Edward Snowden, in support of the Catalan people's right of self-determination, actually

---

[489] See, for instance its overview: Real Instituto Elcano (2019). *The independence conflict in Catalonia.* Real Instituto Elcano - 2019 http://www.realinstitutoelcano.org/wps/wcm/connect/d8496562-e096-44a1-81da-b871c91ccf62/Catalonia-dossier-elcano-october-2019.pdf

[490] Europa Press (2013). "El PP garantiza que no habrá un referéndum ilegal en Cataluña y no opina del castigo penal que pide Aznar", *El Diario.es*, 13 NOV 2013. https://www.eldiario.es/politica/pp-garantiza-referendum-cataluna-aznar_1_5159711.html

[491] E-noticies (2013). "La Generalitat planea utilizar las tarjetas sanitarias como censo para la consulta", *E-noticies*, 13 MAR 2013. https://sociedad.e-noticies.es/la-generalitat-planea-utilizar-las-tarjetas-sanitarias-como-censo-para-la-consulta-73817.html

swayed any significant number of voters during the referendum on 1 October 2017.

5. We have found evidence that in the media there was more activity in favour a "No" vote, or abstention, than in favour of a "Yes" vote.

6. We have found compelling evidence that Spain has made a concerted effort to demonize both the leaders of the independence movement (and in particular, the exiled President, Carles Puigdemont) and the aspirations of the Catalan people: to decide their political future at the ballot box.

7. We have found compelling empirical evidence that, all in all, as regards the Catalan independence process, there is a far greater bias in nearly all the Spanish audiovisual media than in the public and private Catalan audiovisual media, which have been more balanced in the choice of their chat shows invitees and participants.

8. We have found compelling evidence that the Spanish media, politicians, researchers and opinion leaders have, in the main, no idea at all about the reasons behind the Catalan people's drive for independence, especially since the 2010 Constitutional court judgment left Catalonia's Statute of Autonomy, and Catalonia itself, in an unresolved legal limbo.

9. We have found evidence of more fake news and disinformation against Catalonia's independence than in favour of it, except for that reported by *Maldito Bulo* related to the October 1 2017 referendum.

10. There is abundant evidence that the issue of fake news and disinformation is of concern not only to Catalan institutions (e.g. CAC) and organisations (e.g. Media.cat and verificat.cat), but also to researchers.

11. We have found no compelling evidence that the Coronavirus pandemic has given rise to a Catalan "strategy" to strengthen the pro-independence camp.

12. On the contrary, as any simple search of the social media will show, the pandemic has for the time being taken the wind out of the sails of the independence movement and public opinion and, in this sense only, suits the Spanish establishment. The imprisoned leaders of the movement have become a secondary issue. The CDRs are largely inactive. The *Tsunami Democràtic* petered out. Public demonstrations have been out of the question for several months during 2020. The "*mesa de diálogo*" ("a dialogue table") which was to thrash out a political solution to the conflict, was postponed *sine die*... until after an election which, as this book goes to press, in by no means certain to take place on Sunday, 14 February 2021.

Alphabetical Index

Printed in Great Britain
by Amazon

72498638R00159